AVIATION MAINTENANCE TECHNICIAN
REFERENCE HANDBOOK

Production Staff
Lead Illustrator Amy Siever
Designer/Photographer Dustin Blyer
Designer/Production Coordinator Roberta Byerly
Production Manager Holly Bonos

International Standard Book Number 1-933189-09-6
ISBN 13: 978-1-933189-09-3
Order # T-AVMARE-0101

For Sale by: Avotek
A Select Aerospace Industries, Inc. company

Mail to:
P.O. Box 219
Weyers Cave, Virginia 24486
USA

Ship to:
200 Packaging Drive
Weyers Cave, Virginia 24486
USA

Toll Free: 1-800-828-6835
Telephone: 1-540-234-9090
Fax: 1-540-234-9399

Revised Edition
Fourth Printing
Printed in the USA

www.avotek.com

Cover photo courtesy of Duncan Aviation

Preface

Every AMT relies on facts and figures in the course of day-to-day work and continuing education; therefore, the need for a comprehensive reference handbook arises. Avotek's Aircraft Maintenance Technician Reference Handbook is a thorough resource wherein an AMT may find conversion tables and other vital information required in today's aviation industry.

This compilation of material is to be used only as reference and should not supersede the manufacturer's documentation. The manufacturer is always the primary source of operation, maintenance, repair and overhaul information.

Our sincere thanks to the many companies, writers and individuals who have contributed to this manual. Those who have contributed have done so in the spirit of cooperation and for the good of the industry. To the best of their abilities, they have provided pertinent and accurate information. However, as with all human endeavors, unintentional errors and omissions are possible. Please bring them to our attention.

At Avotek we welcome your input. If you have ideas or suggestions for material to include in future editions, please contact us at comments@avotek.com.

Acknowledgements

Avotek would like to thank the following companies and individuals:

Academy of Infrared Training	Genuine Aircraft Hardware
The Boeing Company	Preferred Airparts
CES Composites	Raytheon Aircraft
Champion	Select Aerospace Industries, Inc.
Classic Aviation Services	Select Airparts
David Jones - AIM	Snap-on Tools
Duncan Aviation	Starrett Tools
Dynamic Aviation	

Table of Contents

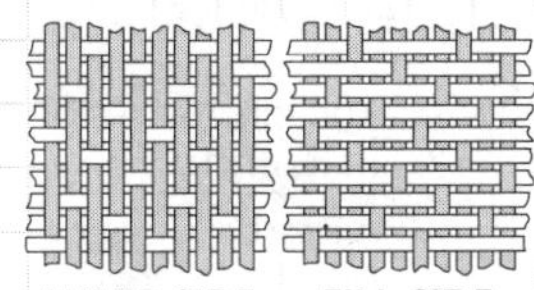

5 HARNESS SATIN WEAVE CONSTRUCTION

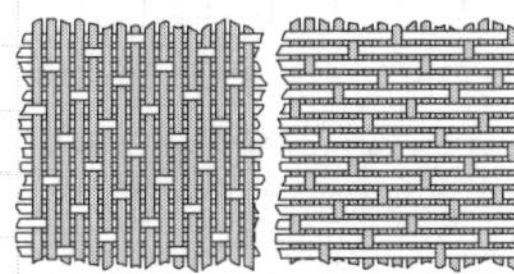

8 HARNESS SATIN WEAVE CONSTRUCTION

1
Composites

1.1 Composite Terms

A-stage	The initial state of the resin as produced by the manufacturer
Adhesive Film	A synthetic resin adhesive, in the form of a thin film of resin
Advanced Composites	Composite materials applicable to aerospace construction made by imbedding high-strength fibers within a matrix
Aramid	A type of highly oriented organic material derived from polyamide (nylon). Kevlar® and nomex are aramids
Autoclave	A closed vessel for producing an environment of pressure, with or without heat
B-stage	An intermediate stage in the reaction of certain thermosetting resins
Balanced Construction	Equal parts of warp and fill in fiber fabric
Bleeder Cloth	A nonstructural layer of material used to allow the escape of excess gas and resin during the cure
Breather Cloth	A loosely woven material that will serve as a continuous vacuum path over a repair area
Carbon Fiber	Fiber produced by the pyrolysis of organic fibers, such as rayon, polyacrylonitrile and pitch in an inert environment
C-stage	The final stage in the reaction of thermosetting resins in which the material is insoluble and infusible
Debond	A separation of a bonded joint or interface
Delamination	Separation of the layers of material in a laminate
Disbond	An area in a bonded interface where an adhesion failure or separation has occurred
E-glass	A general purpose fiberglass cloth suitable for electrical laminates because of its high resistivity
Epoxy Resin	An important matrix resin in composites and structural adhesives
Fabric Fill Face	That side of the woven fabric where the majority of the exposed yarns are perpendicular to the selvage edge
Fabric Warp Face	That side of the fabric where the majority of the exposed yarns are parallel to the selvage edge
Fill	Yarns perpendicular to the selvage edge
Hybrid	A composite laminate consisting of two or more composite material systems

Interply Hybrid	A composite in which adjacent layers are composed of different materials
Intraply Hybrid	A composite in which different materials are used within a specific layer
Isotropic	Having uniform properties in all directions
Kevlar®	Dupont company name for an aramid fiber. Has good impact resistance, low density and high strength
Matrix	The essentially homogeneous resin or polymer material in which the fiber of a composite is imbedded
Modulus	The stiffness of a material
Nested Laminate	The placing of plies of fabric so that the yarns of one ply lie in the valleys between the yarns of the adjacent ply
Plain Weave	A weaving pattern in which the warp and fill fibers alternate
Prepreg	Ready-to-mold material which may be cloth, mat, uni-directional fiber, or paper impregnated with resin and stored for use
Selvage	The woven-edge portion of a fabric parallel to the warp, finished off so as to prevent the yarns from unraveling
S-glass	Structural glass, used as fiber reinforcement, designed to give high tensile strength
Stacking	The lamination sequence in which the warp surface of one ply is laid against the fill surface of the preceding ply
Tap Test	Using a coin, or special hammer, to tap a laminate in different spots, listening for a change in sound, which would indicate the presence of a defect
Thermoplastic	Capable of being repeatedly softened by an increase of temperature and hardened by a decrease in temperature
Thermoset	A plastic that when cured by application of heat or chemical means, changes into a substantially infusible and insoluble material
Tracer	A fiber or yarn added to a prepreg for verifying fiber alignment and, in the case of woven materials, for distinguishing warp fibers from fill fibers
Warp	The yarn running lengthwise in a woven fabric
Warp Clock	A composite fabrication and engineering symbol used as reference for aligning the warp yarns or tows in the desired direction

1.2 Material Storage and Handling

All dry fabrics should be stored in a dry clean area that is protected from oils and chemicals. Kevlar should not be exposed to sunlight or ultraviolet rays due to possible deterioration.

Prepreg fabrics and film adhesives should be stored in a controlled freezer at 0°F or below. A record of time out of freezer should be kept to track shelf life.

All composite fabrics dry and prepreg should be handled with gloves only, to avoid contamination by skin oils and to guard against personal contamination from chemicals.

1.3 Adhesives and Resins

Bulk resins should be stored in a dry area away from ignition sources. Containers should be tightly closed when not in use. Use separate containers for each ingredient.

Film adhesives should be kept in a controlled freezer at 0°F or lower. A record of the time out of the freezer should be kept to track shelf life.

Adhesive films and bulk resins should be handled with gloves only to avoid contamination from skin oils and to guard against personal contamination from chemicals. Mix in accordance with the manufacturer's instructions.

1.4 Warp Clock

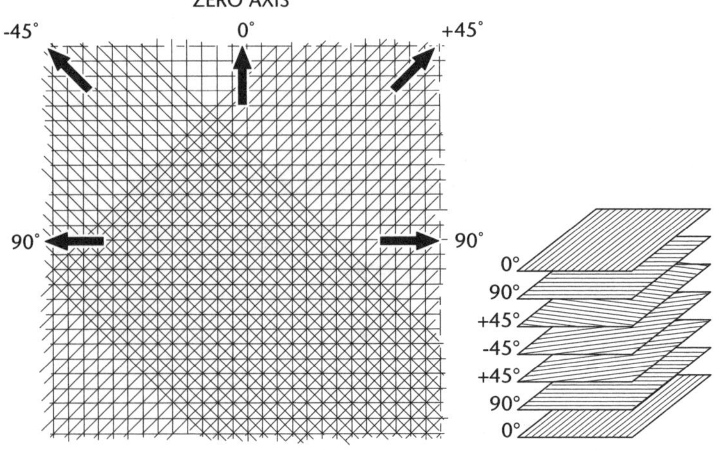

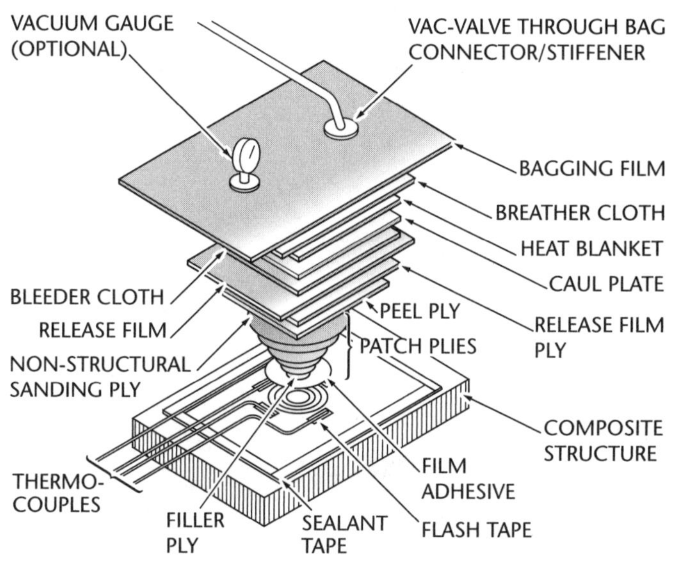

1.6 **Composite Inspection**

Type	Method
Visual	A methodical search for defects using a strong light held at an angle to the surface being inspected.
Tap Test	Used in conjunction with visual inspection. Conducted by tapping on the surface with a coin or special hammer. A dull or dead sound may indicate a defect.
Ultrasonic	Measures the time a transmitted sound wave takes to travel through an object and return. Accurate results depend on experienced operators and known standards.
X-ray	Defects in the material change the degree of radiation absorption and show up on the film as varying areas of dark and light.

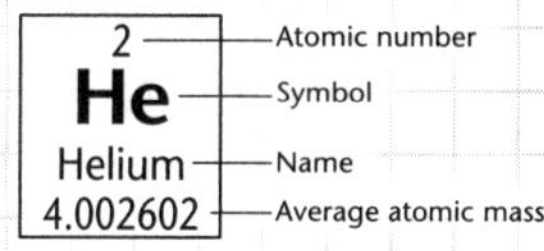

2
Common Reference Tables

2.1 **Decimal Inch Equivalents**

Drill Size	Decimal	Drill Size	Decimal	Drill Size	Decimal
80	0.0135	53	0.0595	28	0.1485
79	0.0145	1/16	0.0625	9/64	0.1406
1/64	0.0156	52	0.0635	27	0.1440
78	0.0160	51	0.0670	26	0.1470
77	0.0180	50	0.0700	25	0.1495
76	0.0200	49	0.0730	24	0.1520
75	0.0210	48	0.0760	23	0.1540
74	0.0225	5/64	0.0781	5/32	0.1562
73	0.0240	47	0.0785	22	0.1570
72	0.0250	46	0.0810	21	0.1590
71	0.0260	45	0.0820	20	0.1610
70	0.0280	44	0.0860	19	0.1640
69	0.0292	43	0.0890	18	0.1695
68	0.0310	42	0.0935	11/64	0.1719
1/32	0.0312	3/32	0.0938	17	0.1730
67	0.0320	41	0.0960	16	0.1770
66	0.0330	40	0.0980	15	0.1800
65	0.0350	39	0.0995	14	0.1820
64	0.0360	38	0.1015	13	0.1850
63	0.0370	37	0.1040	3/16	0.1875
62	0.0380	36	0.1065	12	0.1890
61	0.0390	7/64	0.1094	11	0.1910
60	0.0400	35	0.1100	10	0.1935
59	0.0410	34	0.1110	9	0.1960
58	0.0420	33	0.1130	8	0.1990
57	0.0430	32	0.1160	7	0.2010
56	0.0165	31	0.1200	13/64	0.2031
3/64	0.0169	1/8	0.1250	6	0.2040
55	0.0520	30	0.1285	5	0.2055
64	0.0550	29	0.1360	4	0.2090

2.1 Decimal Inch Equivalents (cont'd)

Drill Size	Decimal	Drill Size	Decimal	Drill Size	Decimal
3	0.2130	S	0.3480	45/64	1.7031
7/32	0.2188	T	0.3580	23/32	0.7188
2	0.2210	23/64	0.3594	47/64	0.7344
1	0.2280	U	0.3680	3/4	0.7500
A	0.2340	3/8	0.3750	49/64	0.7656
15/64	0.2344	V	0.3770	25/32	0.7812
B	0.2380	W	0.3860	51/64	0.7969
C	0.2120	25/64	0.3906	13/16	0.8125
D	0.2460	X	0.3970	53/64	0.8281
1/4	0.2500	Y	0.4040	27/32	0.8438
E	0.2500	13/32	0.4062	55/64	0.8594
F	0.2570	Z	0.4130	7/8	0.8750
G	0.2610	27/64	0.4219	57/64	0.8906
17/64	0.2656	7/16	0.4375	29/22	0.9062
H	0.2660	29/64	0.4531	59/64	0.9219
I	0.2720	15/32	0.4688	15/16	0.9375
J	0.2770	31/64	0.4844	61/64	0.9531
K	0.2810	1/2	0.5000	31/32	0.9688
9/32	0.2812	33/64	0.5156	63/64	0.9844
L	0.2900	17/32	0.5312	1	1.0000
M	0.2950	35/64	0.5669		
19/64	0.2969	9/16	0.5625		
N	0.3020	37/64	0.5781		
5/16	0.3125	19/32	0.5938		
O	0.3160	39/64	0.6094		
P	0.3230	5/8	0.6250		
21/64	0.3281	41/64	0.6406		
Q	0.3320	21/32	0.6562		
R	0.3390	43/64	0.6719		
11/32	0.3438	11/16	0.6875		

2.2 Conversion Table

Multiply:	By:	To Obtain:
Acceleration Due To Gravity (G)	32.174	Feet / Second^2
	980.6	Centimeters / Second^2
Acres	0.4047	Hectares
	43,560	Square Feet
	4,047	Square Meters
	0.001562	Square Miles
	4,840	Square Yards
Acre-feet	60	Cubic Feet
	325,851	Gallons (US)
	1,233.49	Cubic Meters
	1,233,490	Liters
Atmospheres	76.0	Cms of Hg at 32° F
	29.921	Inches of Hg at 32° F
	33.94	Feet of Water at 62° F
	10,333	Kgs / Square Meter
	14.6963	Pounds / Square Inch
	1.058	Tons / Square Foot
	1,013.15	Millibars
	235.1408	Ounces / Square Inch
BTU	252.016	Calories (Gm)
	0.252	Calories (Kg)
	777.54	Foot Pounds
	0.0003927	Horse Power Hours
	1,054.2	Joules
	107.5	Kilogram Meters
	0.0002928	Kilowatt Hours
Calories (Kg)	3.968	BTU
	1,000	Calories (Gm)
	3,088	Foot Pounds
	0.001558	Horse Power Hours
	4,185	Joules
	426.5	Kilogram Meters
	0.0011628	Kilowatt Hours
	1.1628	Watt Hours

Multiply:	By:	To Obtain:
Calories(Kg) / Minute	51.43	Foot Pounds / Second
	0.09351	Horse Power
	0.06972	Kilowatts
Celsius	$°F = \dfrac{°C \times 9}{5} + 32$	Fahrenheit
	$°K = °C + 273$	Kelvin
Centimeters	0.3937	Inches
	0.032808	Feet
	0.01	Meters
	10	Millimeters
Centimeters / Second	1.969	Feet / Minute
	0.03281	Feet / Second
	0.036	Kilometers / Hour
	0.6	Meters / Minute
	002237	Miles / Hour
	0.0003728	Miles / Minute
	0.03281	Feet / Second^2
Circular Inches	1,000,000	Circular Mils
	0.7854	Square Inches
	785,400	Square Mils
Circular Mils	0.7854	Square Mils
	10^{-6}	Circular Inches
	7.854×10^{-7}	Square Inches
Cubic Feet	28,320	Cubic Centimeters
	1,728	Cubic Inches
	0.02832	Cubic Meters
	0.03704	Cubic Yards
	7.48052	Gallons (US)
	28.32	Liters
	59.84	Pints (Liquid US)
	29.92	Quarts (Liquid US)
	2.296×10^{-5}	Acre Feet
Cubic Feet of Water	62.4266	Pounds at 39.2°F
	62.3554	Pounds at 62°F

2.2 Conversion Table (cont'd)

Multiply:	By:	To Obtain:
Cubic Feet / Minute	472	Cubic Centimeters / Second
	0.1247	Gallons (US) / Second
	0.472	Liters / Second
	7.4805	Gallons (US) / Minute
Cubic Feet / Second	646,317	Gallons (US) / 24 Hours
	448.831	Gallons / Minute
	1.98347	Acre Feet / 24 Hours
Cubic Inches	16.387	Cubic Centimeters
	5.787×10^{-4}	Cubic Feet
	1.639×10^{-5}	Cubic Meters
	2.143×10^{-5}	Cubic Yards
	0.004329	Gallons (US)
	0.01639	Liters
	0.03463	Pints (Liquid US)
	0.01732	Quarts (Liquid US)
Cubic Meters	1,000,000	Cubic Centimeters
	35.31	Cubic Feet
	61,023	Cubic Inches
	1.308	Cubic Yards
	264.2	Gallons (US)
	1,000	Liters
	2,113	Pints (Liquid US)
	1,057	Quarts (Liquid US)
Cubic Yards / Minute	0.45	Cubic Feet / Second
	3.367	Gallons (US) / Second
	12.74	Liters / Second
Days (Mean)	1,440	Minutes
	24	Hours
	86,400	Seconds
Days (Sidereal)	86,164.1	Solar Seconds
Degrees F (Less 32)	0.5556	Degrees C
Degrees F	1 (plus 460)	Degrees F Above Absolute 0

Multiply:	By:	To Obtain:
Degrees C	1.8 (x 32)	Degrees F
	1 (x 273)	Degrees C Above Absolute 0
Fahrenheit	$°C = \dfrac{°F - 32}{9} \times 5$	Celsius
	$°R = °F + 460$	Rankine
Feet	30.48	Centimeters
	12	Inches
	0.3048	Meters
	1/3	Yards
Feet of Water at 62°F	0.029465	Atmospheres
	0.88162	Inches of Hg at 32°F
	62.3554	Pounds / Square Foot
	0.43302	Pounds / Square Inch
	304.44	Kilogram / Square Meter
Feet / Minute	0.5080	Centimeters / Second
	0.01667	Feet / Second
	0.01829	Kilometers / Hour
	0.3048	Meters / Minute
	0.01136	Miles / Hour
Feet / Second	30.48	Centimeters / Second
	1.097	Kilometers / Hour
	0.5921	Knots
	18.29	Meters / Minute
	0.6818	Miles / Hour
	0.01136	Miles / Minute
	30.48	Centimeters / Second^2
	0.3048	Meters / Second

2.2 **Conversion Table (cont'd)**

Multiply:	By:	To Obtain:
Foot Pounds	0.0012861	BTU
	0.32412	Calories (Gm)
	0.0003241	Calories (Kg)
	5.05×10^{-7}	Horse Power Hours
	1.3558	Joules
	0.13826	Kilogram Meters
	3.766×10^{-7}	Kilowatt Hours
	0.0003766	Watt Hours
Foot Pounds / Minute	0.001286	BTU / Minute
	0.01667	Foot Pounds / Second
	3.03×10^{-5}	Horse Power
	0.0003241	Calories (Kg) / Minute
	2.26×10^{-5}	Kilowatts
Foot Pounds / Second	0.07717	BTU / Minute
	0.001818	Horse Power
	0.01945	Calories (Kg) / Minute
	0.001356	Kilowatts
Gallons (Imperial)	277.42	Cubic Inches
	4.543	Liters
	1.20095	Gallons (US)
Gallons (US)	3,785	Cubic Centimeters
	0.13368	Cubic Feet
	231	Cubic Inches
	0.003785	Cubic Meters
	0.004951	Cubic Yards
	3.785	Liters
	8	Pints (Liquid US)
	4	Quarts (Liquid US)
	0.83267	Gallons (Imperial)
	3.069×10^{6}	Acre Feet

Multiply:	By:	To Obtain:
	0.002228	Cubic Feet / Second
	0.13368	Cubic Feet / Minute
	8.0208	Cubic Feet / Hour
Gallons (US) / Minute	0.06309	Liters / Second
	3.78533	Liters / Minute
	0.0044192	Acre Feet / 24 Hours
	0.227	Cubic Meters / Hour
	1000	Milligrams
	0.03527	Ounces (Avoir.)
Grams	0.03215	Ounces (Troy)
	0.002205	Pounds
	42.44	BTU / Minute
	33,000	Foot Pounds / Minute
	550	Foot Pounds / Second
Horse Power	1.014	Metric Horse Power (CV)
	10.7	Calories (Kg) / Min
	0.7457	Kilowatts
	745.7	Watts
	2,546.5	BTU
	641,700	Calories (Gm)
	641.7	Calories (Kg)
Horse Power Hours	1,980,000	Foot Pounds
	2,684,500	Joules
	273,740	Kilogram Meters
	0.7455	Kilowatt Hours
	745.5	Watt Hours
	0.08333	Feet
	1,000	Mils
Inches	12	Lines
	72	Points
	25.4	Millimeters (Mm)

2.2 Conversion Table (cont'd)

Multiply:	By:	To Obtain:
	0.03342	Atmospheres
	345.3	Kilograms / Square Meter
Inches of Hg at 32° F	70.73	Pounds / Square Foot
	0.49117	Pounds / Square Inch
	1.1343	Feet of Water at 62° F
	13.6114	Inches of Water at 62° F
	7.85872	Ounces / Square Inch
	0.00094869	BTU
	0.239	Calories (Gm)
	0.000239	Calories (Kg)
	0.73756	Foot Pounds
Joules	3.72×10^{-7}	Horse Power Hours
	0.10197	Kilogram Meters
	2.778×10	Kilowatt Hours
	0.0002778	Watt Hours
	1	Watt Second
Kelvin	$°C = °K - 273$	Celsius
	2.205	Pounds
	0.001102	Tons (Short)
Kilograms	1,000	Grams
	35.274	Ounces (Avoir.)
	32.1507	Ounces (Troy)
	0.009302	BTU
	2.344	Calories (Gm)
	0.002344	Calories (Kg)
	7.233	Foot Pounds
Kilogram Meters	3.653×10^{-6}	Horse Power Hours
	9.806	Joules
	2.724×10^{-6}	Kilowatt Hours
	0.002724	Watt Hours
Kilopascals (Kpa)	0.1450377	Lb. / In² (Psi)
Kilograms / Cubic Meter	0.06243	Pounds / Cubic Foot

Multiply:	By:	To Obtain:
Kilograms / Hour	4.4/density (kg/m3)	GPM
Kilograms / Meter	0.6720	Pounds / Foot
Kilograms / Square Centimeter	14.223	Pounds / Square Inch
Kilogram / Square Meter	9.678×10^{-5}	Atmospheres
	0.003285	Feet of Water at 62° F
	0.002896	Inches of Hg at 32° F
	0.2048	Pounds / Square Foot
	0.001422	Pounds / Square Inch
	0.007356	Centimeters of Hg at 32° F
Kilometers	100,000	Centimeters
	1,000	Meters
	3,281	Feet
	0.6214	Miles
	1,094	Yards
Kilometers / Hour	27.78	Centimeters / Second
	54.68	Feet / Minute
	0.9113	Feet / Second
	16.67	Meters / Minute
	0.6214	Miles / Hour
	0.5396	Knots
Kilowatts	56.92	BTU / Minute
	44,250	Foot Pounds / Minute
	737.6	Foot Pounds / Second
	1.341	Horse Power
	14.34	Calories (Kg) / Minute
	1,000	Watts

2.2 **Conversion Table (cont'd)**

Multiply:	By:	To Obtain:
Kilowatt Hours	3,413	BTU
	860,500	Calories (Gm)
	860.5	Calories (Kg)
	2,655,200	Foot Pounds
	1.341	Horse Power Hours
	3,600,000	Joules
	367,100	Kilogram Meters
	1,000	Watt Hours
Knots	1	Nautical Miles / Hour
	1.1516	Miles / Hour
	1.8532	Kilometers / Hour
Liters	1,000	Cubic Centimeters
	0.03531	Cubic Feet
	61.02	Cubic Inches
	0.001	Cubic Meters
	0.001 308	Cubic Yards
	0.2642	Gallons (US)
	0.22	Gallons (Imp)
	2.113	Pints (Liq. US)
	1.057	Quarts (Liq. US)
	8.11×10^{-7}	Acre Feet
	2.2018	Pounds of Water at 62° F
Meters	100	Centimeters
	3.281	Feet
	39.37	Inches
	1.094	Yards
	0.001	Kilometers
	1,000	Millimeters
Meters / Minute	1.667	Centimeters / Second
	3.281	Feet / Minute
	0.05468	Feet / Second
	0.06	Kilometers / Hour
	0.03728	Miles / Hour

Multiply:	By:	To Obtain:
Meters / Second	196.8	Feet / Minute
	3.281	Feet / Second
	3.6	Kilometers / Hour
	0.06	Kilometers / Minute
	2.237	Miles / Hour
	0.03728	Miles / Minute
Miles	160,934	Centimeters
	5,280	Feet
	63,360	Inches
	1.609	Kilometers
	1,760	Yards
	0.8684	Nautical Miles
Miles / Hour	44.70	Centimeters / Second
	88	Feet / Minute
	1.467	Feet / Second
	1.609	Kilometers / Hour
	0.8684	Knots
	26.82	Meters / Minute
Miles / Minute	2,682	Centimeters / Second
	88	Feet / Second
	1.609	Kilometers / Minute
	60	Miles / Hour
Millibars	0.000987	Atmosphere
Milligrams	0.001	Grams
	0.01543	Grains
Millimeters	0.1	Centimeters
	0.03937	Inches
	39.37	Mils
	1,000	Microns
Nautical Miles	6,080.2	Feet
	1.1516	Miles

2.2 **Conversion Table (cont'd)**

Multiply:	By:	To Obtain:
Ounces (Avoirdupois)	16	Drams (Avoir.)
	437.5	Grains
	0.0625	Pounds (Avoir.)
	28.349527	Grams
	0.9115	Ounces (Troy)
Ounces (Fluid)	1.805	Cubic Inches
	0.02957	Liters
	29.57	Cubic Centimeters
	0.25	Gills
Ounces (Troy)	480	Grains
	20	Pennyweights (Troy)
	0.08333	Pounds (Troy)
	31.103481	Grams
	1.09714	Ounces (Avoir.)
Ounces / Square Inch	0.0625	Pounds / Square Inch
	1.732	Inches of Water at 62° F
	4.39	Centimeters of Water at 62° F
	0.12725	Inches of Hg at 32° F
	0.004253	Atmospheres
Parts / Million	0.0584	Grains / Gallon (US)
	0.07016	Grains / Gallon (Imp)
	8.345	Pounds / Million Gal (US)
Pints (Liquid US)	16	Ounces (Fluid)
	0.5	Quarts (Liquid US)
	28.875	Cubic Inches
	473.1	Cubic Centimeters
Pounds (Avoirdupois)	16	Ounces (Avoir.
	256	Drams (Avoir.)
	0.0005	Tons (Short)
	453.5924	Grams
	1.21528	Pounds (Troy)
	14.5833	Ounces (Troy)

Multiply:	By:	To Obtain:
Pounds (Troy)	12	Ounces (Troy)
	373.24177	Grams
	0.822857	Pounds (Avoir.)
	13.1657	Ounces (Avoir.)
	0.00036735	Tons (Long)
	0.00041143	Tons (Short)
	0.00037324	Tons (Metric)
Pounds of Water at 62°F	0.01604	Cubic Feet
	27.72	Cubic Inches
	0.120	Gallons (US)
Pounds / Foot	1.488	Kilograms / Meter
Pounds / Inch	178.6	Grams / Centimeter
Pounds / Square Foot	0.016037	Feet of Water at 62°F
	4.882	Kilograms / Square Meter
	0.006944	Pounds / Square Inch
	0.014139	Inches of Hg at 32°F
	0.0004725	Atmospheres
Pounds / Square Inch	6.894759	Kilopascals (Kpa)
	0.068044	Atmospheres
	2.30934	Feet of Water at 62°F
	2.0360	Inches of Hg at 32°F
	703.067	Kilograms / Square Meter
	27.912	Inches of Water at 62°F
	0.06894757	Bar
	52.16	Millimeters Hg
Quarts (Dry)	67.20	Cubic Inches
Quarts (Liquid US)	0.9463	Liters
	32	Ounces (Fluid)
	57.75	Cubic Inches
	946.3	Cubic Centimeters

2.2 Conversion Table (cont'd)

Multiply:	By:	To Obtain:
Radians	57.30	Degrees
	3,438	Minutes
	206,625	Seconds
	0.637	Quadrants
Rankine	$°F = °R - 460$	Fahrenheit
Revolutions	360	Degrees
	4	Quadrants
	6.283	Radians
Revolutions / Minute	6	Degrees / Second
	0.001745	Radians / Second
	0.0002778	Revolutions / Second
Revolutions / Second	360	Degrees / Second
	6.283	Radians / Second
	60	Revolutions / Minute
Sections	1	Square Miles
Square Centimeters	0.001076	Square Feet
	0.1550	Square Inches
	0.001	Square Meters
	100	Square Millimeters
Square Feet	2.296×10^{-5}	Acres
	929.0	Square Centimeters
	144	Square Inches
	0.0929	Square Meters
	3.587×10^{-8}	Square Miles
	0.1111	Square Yards
Square Inches	6.452	Square Centimeters
	0.006944	Square Feet
	645.2	Square Millimeters
	1.27324	Circular Inches
	1,273,239	Circular Mils
	1,000,000	Square Mils

Multiply:	By:	To Obtain:
Square Kilometers	247.1	Acres
	10,760,000	Square Feet
	1,000,000	Square Meters
	0.3861	Square Miles
	1,196,000	Square Yards
Square Meters	0.0002471	Acres
	10.764	Square Feet
	1.196	Square Yards
Square Miles	640	Acres
	27,878,400	Square Feet
	2.590	Square Kilometers
	3,097,600	Square Yards
Square Millimeters	0.01	Square Centimeters
	0.00155	Square Inches
	1,550	Square Mils
	1,973	Circular Mils
Square Mils	1.27324	Circular Mils
	0.0006452	Square Millimeters
	10^{-6}	Square Inches
Square Yards	0.0002066	Acres
	9	Square Feet
	0.8361	Square Meters
	3.228×10^{-7}	Square Miles
Tons (Long)	1,016	Kilograms
	2,240	Pounds
	1.12	Tons (Short)
Tons (Metric)	1,000	Kilograms
	2,205	Pounds
	1.1023	Tons (Short)
Tons (Short)	2,000	Pounds
	32,000	Ounces
	907.185	Kilograms
	0.90718	Tons (Metric)
	0.89286	Tons (Long)

2.2 Conversion Table (cont'd)

Multiply:	By:	To Obtain:
	0.05692	BTU / Minute
	44.26	Foot Pounds / Minute
	0.7376	Foot Pounds / Second
Watts	0.001341	Horse Power
	0.01434	Calories (Kg) / Minute
	0.001	Kilowatts
	1	Joule / Second
	3.413	BTU
	860.5	Calories (Gm)
	0.8605	Calories (Kg)
	2,655	Foot Pounds
Watt Hours	0.001341	Horse Power Hours
	3,600	Joules
	367.1	Kilogram Meters
	0.001	Kilowatt Hours
	91.44	Centimeters
	3	Feet
Yards	36	Inches
	0.9144	Meters
	0.1818	Rods

2.3 ATA 100 System Codes

General Aircraft Information

00 Introduction

05 Periodic Inspections

06 Dimension and Arrangement

07 Lifting and Hoisting

08 Leveling-Weighting-Alignment

09 Towing and Taxiing

10 Parking and Mooring

11 Nameplates

12 Servicing-Routine Maintenance

Airframe Systems

21 Air Conditioning

- 00 General
- 10 Compression
- 20 Distribution
- 30 Pressurization Control
- 40 Heating
- 50 Cooling
- 60 Temperature Control
- 70 Moisture / Air Contaminant Control

22 Auto Flight

- 00 General
- 10 Auto Pilot
- 20 Speed / Attitude Correction
- 30 Auto Throttle
- 40 System Monitor

23 Communications

- 00 General
- 10 HF
- 20 VHF-UHF
- 30 Passenger Addressing and Entertainment
- 40 Intercom
- 50 Audio Integrating
- 60 Static Discharging
- 70 Audio and Video Monitoring

24 Electrical Power

- 00 General
- 10 Generator Drive
- 20 AC Generation
- 30 DC Generation
- 40 External Power
- 50 Electrical Load Distribution

25 Equipment and Furnishing

- 00 General
- 10 Flight Compartment
- 20 Passenger Compartment
- 30 Buffet-Galley
- 40 Lavatories
- 50 Cargo Compartment
- 60 Emergency
- 70 Accessory Compartments

26 Fire Protection

- 00 General
- 10 Detection
- 20 Extinguishing
- 30 Explosion Suppression

27 Flight Controls

- 00 General
- 10 Aileron & Tab
- 20 Rudder-Ruddervator & Tab
- 30 Elevator & Tab
- 40 Horizontal Stabilizer-Stabilator
- 50 Flaps
- 60 Spoilers, Drag Devices & Variable Aerodynamic Fairings
- 70 Gust Lock & Dampener

2.3 ATA 100 System Codes (cont'd)

80 Lift Augmenting

28 Fuel

00 General

10 Storage

20 Distribution-Drain Valves

30 Dump

40 Indicating

29 Hydraulic Power

00 General

10 Main

20 Auxiliary

30 Indicating

30 Ice & Rain Protection

00 General

10 Airfoil

20 Air Intakes

30 Pitot & Static

40 Windows & Windshields

50 Antennas & Radomes

60 Propellers & Rotor

70 Water Lines

80 Detection

31 Indicating and Recording Systems

00 General

10 Unassigned

20 Unassigned

30 Recorders

40 Central Computers

50 Central Warning System

32 Landing Gear

00 General

10 Main Gear

20 Nose Gear-Tail Gear

30 Extension & Retraction, Level Switch

40 Wheels & Brakes

50 Steering

60 Position, Warning & Ground Safety Switch

70 Supplementary Gear-Skis, Floats

33 Light

00 General

10 Flight Compartment & Annunciator Panel

20 Passenger Compartments

30 Cargo & Service Compartment

40 Exterior Lighting

50 Emergency Lighting

34 Navigation

00 General

10 Flight Environment Data

20 Attitude & Direction

30 Landing & Taxi Aids

40 Independent Position Determining

50 Dependent Position Determining

60 Position Computing

35 Oxygen

00 General

10 Crew

20 Passengers

30 Portable

36 Pneumatic

00 General

10 Distribution

20 Indicating

37 Vacuum-pressure

00 General

10 Distribution

20 Indicating

38 Water - Waste

00 General

10 Potable

20 Wash

30 Waste Disposal

40 Air Supply

39 Electrical-Electronic Panels and multi-purpose components

00 General

10 Instrument & Control Panels

20 Electrical & Electronic Equipment Racks

30 Electrical & Electronic Junction Boxes

40 Multipurpose Electronic Components

50 Integrated Circuits

60 Printed Circuit Card Assemblies

46 Armament

47 Weapons Electronics

49 Airborne Auxiliary Power

00 General

10 Instrument & Control Panels

20 Electrical & Electronic Equipment Racks

30 Electrical & Electronic Junction Boxes

40 Multipurpose Electronic Components

50 Integrated Circuits

60 Printed Circuit Card Assemblies

51 Structures

01 General

52 Doors and Openings

00 General

10 Passenger / Crew

20 Emergency Exit

30 Cargo

40 Service

50 Fixed Interior

60 Entrance Stairs

70 Door Warning

80 Landing Gear

53 Fuselage

00 General

10 Main Frame

20 Auxiliary Structure

30 Plates / Skin

40 Attach Fittings

50 Aerodynamic Fairings

54 Nacelles-Pylons

01 General

11 Main Frame

21 Auxiliary Structure

31 Plates-Skin

41 Attach Fittings

51 Fillets-Fairings

55 Stabilizers - Tail Unit

00 General

10 Horizontal Stabilizer-Stabilator

20 Elevator-Elevon

30 Vertical Stabilizer

40 Rudder-Ruddevator

50 Attach Fittings

55 Stabilizers

00 General

2.3 ATA 100 System Codes (cont'd)

10	Horizontal Stabilizer / Stabilator
20	Elevator / Elevon
30	Vertical Stabilizer
40	Rudder / Ruddervator
50	Attach Fittings

56 Windows

00	General
10	Flight Compartment
20	Cabin
30	Door
40	Inspection & Observation

57 Wings

00	General
10	Main Frame
20	Auxiliary Structure
30	Plates-Skin
40	Attach Fittings
50	Flight Surfaces

Propellers and Rotors

60 Indicating Variant for Helicopters

60	Rotor Standard Practices
62	Main Rotor
63	Main Rotor Drive
64	Tail Rotor
65	Tail Rotor Drive
66	Rotor Blade And Tail Pylon Folding
67	Rotor Controls

61 Propellers

00	General
10	Propeller
20	Controlling
30	Braking

40	Indicating

65 Rotors

00	General
10	Main Rotor
20	Anti-torque Rotor Assembly
30	Accessory Driving
40	Controlling
50	Braking

Powerplant

71 Powerplant

00	General
10	Cowling
20	Mounts
30	Fireseals & Shrouds
40	Attach Fittings
50	Electrical Harness
60	Engine Air Intakes
70	Engine Drains

72 Engine Turbine - Turboprop

00	General
10	Reduction Gear & Shaft Section
20	Air Inlet Section
30	Compressor Section
40	Combustion Section
50	Turbine Section
60	Accessory Drives
70	By-pass Section

72 Engine - Reciprocating

00	General
10	Front Section
20	Power Section
30	Cylinder Section
40	Supercharger Section
50	Lubrication

73 Engine Fuel & Control

- 00 General
- 10 Distribution
- 20 Controlling-Governing
- 30 Indicating

74 Ignition

- 00 General
- 10 Electrical Power Supply
- 20 Distribution
- 30 Switching

75 Bleed Air

- 00 General
- 10 Engine Anti-icing
- 20 Engine Cooling
- 30 Compressor Control
- 40 Indicating

76 Engine Controls

- 00 General
- 10 Power Control
- 20 Emergency Shutdown

77 Engine Indicating

- 00 General
- 10 Power
- 20 Temperature
- 30 Analyzers

78 Engine Exhaust

- 00 General
- 10 Collector-Nozzle
- 20 Noise Suppressor
- 30 Thrust Reverser
- 40 Supplemental Air

79 Engine Oil

- 00 General
- 10 Storage (dry sump)
- 20 Distribution
- 30 Indicating

80 Starting

- 00 General
- 10 Cranking

81 Turbines (Reciprocating Engines)

- 00 General
- 10 Power Recovery
- 20 Turbo-supercharger

82 Water Injection

- 00 General
- 10 Storage
- 20 Distribution
- 30 Dumping & Purging
- 40 Indicating

83 Remote Gear Boxes (Engine Driven)

- 00 General
- 10 Drive Shaft Section
- 20 Gearbox Section

2.4 Nationality Markings

(Alphabetical by Country)

Country	Code
Afghanistan	YA
Algeria	7T
Angola	D2
Antigua & Barbuda	V2
Argentina	LQ
Argentina	LV
Armenia	EK
Aruba	P4
Australia	VH
Austria	OE
Azerbaijan	4K
Bahamas	C6
Bahrain	A9C
Bangladesh	S2
Barbados	8P
Belarus	EW
Belgium	OO
Belize	V3
Benin	TY
Bhutan	A5
Bolivia	CP
Bosnia/ Herzegovina	T9
Botswana	A2
Brazil	PP
Brazil	PR
Brazil	PT
Brazil	PU
Brunei Darussalam	V8
Bulgaria	LZ
Burkina Faso	XT
Burundi	9U
Cambodia	XU
Cameroon	TJ
Canada	C
Canada	CF
Cape Verde	D4
Central African Republic	TL
Chad	TT
Chile	CC
China	B
Columbia	HK
Comoros	D6
Congo	TN
Cook Islands	E5
Costa Rica	TI
Côte d'Ivoire	TU
Croatia	9A
Cuba	CU
Cyprus	5B
Czech Republic	OK
Democratic People's Republic of Korea	P
Democratic Republic of the Congo	9Q
Denmark	OY
Djibouti	J2
Dominica	J7
Dominican Republic	HI
Ecuador	HC
Egypt	SU
El Salvador	YS
Equatorial Guinea	3C
Eritrea	E3
Estonia	ES
Ethiopia	ET
Fiji	DQ
Finland	OH
France	F
Gabon	TR
Gambia	C5
Georgia	4L
Germany	D
Ghana	9G
Greece	SX
Grenada	J3
Guatemala	TG
Guinea	3X
Guinea Bissau	J5
Guyana	8R
Haiti	HH
Honduras	HR
Hungary	HA
Iceland	TF
India	VT
Indonesia	PK
Iran, Islamic Republic of	EP
Iraq	YI
Ireland	EI
Ireland	EJ
Israel	4X
Italy	I
Jamaica	6Y
Japan	JA
Jordan	JY
Kazakhstan	UP
Kenya	5Y
Kuwait	9K
Kyrgyzstan	EX
Laos	RDPL
Latvia	YL

Country	Code	Country	Code	Country	Code
Lebanon	OD	Nepal	9N	Senegal	6V
Lesotho	7P	Netherlands	PH	Senegal	6W
Liberia	A8	Netherlands Antilles	PI	Serbia	YU
Libya Arab Jamahiriya	5A	New Zealand	ZK	Seychelles	S7
Liechtenstein (plus national emblem)	HB	New Zealand	ZL	Sierra Leone	9L
		New Zealand	ZM	Singapore	9V
Lithuania	LY	Nicaragua	YN	Slovakia	OM
Luxembourg	LX	Niger	5U	Slovenia	S5
Macedonia, The Former Yugoslav Republic of	Z3	Nigeria	5N	Solomon Islands	H4
		Norway	LN	Somalia	6O
		Oman	A40	South Africa	ZS
Madagascar	5R	Pakistan	AP	South Africa	ZT
Malawi	7QY	Palau	T8	South Africa	ZU
Malaysia	9M	Panama	HP	Spain	EC
Maldives	8Q	Papua New Guinea	P2	Sri Lanka	4R
Mali	TZ	Paraguay	ZP	St. Kitts & Nevis	V4
Malta	9H	Peru	OB	St. Lucia	J6
Marshall Islands	V7	Philippines	RP	St. Vincent and the Grenadines	J8
Mauritania	5T	Poland	SP		
Mauritius	3B	Portugal	CR	Sudan	ST
Mexico	XA	Portugal	CS	Surinam	PZ
Mexico	XB	Qatar	A7	Swaziland	3D
Mexico	XC	Republic of Korea (South Korea)	HL	Sweden	SE
Micronesia, Federated States of	V6			Switzerland (plus national emblem)	HB
Monaco	3A	Republic of Moldova	ER	Syrian Arab Republic	YK
Mongolia	JU	Romania	YR	Tajikistan	EY
Montenegro	4O	Russian Federation	RA	Tanzania, United Republic of	5H
Morocco	CN				
Mozambique	C9	Rwanda	9XE	Thailand	HS
Myanmar	XY	Samoa	5W	Togo	5V
Myanmar	XZ	San Marino	T7	Tonga	A3
Namibia	V5	Sao Tome & Principe	S9	Trinidad & Tobago	9Y
Nauru	C2	Saudi Arabia	HZ	Tunisia	TS

Nationality Markings (cont'd)

Country	Code
Turkey	TC
Turkmenistan	EZ
Uganda	5X
Ukraine	UR
United Arab Emirates	A6
United Kingdom	G
United Kingdom Colonies & Protectorates	VP
United Kingdom Colonies & Protectorates	VQ
United Kingdom Colonies & Protectorates	VR
United States of America	N
Uruguay	CX
Uzbekistan	UK
Vanuatu	YJ
Venezuela	YV
Vietnam	XV
Yemen	7O
Zambia	9J
Zimbabwe	Z

(Alphabetical by Code)

Code	Country
3A	Monaco
3B	Mauritius
3C	Equatorial Guinea
3D	Swaziland
3X	Guinea
4K	Azerbaijan
4L	Georgia
4O	Montenegro
4R	Sri Lanka
4X	Israel
5A	Libya Arab Jamahiriya
5B	Cyprus
5H	Tanzania, United Republic of
5N	Nigeria
5R	Madagascar
5T	Mauritania
5U	Niger
5V	Togo
5W	Samoa
5X	Uganda
5Y	Kenya
6O	Somalia
6V	Senegal
6W	Senegal
6Y	Jamaica
7O	Yemen
7P	Lesotho
7QY	Malawi
7T	Algeria
8P	Barbados
8Q	Maldives
8R	Guyana

Code	Country
9A	Croatia
9G	Ghana
9H	Malta
9J	Zambia
9K	Kuwait
9L	Sierra Leone
9M	Malaysia
9N	Nepal
9Q	Democratic Republic of the Congo
9U	Burundi
9V	Singapore
9XE	Rwanda
9Y	Trinidad & Tobago
A2	Botswana
A3	Tonga
A4O	Oman
A5	Bhutan
A6	United Arab Emirates
A7	Qatar
A8	Liberia
A9C	Bahrain
AP	Pakistan
B	China
C	Canada
C2	Nauru
C5	Gambia
C6	Bahamas
C9	Mozambique
CC	Chile
CF	Canada
CN	Morocco
CP	Bolivia
CR	Portugal

Code	Country
CS	Portugal
CU	Cuba
CX	Uruguay
D	Germany
D2	Angola
D4	Cape Verde
D6	Comoros
DQ	Fiji
E3	Eritrea
E5	Cook Islands
EC	Spain
EI	Ireland
EJ	Ireland
EK	Armenia
EP	Iran, Islamic Republic of
ER	Republic of Moldova
ES	Estonia
ET	Ethiopia
EW	Belarus
EX	Kyrgyzstan
EY	Tajikistan
EZ	Turkmenistan
F	France
G	United Kingdom
H4	Solomon Islands
HA	Hungary
HB	Liechtenstein (plus national emblem)
HB	Switzerland (plus national emblem)
HC	Ecuador
HH	Haiti

Code	Country
HI	Dominican Republic
HK	Columbia
HL	Republic of Korea
HP	Panama
HR	Honduras
HS	Thailand
HZ	Saudi Arabia
I	Italy
J2	Djibouti
J3	Grenada
J5	Guinea Bissau
J6	St. Lucia
J7	Dominica
J8	St. Vincent and the Grenadines
JA	Japan
JU	Mongolia
JY	Jordan
LN	Norway
LQ	Argentina
LV	Argentina
LX	Luxembourg
LY	Lithuania
LZ	Bulgaria
N	United States of America
OB	Peru
OD	Lebanon
OE	Austria
OH	Finland
OK	Czech Republic
OM	Slovakia
OO	Belgium
OY	Denmark

Code	Country
P	Democratic People's Republic of Korea
P2	Papua New Guinea
P4	Aruba
PH	Netherlands
PI	Netherlands Antilles
PK	Indonesia
PP	Brazil
PT	Brazil
PZ	Surinam
RA	Russian Federation
RDPL	Laos
RP	Philippines
S2	Bangladesh
S5	Slovenia
S7	Seychelles
S9	Sao Tome & Principe
SE	Sweden
SP	Poland
ST	Sudan
SU	Egypt
SX	Greece
T7	San Marino
T8	Palau
T9	Bosnia/ Herzegovina
TC	Turkey
TF	Iceland
TG	Guatemala
TI	Costa Rica
TJ	Cameroon
TL	Central African Republic

2.4 Nationality Markings (cont'd)

Code	Country	Code	Country	Code	Country
TN	Congo	VP	United Kingdom Colonies & Protectorates	YK	Syrian Arab Republic
TR	Gabon			YL	Latvia
TS	Tunisia	VQ	United Kingdom Colonies & Protectorates	YN	Nicaragua
TT	Chad			YR	Romania
TU	Côte d'Ivoire			YS	El Salvador
TY	Benin	VR	United Kingdom Colonies & Protectorates	YU	Senegal
TZ	Mali			YV	Venezuela
UK	Uzbekistan			Z	Zimbabwe
UP	Kazakhstan	VT	India	Z3	Macedonia
UR	Ukraine	XA	Mexico	ZK	New Zealand
V2	Antigua & Barbuda	XB	Mexico	ZL	New Zealand
V3	Belize	XC	Mexico	ZM	New Zealand
V4	St. Kitts & Nevis	XT	Burkina Faso	ZP	Paraguay
V5	Namibia	XU	Cambodia	ZS	South Africa
V6	Micronesia	XV	Vietnam	ZT	South Africa
V7	Marshall Islands	XY	Myanmar	ZU	South Africa
V8	Brunei Darussalam	XZ	Myanmar		
VH	Australia	YA	Afghanistan		
		YI	Iraq		
		YJ	Vanuatu		

2.5 Phonetic Alphabet

A	Alpha	J	Juliet	S	Sierra
B	Bravo	K	Kilo	T	Tango
C	Charlie	L	Lima	U	Uniform
D	Delta	M	Mike	V	Victor
E	Echo	N	November	W	Whiskey
F	Foxtrot	O	Oscar	X	X Ray
G	Golf	P	Papa	Y	Yankee
H	Hotel	Q	Quebec	Z	Zulu
I	India	R	Romeo		

Key:

Atomic number	2
Symbol	He
Name	Helium
Average atomic mass	4.002602

Periodic Table

Period	Group 1	Group 2	Group 3	Group 4	Group 5	Group 6	Group 7	Group 8	Group 9	Group 10	Group 11	Group 12	Group 13	Group 14	Group 15	Group 16	Group 17	Group 18
1	1 H Hydrogen 1.008																	2 He Helium 4.003
2	3 Li Lithium 6.941	4 Be Beryllium 9.012											5 B Boron 10.81	6 C Carbon 12.01	7 N Nitrogen 14.01	8 O Oxygen 16.00	9 F Fluorine 19.00	10 Ne Neon 20.18
3	11 Na Sodium 22.99	12 Mg Magnesium 24.31											13 Al Aluminum 26.98	14 Si Silicon 28.09	15 P Phosphorus 30.97	16 S Sulfur 32.07	17 Cl Chlorine 35.45	18 Ar Argon 39.95
4	19 K Potassium 39.10	20 Ca Calcium 40.08	21 Sc Scandium 44.96	22 Ti Titanium 47.87	23 V Vanadium 50.94	24 Cr Chromium 52.00	25 Mn Manganese 54.94	26 Fe Iron 55.85	27 Co Cobalt 58.93	28 Ni Nickel 58.69	29 Cu Copper 63.55	30 Zn Zinc 65.38	31 Ga Gallium 69.72	32 Ge Germanium 72.64	33 As Arsenic 74.92	34 Se Selenium 78.96	35 Br Bromine 79.90	36 Kr Krypton 83.80
5	37 Rb Rubidium 85.47	38 Sr Strontium 87.61	39 Y Yttrium 88.91	40 Zr Zirconium 91.22	41 Nb Niobium 92.91	42 Mo Molybdenum 95.96	43 Tc Technetium (98)	44 Ru Ruthenium 101.1	45 Rh Rhodium 102.9	46 Pd Palladium 106.4	47 Ag Silver 107.9	48 Cd Cadmium 112.4	49 In Indium 114.8	50 Sn Tin 118.7	51 Sb Antimony 121.8	52 Te Tellurium 127.6	53 I Iodine 126.9	54 Xe Xenon 131.3
6	55 Cs Cesium 132.9	56 Ba Barium 137.3	57 La Lanthanum 138.9	72 Hf Hafnium 178.5	73 Ta Tantalum 180.9	74 W Tungsten 183.9	75 Re Rhenium 186.2	76 Os Osmium 190.2	77 Ir Iridium 192.2	78 Pt Platinum 195.1	79 Au Gold 197.0	80 Hg Mercury 200.6	81 Tl Thallium 204.4	82 Pb Lead 207.2	83 Bi Bismuth 209.0	84 Po Polonium (209)	85 At Astatine (210)	86 Rn Radon (222)
7	87 Fr Francium (223)	88 Ra Radium (226)	89 Ac Actinium (227)	104 Rf Rutherfordium (261)	105 Db Dubnium (262)	106 Sg Seaborgium (263)	107 Bh Bohrium (264)	108 Hs Hassium (265)†	109 Mt Meitnerium (268)†	110 Ds Darmstadtium (281)†	111 Rg Roentgenium (280)†	112 Cn Copernicum (285)†	113 Uut* Ununtrium (284)†	114 Uuq* Ununquadium (289)†	115 Uup* Ununpentium (288)†	116 Uuh* Ununhexium (293)†	117 Uus* Ununseptium (294)†	118 Uuo* Ununoctium (294)†

Lanthanide Series

58 Ce Cerium 140.1	59 Pr Praseodymium 140.9	60 Nd Neodymium 144.2	61 Pm Promethium (145)	62 Sm Samarium 150.4	63 Eu Europium 152.0	64 Gd Gadolinium 157.3	65 Tb Terbium 158.9	66 Dy Dysprosium 162.5	67 Ho Holmium 164.9	68 Er Erbium 167.3	69 Tm Thulium 168.9	70 Yb Ytterbium 173.1	71 Lu Lutetium 175.0

Actinide Series

90 Th Thorium 232.0	91 Pa Protactinium 231.0	92 U Uranium 238.0	93 Np Neptunium (237)	94 Pu Plutonium (244)	95 Am Americium (243)	96 Cm Curium (247)	97 Bk Berkelium (247)	98 Cf Californium (251)	99 Es Einsteinium (252)	100 Fm Fermium (257)	101 Md Mendelevium (258)	102 No Nobelium (259)	103 Lr Lawrencium (262)

Categories indicated on the table: Noble Gases, Halogens, Nonmetals, Semiconductors, Light Metals, Transition Metals, Rare Earth Elements.

The atomic masses listed in this table reflect the precision of current measurements. (Values listed in parentheses are those of the element's most stable or most common isotope.)

† Estimated from currently available IUPAC data.

*The systematic names and symbols for elements greater than 112 will be used until the approval of trivial names by IUPAC.

2.7 Density of Solids and Liquids

Material	Specific Gravity (lbs/cu.in.)	Density (lbs/cu.ft.)	Material	Specific Gravity (lbs/cu.in.)	Density (lbs/cu.ft.)
Gas/Vapor			Glue, casein	0.56	35
Ammonia	0.00	0.048	Glycerine	1.26	63
Carbon Dioxide	0.00	0.1234	Iron, cost	7.21	450
Helium	0.138	0.01054	Iron, wrought	7.71	485
Hydrogen	0.0695	0.00531	Lead	11.35	708
Methane	0.555	0.0424	Leather	0.95	59
Methyl Chloride	1.785	0.1356	Magnesium	1.75	109
Nitrogen	0.00	0.0784	Mercury	13.61	849
Oxygen	0.00	0.0892	Molybdenum	10.19	636
Solids			Nickel	8.67	541
Aluminum	2.64	165.0	Pine, white	0.42	26
Asbestos	2.45	153.0	Platinum	21.51	1,342
Bakelite	1.36	85.0	Tin	7.36	459
Brass, sheet	8.5	534	Tungsten	19.62	1,224
Bronze, Aluminum	7.7	498	Vanadium	5.50	343
Cadmium	8.65	540	Zinc	7.65	440
Chromium	7.19	428	**Liquids**		
Copper	8.69	542	Alcohol	0.789	49.0
Cork	0.24	15	Water, fresh	1.00	62.4
Glass, shatterproof	2.58	161	Water, salt	1.03	64.08
			Oil	0.88	55

2.8 Estimating Quantity of Liquid in a Drum

55 Gallon Drum Upright

Depth (inches)	Gallons (approx.)	Depth (inches)	Gallons (approx.)	Depth (inches)	Gallons (approx.)
1	2.0	12	21.0	23	40.0
2	3.5	13	22.5	24	41.5
3	5.0	14	24.5	25	43.5
4	7.0	15	26.0	26	45.0
5	8.5	16	27.5	27	47.0
6	10.5	17	29.5	28	48.5
7	12.0	18	31.5	29	50.0
8	14.0	19	33.0	30	52.0
9	15.5	20	34.5	31	54.0
10	17.5	21	36.5		
11	19.0	22	38.0		

55 Gallon Drum on Side

Depth (inches)	Gallons (approx.)	Depth (inches)	Gallons (approx.)	Depth (inches)	Gallons (approx.)
1	0.8	8	18.5	15	41.5
2	2.5	9	22.0	16	44.5
3	4.5	10	25.0	17	47.5
4	7.0	11	28.5	18	50.0
5	9.5	12	32.0	19	52.5
6	12.5	13	35.0	20	55.0
7	15.5	14	38.5		

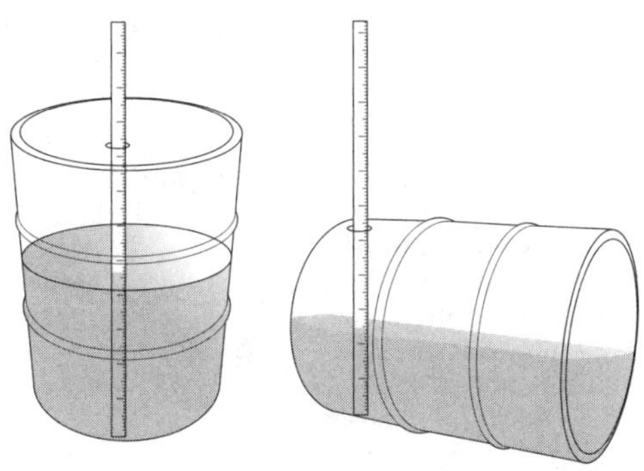

2.9 Cylinder Identification Color Code

Color	Indication
Engine Gray or Unpainted	Standard Steel Cylinder Barrels
Orange Stripe	Chrome Plated Cylinder Barrels
Blue Stripe	Nitride Hardened Cylinder Barrels
*Green Stripe	Steel Cylinder 0.010 Oversize
*Yellow Stripe	Steel Cylinder 0.020 Oversize
White	Rebarreled Cylinder
Platinum	CermiNil® Cylinder Barrels
Two Orange Bands	CermiChrome® Cylinder Barrels

NOTE: Found between push rods on head, or band around base of barrel
*Color code applicable only to engines overhauled in the field.

2.10 Spark Plug Identification Color Code

Color	Indication
Engine Gray or Unpainted	Short Reach Spark Plugs
Yellow	Long Reach Spark Plugs

NOTE: Located on fin area between spark plug and rocker box.

2.11 In-service Spark Plug Identification

Massive Electrode Spark Plug

Fine Wire Spark Plug

Normal  Indicates short service time and correct heat range. Clean, regap and test before reinstalling.

Normal 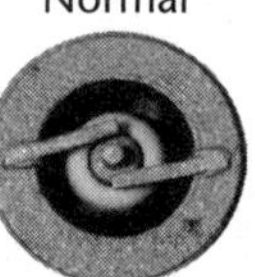 Indicates short service time and correct heat range. Clean, regap and test before reinstalling.

Worn Out Normal 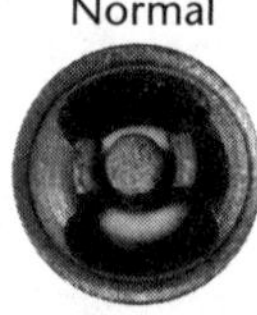 Indicates normal service life, electrodes show normal erosion, ground electrodes about half original thickness. Install new plugs.

Worn Out Normal 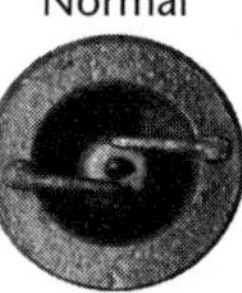 Indicates normal service life, electrodes show normal erosion, ground electrodes about half original thickness. Install new plugs.

Massive Electrode Spark Plug

Fine Wire Spark Plug

Worn Out Severe 	Extensive necking of ground electrodes indicate abnormal engine power operation. Check fuel metering. Install new plugs.	**Worn Out Severe** 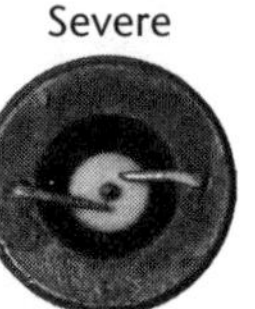	Excessively eroded center and ground electrodes indicate abnormal engine power operation. Check fuel metering. Install new plugs.
Lead Fouled 	Hard, cinderlike deposits from poor fuel vaporization, high T.E.L. content in fuel or engine operating too cold. Clean regap, test and reinstall.	**Lead Fouled** 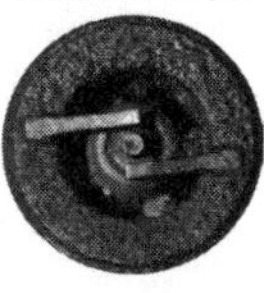	Hard, cinderlike deposits from poor fuel vaporization, high T.E.L. content in fuel or engine operating too cold. Install new plugs.
Carbon Fouled 	Black, sooty deposits from excessive ground idling, idle mixture too rich or plug type too cold. If heat range is correct, clean, regap, test and reinstall.	**Carbon Fouled** 	Black, sooty deposits from excessive ground idling, idle mixture too rich or plug type too cold. If heat range is correct, clean, regap, test and reinstall.
Oil Fouled 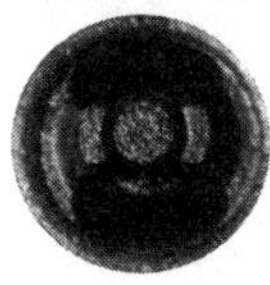	Wet, oily deposits may be caused by broken or worn piston rings, excessive valve guide clearances, leaking impeller seal or engine still in break-in period. Repair engine as required. Clean, regap, test and reinstall plugs.	**Oil Fouled** 	Wet, oily deposits may be caused by broken or worn piston rings, excessive valve guide clearances, leaking impeller seal or engine still in break-in period. Repair engine as required. Clean, regap, test and reinstall plugs.

2.12 Math Symbols

Symbol	Meaning	Symbol	Meaning
π	Pi or 3.14 (approx.)	$>$	Greater than
Δ	Delta (Rate of Change)	$\neq$	Not Equal to
∞	Infinity	$\sqrt{}$	Square Root
$+$	Plus or Positive	$\sqrt[3]{}$	Cube Root
$-$	Minus or Negative	$\equiv$	Identical with
$\pm$	Plus or Minus	$|x|$	Absolute Value
x or $\bullet$	Multiply	$:$	Ratio
$\div$	Divide	$\therefore$	Therefore
$=$	Equals	$\exists$	There Exists
$\approx$	Approximately Equal to	$\perp$	Perpendicular to
$\leq$	Less than or Equal to	$\parallel$	Parallel with
$\geq$	Greater than or Equal to	$\angle$	Angle
$<$	Less than	Δ	Increment

2.13 Mathematical Constants

$$\pi = 3.1416 \qquad\qquad 4\pi = 12.5664$$

$$\pi^2 = 9.8696 \qquad\qquad \frac{\pi}{2} = 1.5708$$

$$\pi^3 = 31.0063$$

$$\frac{1}{\pi} = 0.3183 \qquad\qquad \sqrt{\frac{\pi}{2}} = 1.253$$

$$\frac{1}{\pi^2} = 0.1013 \qquad\qquad \sqrt{2} = 1.4142$$

$$\sqrt{3} = 1.7321$$

$$\sqrt{\pi} = 1.7725$$

$$\frac{1}{\sqrt{\pi}} = 0.5642 \qquad\qquad \frac{1}{\sqrt{2}} = 0.7071$$

$$\frac{1}{2\pi} = 0.1592 \qquad\qquad \frac{1}{\sqrt{3}} = 0.5773$$

$$\left[\frac{1}{2\pi}\right]^2 = 0.0253 \qquad\qquad \log\pi = 0.4971$$

$$2\pi = 6.2832 \qquad\qquad \log\pi^2 = 0.9943$$

$$\log\sqrt{\pi} = 0.2486$$

$$2\pi^2 = 39.4784 \qquad\qquad \log\frac{\pi}{2} = 1.5708$$

Area of a Rectangle
$$A = LW$$

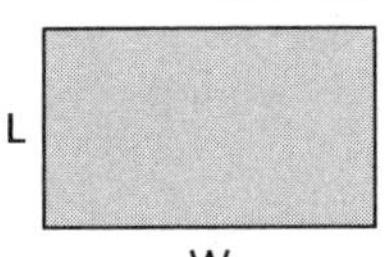

A = Area
L = Length
W = Width

A rectangle is a four sided figure whose opposite sides are of equal length. All angles of the rectangle are 90° and equal 360°.

Area of a Parallelogram
$$A = LW$$

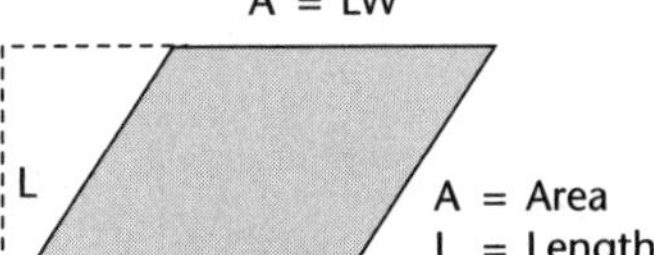

A = Area
L = Length
W = Width

A parallelogram is a rectangle whose angles are not 90°; the opposite sides are of equal length, and are parallel.

Area of a Triangle
$$A = \tfrac{1}{2}HB$$

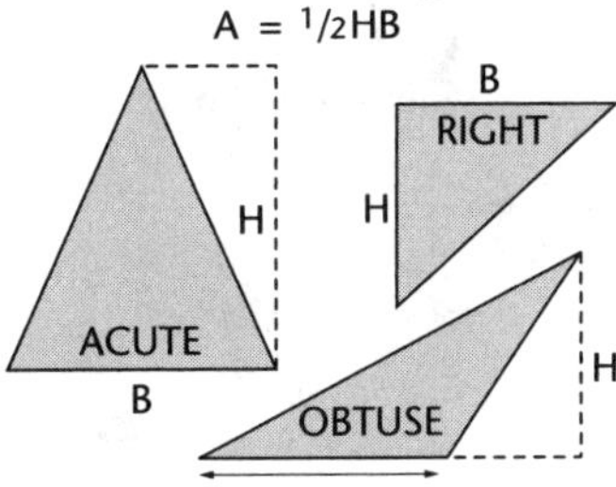

A = Area
H = Triangle Altitude
B = Triangle Base
$\tfrac{1}{2}$ = Given

A triangle is a three sided figure whose angles are all less than 90° and equal 180°.

Area of a Circle
$$A = \pi r^2$$

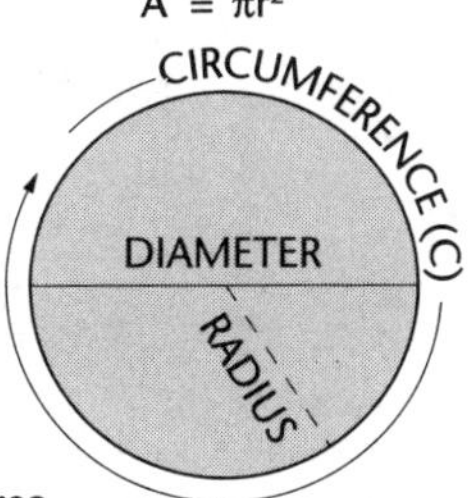

A = Area
π = 3.1416
r = Radius

A circle's boundaries consist of points which are all equidistant from a fixed point in space.

Area of a Square
$$A = S^2$$

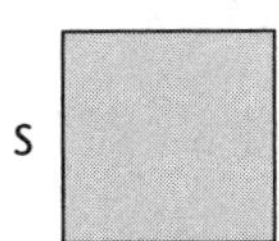

S = Length of a Side

A square is a figure that has four equal side and four right angles. All angles in a square equal 360°.

Area of a Trapezoid
$$A = \tfrac{1}{2}(B_1 + B_2)H$$

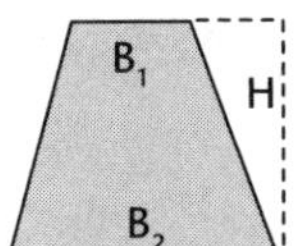

A = Area
B_1 = Parallel Side
B_2 = Parallel Side
H = Height

A trapezoid is a four sided polygon with only two parallel sides. The sum of all corner angles is 360°. Diametrically opposite corner angles are not equal.

2.15 **Computation of Volume**

Volume of a Rectangular Solid
$$V = LWH$$

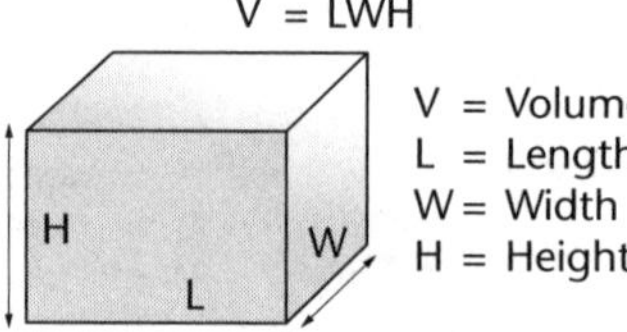

V = Volume
L = Length
W = Width
H = Height

A rectangular solid is a solid bounded entirely by rectangles.

Volume of a Cube
$$V = S^3$$

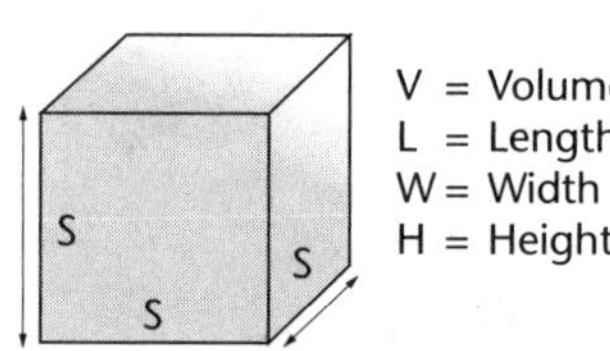

V = Volume
L = Length
W = Width
H = Height

A cube is a solid bounded entirely by rectangles of equal sides and dimensions.

Volume of a Cone
$$V = \pi/3 \times R^2 \times H$$
$$A = \pi R \sqrt{R^2 + H^2}$$

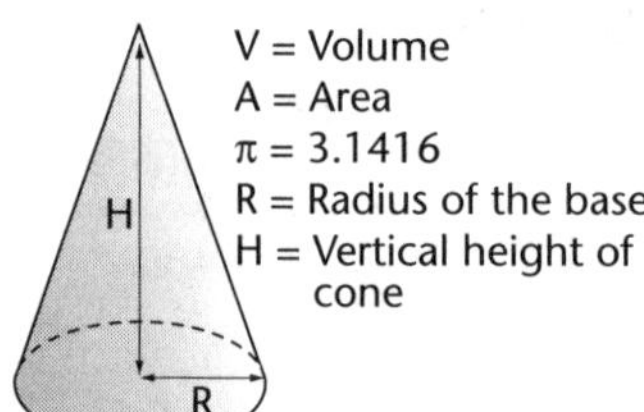

V = Volume
A = Area
π = 3.1416
R = Radius of the base
H = Vertical height of cone

A cone is a solid with a circular base and sides that taper to a point.

Volume of a Cylinder
$$V = \pi r^2 H$$

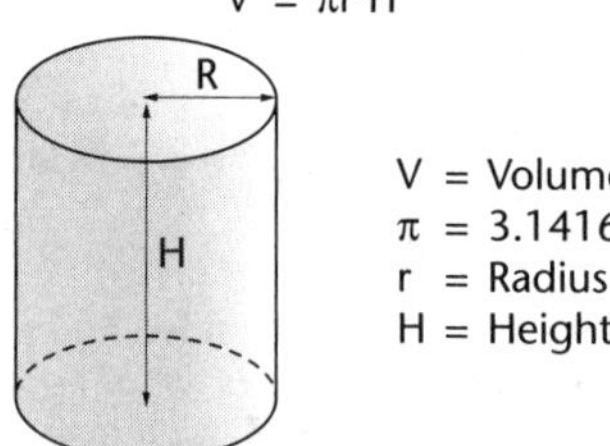

V = Volume
π = 3.1416
r = Radius
H = Height

A cylinder is a solid that has circular ends of equal size that are connected circumferentially by a perpendicular plane.

Volume of a Sphere
$$V = D^3(^1/_6\pi)$$

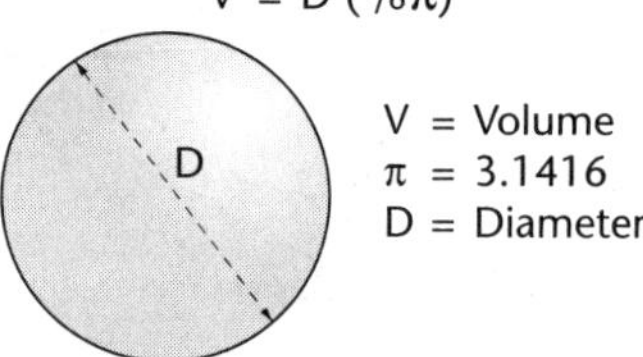

V = Volume
π = 3.1416
D = Diameter

A sphere is a three dimensional solid whose entire surface is located an equal distance from one point.

To Find Circumference:
• Multiply diameter by 3.1416
• Or divide diameter by 0.3183

To Find Diameter:
• Multiply circumference by 0.3183
• Or divide circumference by 3.1416

To Find Radian:
• Multiply circumference by 0.15915
• Or divide circumference by 6.28318

To Find Side of an Inscribed Square:
• Multiply diameter by 0.7071
• Or multiply circumference by 0.2251   Or divide circumference by 4.4428

To Find Side of an Equal Square:
• Multiply diameter by 0.8862
• Or divide diameter by 1.1284
• Or multiply circumference by 0.2821   Or divide circumference by 3.545

Square:
• A side multiplied by 1.4142 equals diameter of its circumscribing circle.
• A side multiplied by 4.443 equals circumference of its circumscribing circle.
• A side multiplied by 1.128 equals diameter of an equal circle.
• A side multiplied by 3.547 equals circumference of an equal circle.

To Find the Area of a Circle:
• Multiply circumference by one-quarter of the diameter.
• Or multiply the square of diameter by 0.7854
• Or multiply the square of circumference by 0.07958
• Or multiply the square of 1/2 diameter by 3.1416

To Find the Surface of a Sphere or Globe:
• Multiply the diameter by the circumference.
• Or multiply the square of diameter by 3.1416
• Or multiply four times the square of radius by 3.1416

2.17 **Right Angle Triangles**

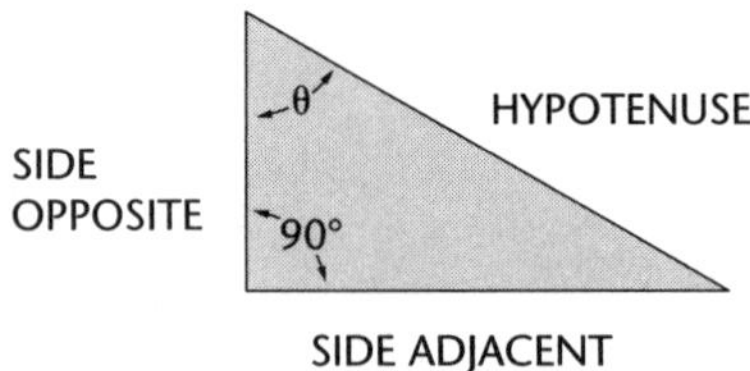

The six basic trigonometric functions, the sine (sin), cosine (cos), tangent (tan), cosecant (csc), secant (sec), and cotangent (cot) are the ratios of the lengths of the three sides of a right triangle.

θ = Acute angle (theta)

$$\text{Sine (sin) } \theta = \frac{\text{side opposite}}{\text{hypotenuse}}$$

$$\text{Cosine (cos) } \theta = \frac{\text{side adjacent}}{\text{hypotenuse}}$$

$$\text{Tangent (tan) } \theta = \frac{\text{side opposite}}{\text{side adjacent}}$$

$$\text{Cosecant (csc) } \theta = \frac{1}{\sin \theta} = \frac{\text{hypotenuse}}{\text{side opposite}}$$

$$\text{Secant (sec) } \theta = \frac{1}{\cos \theta} = \frac{\text{hypotenuse}}{\text{side adjacent}}$$

$$\text{Cotangent (cot) } \theta = \frac{1}{\tan \theta} = \frac{\text{side adjacent}}{\text{side opposite}}$$

2.18 Binary, Hexadecimal, Decimal Equivalents

Binary	Hexidecimal	Decimal
0000	0	0
0001	1	1
0100	2	2
0011	3	3
0100	4	4
0101	5	5
0110	6	6
0111	7	7
1000	8	8
1001	9	9
1010	A	10
1011	B	11
1100	C	12
1101	D	13
1110	E	14
1111	F	15

Binary Numbers							Decimal Numbers
64	32	16	8	4	2	1	
0	0	0	0	0	0	1	1
0	0	0	0	0	1	0	2
0	0	0	0	0	1	1	3
0	0	0	0	1	0	0	4
0	0	0	0	1	0	1	5
0	0	1	1	0	1	1	27
0	1	1	0	0	0	0	48
1	0	1	1	1	0	0	92
1	1	1	0	1	0	1	117

2.19 **Powers of 10**

Power of 10	Expansion	Value
10^6	10 x 10 x 10 x 10 x 10 x 10	1,000,000
10^5	10 x 10 x 10 x 10 x 10	100,000
10^4	10 x 10 x 10 x 10	10,000
10^3	10 x 10 x 10	1,000
10^2	10 x 10	100
10^1	10	10
10^0		1

NOTE: The velocity of light, 30,000,000,000 centimeters per second, simplifies to 3×10^{10} centimeters per second.

$$10^{-1} = \frac{1}{10} \qquad \frac{1}{10} \qquad \frac{1}{10} \qquad = 0.1$$

$$10^{-2} = \frac{1}{10^2} \qquad \frac{1}{10 \times 10} \qquad \frac{1}{100} \qquad = 0.01$$

$$10^{-3} = \frac{1}{10^3} \qquad \frac{1}{10 \times 10 \times 10} \qquad \frac{1}{1,000} \qquad = 0.001$$

$$10^{-4} = \frac{1}{10^4} \qquad \frac{1}{10 \times 10 \times 10 \times 10} \qquad \frac{1}{10,000} \qquad = 0.0001$$

$$10^{-5} = \frac{1}{10^5} \qquad \frac{1}{10 \times 10 \times 10 \times 10 \times 10} \qquad \frac{1}{100,000} \qquad = 0.00001$$

$$10^{-6} = \frac{1}{10^6} \qquad \frac{1}{10 \times 10 \times 10 \times 10 \times 10 \times 10} \qquad \frac{1}{1,000,000} \qquad = 0.000001$$

NOTE: The mass of an electron, 0.000,000,000,000,000,000,000,000,000,911 gram becomes 9.11×10^{-28} gram.

No.	Square	Cube	Square Root	Cube Root
1	1	1	1.0000	1.0000
2	4	8	1.4142	1.2599
3	9	27	1.7321	1.4422
4	16	64	2.0000	1.5874
5	25	125	2.2361	1.7100
6	36	216	2.4495	1.8171
7	49	343	2.6458	1.9129
8	64	512	2.8284	2.0000
9	81	729	3.0000	2.0801
10	100	1,000	3.1623	2.1544
11	121	1,331	3.3166	2.2240
12	144	1,728	3.4641	2.2894
13	169	2,197	3.6056	2.3513
14	196	2,744	3.7417	2.4101
15	225	3375	3.8730	2.4662
16	256	4,096	4.0000	2.5198
17	289	4,913	4.1231	2.5713
18	324	5,832	4.2426	2.6207
19	361	6,859	4.3589	2.6684
20	400	8,000	4.4721	2.7144
30	900	27,000	5.4772	3.1072
35	1,225	42,875	5.9161	3.2711
40	1,600	64,000	6.3246	3.4200
45	2,025	91,125	6.7082	3.5569
50	2,500	125,000	7.0711	3.6840
55	3,025	166,375	7.4162	3.8030
60	3,600	216,000	7.7460	3.9149
65	4,225	274,625	8.0623	4.0207
70	4,900	343,000	8.3666	4.1213
75	5,625	421,875	8.6603	4.2172
80	6,400	512,000	8.9443	4.3089
85	7,225	614,125	9.2195	4.3968
90	8,100	729,000	9.4868	4.4814
95	9,025	857,375	9.7468	4.5629
100	10,000	1,000,000	10.0000	4.6416

2.21 Weight of Steel Bars

Size	Round	Hexagon	Square
1/4	0.167	0.184	0.213
5/16	0.261	0.288	0.332
3/8	0.376	0.414	0.478
7/16	0.511	0.564	0.651
1/2	0.668	0.736	0.850
9/16	0.845	0.932	1.080
5/8	1.040	1.150	1.330
11/16	1.260	1.390	1.610
3/4	1.500	1.660	1.910
7/8	2.040	2.250	2.600
1	2.670	2.940	3.400
1-1/8	3.380	3.730	4.300
1-1/4	4.170	4.600	5.310
1-3/8	5.050	5.570	6.430
1-1/2	6.010	6.630	7.650
1-5/8	7.050	7.780	8.980
1-3/4	8.180	9.020	10.410
1-7/8	9.390	10.350	11.950
2	10.680	11.780	13.600
2-1/2	16.690	18.400	21.250
2-5/8	18.400	20.290	23.430
2-3/4	20.190	22.270	25.710
3	24.030	26.500	30.600
3-1/4	28.210	31.100	35.910
3-1/2	32.710	36.070	41.650
3-3/4	37.550	41.410	47.810
4	42.730	47.110	54.400

NOTE: Weight in pounds of a linear foot of round, hexagon, and square steel bars.
All dimensions are in inches

Gauge Number[1]	Approx. Thickness	Pounds per Sq. Foot
7	0.188	7.500
8	0.172	6.875
9	0.156	6.250
10	0.141	5.625
11	0.125	5.000
12	0.109	4.375
13	0.094	3.750
14	0.078	3.125
15	0.070	2.812
16	0.063	2.500
17	0.056	2.250
18	0.050	2.000
19	0.044	1.750
20	0.038	1.500
21	0.034	1.375
22	0.031	1.250
23	0.028	1.125
24	0.025	1.000
25	0.022	0.875
26	0.019	0.750
27	0.017	0.687
28	0.016	0.625

NOTE: All dimensions are in inches
[1]United States Standard Gauge

2.23 Steel Temperatures as Judged by Color

Degrees (°C)	Degrees (°F)	High Temperatures Judged by Color
400	752	Red heat, visible in the dark
474	885	Red heat, visible in twilight
525	975	Red heat, visible in daylight
581	1,077	Red heat, visible in sunlight
700	1,292	Dark red
800	1,472	Dull cherry-red
900	1,652	Cherry-red
1,000	1,832	Bright cherry-red
1,100	2,012	Orange-red
1,200	2,192	Orange-yellow
1,300	2,372	Yellow-white
1,400	2,552	White welding heat
1,500	2,732	Brilliant white
1,600	2,912	Dazzling white (bluish-white)

2.24 Colors for Steel Tempering

Degrees (°C)	Degrees (°F)	Colors for Tempering
221.1	430	Very pale yellow
226.7	440	Light yellow
232.2	450	Pale straw-yellow
237.8	460	Straw-yellow
243.3	470	Deep straw-yellow
248.9	480	Dark yellow
254.4	490	Yellow-brown
260.0	500	Brown-yellow
265.6	510	Spotted red-brown
271.1	520	Brown-purple
276.7	530	Light purple
282.2	540	Full purple
287.8	550	Dark purple
293.3	560	Full blue
298.9	570	Dark blue

8ths		
$1/8 = 0.125$	$11/32 = 0.34375$	$23/64 = 0.359375$
$1/4 = 0.250$	$13/32 = 0.40625$	$25/64 = 0.390625$
$3/8 = 0.375$	$15/32 = 0.46875$	$27/64 = 0.421875$
$1/2 = 0.500$	$17/32 = 0.53125$	$29/64 = 0.453125$
$5/8 = 0.625$	$19/32 = 0.59375$	$31/64 = 0.484375$
$3/4 = 0.750$	$21/32 = 0.65625$	$33/64 = 0.515625$
$7/8 = 0.875$	$23/32 = 0.71875$	$35/64 = 0.546875$
16ths	$25/32 = 0.78125$	$37/64 = 0.578125$
$1/16 = 0.0625$	$27/32 = 0.84375$	$39/64 = 0.609375$
$3/16 = 0.1875$	$29/32 = 0.90625$	$41/64 = 0.640625$
$5/16 = 0.3125$	$31/32 = 0.96875$	$43/64 = 0.671875$
$7/16 = 0.4375$	**64ths**	$45/64 = 0.703125$
$9/16 = 0.5625$	$1/64 = 0.015625$	$47/64 = 0.734375$
$11/16 = 0.6875$	$3/64 = 0.046875$	$49/64 = 0.765625$
$13/16 = 0.8125$	$5/64 = 0.078125$	$51/64 = 0.796875$
$15/16 = 0.9375$	$7/64 = 0.109375$	$53/64 = 0.828125$
32nds	$9/64 = 0.140625$	$55/64 = 0.859375$
$1/32 = 0.03125$	$11/64 = 0.171875$	$57/64 = 0.890625$
$3/32 = 0.09375$	$13/64 = 0.203125$	$59/64 = 0.921875$
$5/32 = 0.15625$	$15/64 = 0.234375$	$61/64 = 0.953125$
$7/32 = 0.21875$	$17/64 = 0.265625$	$63/64 = 0.984375$
$9/32 = 0.28125$	$19/64 = 0.296875$	
	$21/64 = 0.328125$	

2.26 Metric to English Conversion Table

mm	Inches	mm	Inches	mm	Inches
0.01	0.00039	0.36	0.01417	0.81	0.03189
0.02	0.00079	0.37	0.01457	0.82	0.03228
0.03	0.00118	0.38	0.01496	0.83	0.03268
0.04	0.00157	0.39	0.01535	0.84	0.03307
0.05	0.00197	0.40	0.01575	0.85	0.03346
0.06	0.00236	0.41	0.01614	0.86	0.03386
0.07	0.00276	0.42	0.01654	0.87	0.03425
0.08	0.00315	0.43	0.01693	0.88	0.03465
0.09	0.00354	0.44	0.01732	0.89	0.03504
0.10	0.00394	0.45	0.01772	0.90	0.03543
0.11	0.00433	0.46	0.01811	0.91	0.03583
0.12	0.00472	0.47	0.01850	0.92	0.03622
0.13	0.00512	0.48	0.01890	0.93	0.03661
0.14	0.00551	0.49	0.01929	0.94	0.03701
0.15	0.00591	0.50	0.01969	0.95	0.03740
0.16	0.00630	0.51	0.02008	0.96	0.03780
0.17	0.00669	0.52	0.02047	0.97	0.03819
0.18	0.00709	0.53	0.02087	0.98	0.03858
0.19	0.00748	0.54	0.02126	0.99	0.03898
0.20	0.00787	0.55	0.02165	1.00	0.03937
0.21	0.00827	0.56	0.02205	1.00	0.03937
0.22	0.00866	0.57	0.02244	2.00	0.07874
0.23	0.00906	0.58	0.02283	3.00	0.11811
0.24	0.00945	0.59	0.02323	4.00	0.15748
0.25	0.00984	0.60	0.02362	5.00	0.19685
0.26	0.01024	0.61	0.02402	6.00	0.23622
0.27	0.01063	0.62	0.02441	7.00	0.27559
0.28	0.01102	0.63	0.02480	8.00	0.31496
0.29	0.01142	0.64	0.02520	9.00	0.35433
0.30	0.01181	0.65	0.02559	10.00	0.39370
0.31	0.01220	0.66	0.02598	11.00	0.43307
0.32	0.01260	0.67	0.02638	12.00	0.47244
0.33	0.01299	0.68	0.02677	13.00	0.51181
0.34	0.01339	0.69	0.02117	14.00	0.55118
0.35	0.01378	0.70	0.02756	15.00	0.59055

 # Metric to English Conversion Table (cont'd)

mm	Inches	mm	Inches	mm	Inches
16.00	0.62992	46.00	1.81102	76.00	2.99213
17.00	0.66929	47.00	1.85039	77.00	3.03150
18.00	0.70866	48.00	1.88976	78.00	3.07087
19.00	0.74803	49.00	1.92913	79.00	3.11024
20.00	0.78740	50.00	1.96850	80.00	3.14961
21.00	0.82677	51.00	2.00787	81.00	3.18898
22.00	0.86614	52.00	2.04724	82.00	3.22835
23.00	0.90551	53.00	2.08661	83.00	3.26772
24.00	0.94488	54.00	2.12598	84.00	3.30709
25.00	0.98425	55.00	2.16535	85.00	3.34646
26.00	1.02362	56.00	2.20472	86.00	3.38583
27.00	1.06299	57.00	2.24409	87.00	3.42520
28.00	1.10236	58.00	2.28346	88.00	3.46457
29.00	1.14173	59.00	2.32283	89.00	3.50394
30.00	1.18110	60.00	2.36220	90.00	3.54331
31.00	1.22047	61.00	2.40157	91.00	3.58268
32.00	1.25984	62.00	2.44094	92.00	3.62205
33.00	1.29921	63.00	2.48031	93.00	3.66142
34.00	1.33858	64.00	2.51969	94.00	3.70079
35.00	1.37795	65.00	2.55906	95.00	3.74016
36.00	1.41732	66.00	2.59843	96.00	3.77953
37.00	1.45669	67.00	2.63780	97.00	3.81890
38.00	1.49606	68.00	2.67717	98.00	3.85827
39.00	1.53543	69.00	2.71654	99.00	3.89764
40.00	1.57480	70.00	2.75591	100.00	3.93701
41.00	1.61417	71.00	2.79528		
42.00	1.65354	72.00	2.83465		
43.00	1.69291	73.00	2.87402		
44.00	1.73228	74.00	2.91339		
45.00	1.77165	75.00	2.95276		

2.27 English to Metric Conversion Table

Inches	mm	Inches	mm	Inches	mm
0.001	0.0254	0.280	7.1120	0.640	16.2560
0.002	0.0508	0.290	7.3660	0.650	16.5100
0.003	0.0762	0.300	7.6200	0.660	16.7640
0.004	0.1016	0.310	7.8740	0.670	17.0180
0.005	0.1270	0.320	8.1280	0.680	17.2720
0.006	0.1524	0.330	8.3820	0.690	17.5260
0.007	0.1778	0.340	8.6360	0.700	17.7800
0.008	0.2032	0.350	8.8900	0.710	18.0340
0.009	0.2286	0.360	9.1440	0.720	18.2880
0.010	0.2540	0.370	9.3980	0.730	18.5420
0.020	0.5080	0.380	9.6520	0.740	18.7960
0.030	0.7620	0.390	9.9060	0.750	19.0500
0.040	1.0160	0.400	10.1600	0.760	19.3040
0.050	1.2700	0.410	10.4140	0.770	19.5580
0.060	1.5240	0.420	10.6680	0.780	19.8120
0.070	1.7780	0.430	10.9220	0.790	20.0660
0.080	2.0320	0.440	11.1760	0.800	20.3200
0.090	2.2860	0.450	11.4300	0.810	20.5740
0.100	2.5400	0.460	11.6840	0.820	20.8280
0.110	2.7940	0.470	11.9380	0.830	21.0820
0.120	3.0480	0.480	12.1920	0.840	21.3360
0.130	3.3020	0.490	12.4400	0.850	21.5900
0.140	3.5560	0.500	12.7000	0.860	21.8440
0.150	3.8100	0.510	12.9540	0.870	22.0980
0.160	4.0640	0.520	13.2080	0.880	22.3520
0.170	4.3180	0.530	13.4620	0.890	22.6060
0.180	4.5720	0.540	13.7160	0.900	22.8600
0.190	4.8260	0.550	13.9700	0.910	23.1140
0.200	5.0800	0.560	14.2240	0.920	23.3680
0.210	5.3340	0.570	14.4780	0.930	23.6220
0.220	5.5880	0.580	14.7320	0.940	23.8760
0.230	5.8420	0.590	14.9860	0.950	24.1300
0.240	6.0960	0.600	15.2400	0.960	24.3840
0.250	6.3500	0.610	15.4940	0.970	24.6380
0.260	6.6040	0.620	15.7480	0.980	24.8920
0.270	6.8580	0.630	16.0020	0.990	25.1460
				1.000	25.4000

2.27 English to Metric Conversion Table (cont'd)

Inches	Inches	mm	Inches	Inches	mm
1/64	0.0156	0.3969	9/16	0.5625	14.2875
1/32	0.0312	0.7938	37/64	0.5781	14.6844
3/64	0.0469	1.1906	19/32	0.5938	15.0812
1/16	0.0625	1.5875	39/64	0.6094	15.4781
5/64	0.0781	1.9844	5/8	0.6250	15.8750
3/32	0.0938	2.3812	41/64	0.6406	16.2719
7/64	0.1094	2.7781	21/32	0.6562	16.6688
1/8	0.1250	3.1750	43/64	0.6719	17.0656
9/64	0.1406	3.5719	11/16	0.6875	17.4625
5/32	0.1562	3.9688	45/64	0.7031	17.8594
11/64	0.1719	4.3656	23/32	0.7188	18.2562
3/16	0.1875	4.7625	47/64	0.7344	18.6531
13/64	0.2031	5.1594	3/4	0.7500	19.0500
7/32	0.2188	5.5562	49/64	0.7656	19.4469
15/64	0.2344	5.9531	25/32	0.7812	19.8438
1/4	0.2500	6.3500	51/64	0.7969	20.2406
17/64	0.2656	6.7469	13/16	0.8125	20.6375
9/32	0.2812	7.1438	53/64	0.8281	21.0344
19/64	0.2969	7.5406	27/32	0.8438	21.4312
5/16	0.3125	7.9375	55/64	0.8594	21.8281
21/64	0.3281	8.3344	7/8	0.8750	22.2250
11/32	0.3438	8.7312	57/64	0.8906	22.6219
23/64	0.3594	9.1281	29/32	0.9062	23.0188
3/8	0.3750	9.5250	59/64	0.9219	23.4156
25/64	0.3906	9.9219	15/16	0.9375	23.8125
13/32	0.4062	10.3188	61/64	0.9531	24.2094
27/64	0.4219	10.7156	31/32	0.9688	24.6062
7/16	0.4375	11.1125	63/64	0.9844	25.0031
29/64	0.4531	11.5094	1	1.0000	25.4000
15/32	0.4688	11.9062			
31/64	0.4844	12.3031			
1/2	0.5000	12.7000			
33/64	0.5156	13.0969			
17/32	0.5312	13.4938			
35/64	0.5469	13.8906			

2.28 Torque Values for Nut and Bolt Combinations

Fine Thread Series: Steel

Nut-Bolt Size	Standard AN & MS Steel Bolts in Tension				High Strength MS & NAS Steel Bolts in Tension			
	Nuts Steel Tension Torque limits (in-lbs.)		Nuts Steel Shear Torque limits (in-lbs.)		Nuts Steel Tension Torque limits (in-lbs.)		Nuts Steel Shear Torque limits (in-lbs.)	
	Min.	Max.	Min.	Max.	Min.	Max.	Min.	Max.
8-36	12	15	7	9	–	–	–	–
10-32	20	25	12	15	25	30	15	20
1/4-28	50	70	30	40	80	100	50	60
5/16-24	100	140	60	85	120	145	70	90
3/8-24	160	190	95	110	200	250	120	150
7/16-20	450	500	270	300	520	630	300	400
1/2-20	480	690	290	410	770	950	450	550
9/16-18	800	1,000	480	600	1,100	1,300	650	800
5/8-18	1,100	1,300	660	780	1,250	1,550	750	950
3/4-16	2,300	2,500	1,300	1,500	2,650	3,200	1,600	1,900
7/8-14	2,500	3,000	1,500	1,800	3,550	4,350	2,100	2,600
1-14	3,700	4,500	2,200	3,300	4,500	5,500	2,700	3,300
1-1/8-12	5,000	7,000	3,000	4,200	6,000	7,300	3,600	4,400
1-1/4-12	9,000	11,000	5,400	6,600	11,000	13,400	6,600	8,000

Fine Thread Series: Aluminum

Nut-Bolt Size	Aluminum Bolts in Tension			
	Nuts Shear Torque limits (in-lbs.)		Nuts Tension Torque limits (in-lbs.)	
	Min.	Max.	Min.	Max.
8-36	5	10	3	6
10-32	10	15	5	10
1/4-28	30	45	15	30
5/16-24	40	65	25	40
3/8-24	75	110	45	70
7/16-20	180	280	110	170
1/2-20	280	410	160	260

2.28 Torque Values for Nut and Bolt Combinations (cont'd)

Coarse Thread Series: Steel

Standard AN & MS Steel Bolts in Tension

Nut-Bolt Size	Nuts Tension Torque Limits (in-lbs.)		Nuts Shear Torque Limits (in-lbs.)	
	Min.	Max.	Min.	Max.
8-32	12	15	7	9
10-24	20	25	12	15
1/4-20	40	50	25	30
5/16-18	80	90	48	55
3/8-16	160	185	95	110
7/16-14	235	255	140	155
1/2-13	400	480	240	290
9/16-12	500	700	300	420
5/8-11	700	900	420	540
3/4-10	1,150	1,600	700	950
7/8-9	2,200	3,000	1,300	1,800
1-8	3,700	5,000	2,200	3,000
1-1/8-8	5,500	6,500	3,300	4,000
1-1/4-8	6,500	8,000	4,000	5,000

2.29 Ground Handling: Fixed Wing Aircraft

START ENGINE
ENGAGE ROTOR
STOP ROTOR
STOP
MOVE BACK
MOVE FORWARD
SWING TAIL TO RIGHT
TAKE OFF
LANDING DIRECTION
MOVE RIGHT
MOVE LEFT
GO UP
GO DOWN
SWING TAIL TO LEFT

2.31 Hydraulic Relationships

In any type of hydraulic system, a relationship exists between pressure, area, and volume.

Any of the values are found when only two of the others are known.

Where:

F = Force in pounds

P= Pressure in pounds per square inch

A= Area in square inches

Force
The amount of force produced by an actuator is found by multiplying the pressure in p.s.i. by the area of the piston in square inches.

F = P x A

Area
To determine the area of the piston, divide the force by the pressure.

A = F/P

Pressure
To find the pressure in an actuator with a piston of a given area and a force in pounds, divide the force by the area.

P = F/A

There is also a relationship between the volume of fluid moved by a piston in a cylinder, the distance that the piston moves and the area of the piston.

Where:

V = Volume in cubic inches

A = Area in square inches

D = Distance the piston moves in inches

Volume
A piston will move a certain volume of fluid when a piston of a given size is moved a certain distance.

$$V = A \times D$$

Area
The area of the piston needed to move a given quantity of fluid is found by dividing the volume of fluid by the distance the piston moves.

$$A = V/D$$

Distance
The distance a piston must move to displace a given volume of fluid is found by dividing the volume by the area of the piston.

$$D = V/A$$

Pascal's Law or Principle
The French mathematician Blaise Pascal developed the law that is fundamental to hydraulics.

It states that when there is an increase in pressure at any point in a confined fluid, there is an equal increase at every other point in the container.

Important applications of Pascal's law are seen in hydraulic jacks, hydraulic brakes and forklifts.

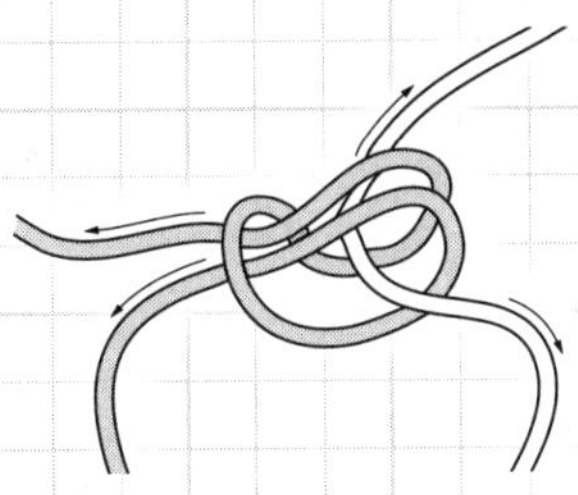

3
Aircraft Fabric

3.1 **Starting Stitch for Rib Lacing**

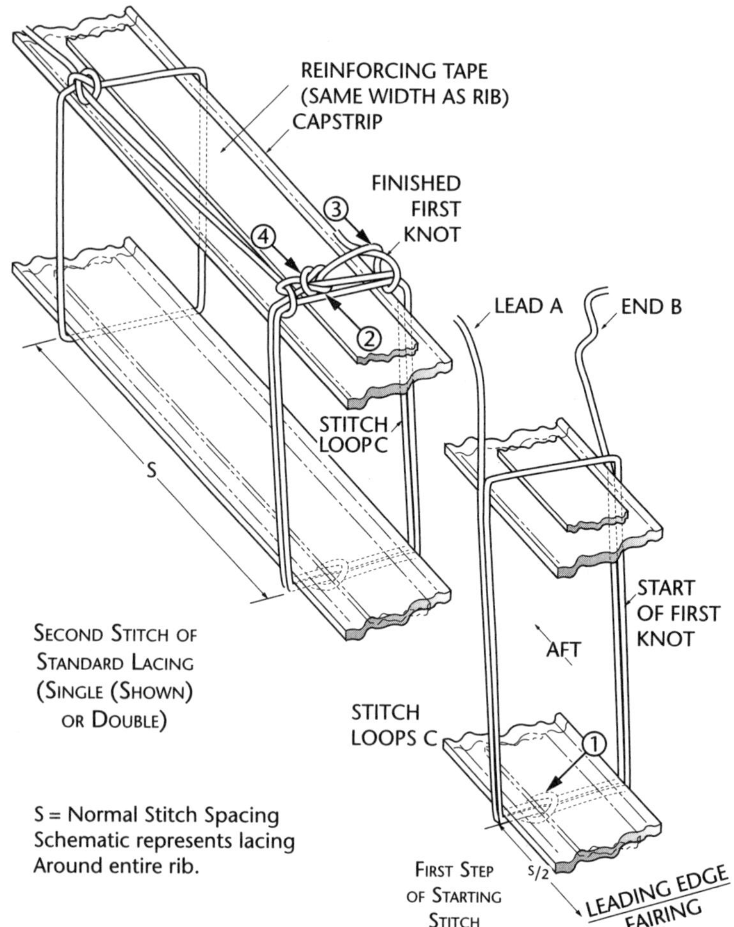

1. Tie square knot on center of capstrip.

2. Tie square knot on capstrip with lead 'A'
   and end 'B'.

3. Lock square knot with half hitch around
   stitch loops C with end B. Cut off
   surplus of end B.

4. Half hitch around stitch loops C.

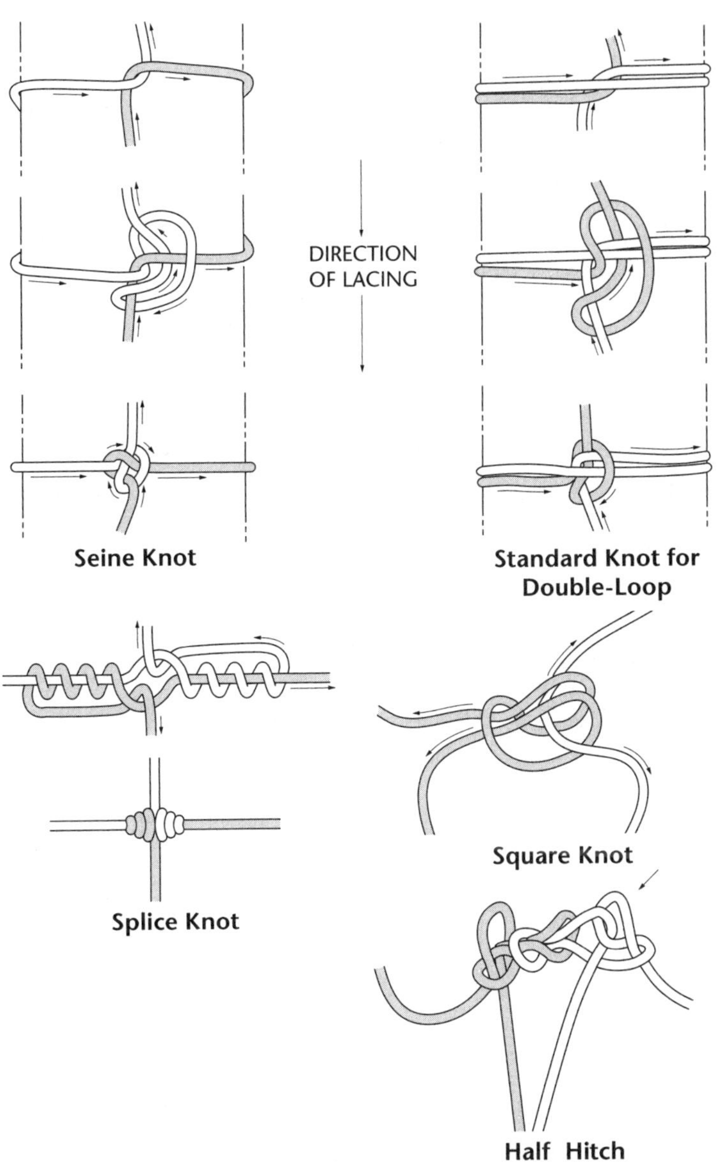
DIRECTION
OF LACING
Seine Knot
Standard Knot for
Double-Loop
Splice Knot
Square Knot
Half Hitch

3.3 Rib Stitch Spacing

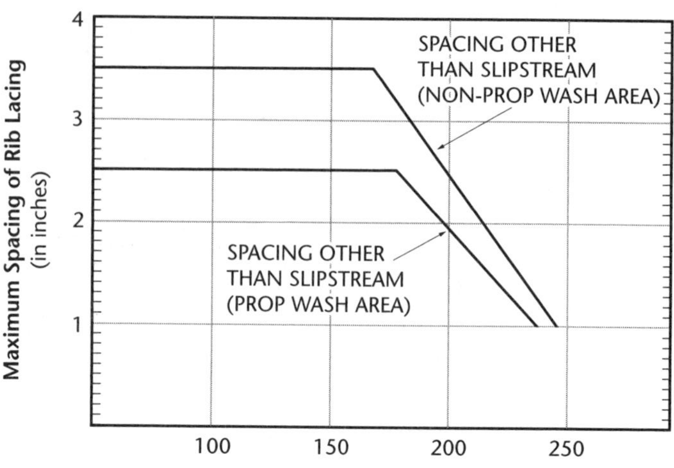

Aircraft Velocity Never Exceed Values (VNE)
(speed, in miles per hour)

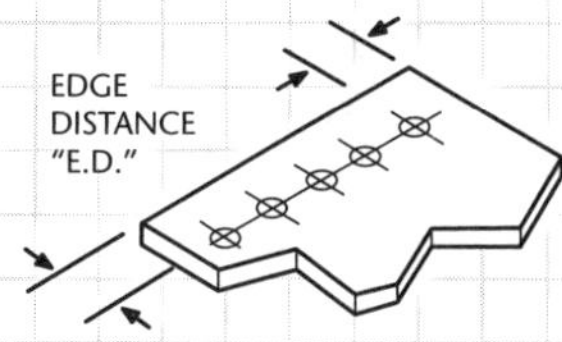

4

Materials for Aircraft

4.1 Numeric Designations for Wrought Aluminum

1xxx	Aluminum (99 percent or greater) non-heat-treatable
2xxx	Copper heat-treatable
3xxx	Manganese non-heat-treatable
4xxx	Silicon non-heat-treatable
5xxx	Magnesium non-heat-treatable
6xxx	Magnesium & silicon heat-treatable
7xxx	Zinc heat-treatable

4.2 Composition of Wrought Alloys

Alloy	Copper	Silicon	Manganese	Magnesium	Zinc	Nickel	Chromium	Lead	Bismuth
1100	–	–	–	–	–	–	–	–	–
3003	–	–	1.2	–	–	–	–	–	–
2011	5.50	–	–	–	–	–	–	0.5	0.5
2014	4.40	0.8	0.8	0.4	–	–	–	–	–
2017	4.00	–	0.5	0.5	–	–	–	–	–
2117	2.50	–	–	0.3	–	–	–	–	–
2018	4.00	–	–	0.5	–	2.0	–	–	–
2024	4.50	–	0.6	1.5	–	–	–	–	–
2025	4.50	0.8	0.8	–	–	–	–	–	–
4032	0.90	12.5	–	1.0	–	0.9	–	–	–
6151	–	1.0	–	0.6	–	–	0.25	–	–
5052	–	–	–	2.5	–	–	0.25	–	–
6053	–	0.7	–	1.3	–	–	0.25	–	–
6061	0.25	0.6	–	1.0	–	–	0.25	–	–
7075	1.60	–	–	2.5	5.6	–	0.30	–	–

NOTE: Percent of alloying elements. Aluminum and normal impurities constitute remainder.

4.3 Chemical Composition Limits

Chemical Composition Limits (WT%)

Alloy Group	Alloy #	Cu	Si	Fe	Mn	Mg	Zn	Cr	Ti	Pb,Bi	Al	Others
Al	1050	0.05	0.25	0.40	0.50	0.05	0.05	–	–	–	99.50 min	–
	1100	0.05–0.50	Si+Fe	1.0 max	0.05	–	0.10	–	–	–	99.0 min	–
Al–Cu	2011	0.50~0.60	0.40	0.70	–	–	0.30	–	–	0.2~0.6, each	rem	–
	2014	3.9~5.0	0.5~1.2	0.70	0.4~1.2	0.2~0.8	0.25	0.10	0.15	–	rem	–
	2017	3.5~4.5	0.2~0.8	0.7	0.4~1.0	0.4~0.8	0.25	0.10	0.15	–	rem	–
	2024	3.8~4.9	0.5	0.5	0.3~0.9	1.2~1.8	0.25	0.10	0.15	–	rem	–
	2218	3.5~4.5	0.9	1.0	0.20	1.2~1.8	0.25	0.10	–	–	rem	Ni 1.7~2.3
	2224	3.8~4.4	0.12	0.15	0.30~0.9	1.2~1.8	0.25	0.10	0.15	–	rem	–
Al–Mn	3003	0.05~0.20	0.6	0.7	1.0~1.5	–	0.10	–	–	–	rem	–
Al–Si	4032	0.5~1.3	11.0–13.5	1.0	–	0.8~1.3	0.25	0.10	–	–	rem	Ni 0.5~1.3
Al–Mg	5052	0.10	0.25	0.40	0.10	2.2~2.8	0.10	0.15~0.35	–	–	rem	–
	5056	0.10	0.30	0.40	0.05~0.20	4.5~5.6	0.10	0.05~0.20	–	–	rem	–
	5083	0.10	0.40	0.40	0.4~1.0	4.0~4.9	0.25	0.05~0.25	0.15	–	rem	–
	5086	0.10	0.40	0.50	0.20~0.7	3.5~4.5	0.25	0.05~0.25	0.15	–	rem	–
Al–Mg–Si	6061	0.15~0.40	0.4~0.8	0.7	0.15	0.8~1.2	0.25	0.25	0.15	–	rem	–

Chemical Composition Limits (WT%)

Alloy Group	Alloy #	Cu	Si	Fe	Mn	Mg	Zn	Cr	Ti	Pb,Bi	Al	Others
Al–Mg–Si	6063	0.10	0.2~0.6	0.35	0.10	0.45~0.9	0.10	0.10	0.10	–	rem	–
	6070	0.15~0.40	1.0~1.7	0.50	0.40~1.0	0.50~1.2	0.25	0.10	0.15	–	rem	–
	6151	0.35	0.6~1.2	1.0	0.2	0.45~0.8	0.25	0.15~0.35	0.15	–	rem	–
	6262	0.15~0.40	0.4~0.8	0.7	0.15	0.8~1.2	0.25	0.04~0.14	0.15	0.40~0.7 each	rem	–
	6351	0.10	0.7~1.3	0.5	0.4~0.8	0.40~0.8	0.20	–	0.20	–	rem	–
	6463	0.20	0.20~0.6	0.15	0.05	0.45~0.9	0.05	–	–	–	rem	–
Al–Zn	7001	1.6~2.6	0.35	0.40	0.20	2.6~3.4	6.8~8.0	0.18~0.35	0.20	–	rem	–
	7003	0.20	0.30	0.35	0.30	0.50~1.0	5.0~6.5	0.20	0.20	–	rem	Zr 0.05~0.25
	7050	2.0~2.6	0.12	0.15	0.10	1.9~2.6	5.7~6.7	0.04	0.06	–	rem	Zr 0.08~0.15
	7075	1.2~2.0	0.4	0.5	0.3	2.1~2.9	5.1~6.1	0.18~0.28	0.20	–	rem	–
	7178	1.6~2.4	0.40	0.50	0.30	2.4~3.1	6.3~7.3	0.18~0.35	0.20	–	rem	–
	7475	1.2~1.9	0.10	0.12	0.06	1.9~2.6	5.2~6.2	0.18~0.25	0.06	–	rem	–
Al–Li	2090	2.4~3.0	1.10	0.12	0.05	0.25	0.10	0.05	0.15	Zr 0.08~0.15	rem	Li 1.9~2.6

4.4 Temper Designations for Aluminum Alloys

Heat-treatable Alloys

Temper	Definition
-O	Annealed recrystallized (wrought products only) applies to softest temper of wrought products
-T1	Cooled from an elevated temperature shaping process (such as extrusion or casting) and naturally aged to a substantially stable condition
-T2	Annealed (castings only)
-T3	Solution heat-treated and cold-worked by the flattening or straightening operation
-T36	Solution heat-treated and cold-worked by reduction of 6 percent
-T4	Solution heat-treated
-T42	Solution heat-treated by the user regardless of prior temper (applicable only to 2014 and 2024 alloys)
-T5	Artificially aged only (castings only)
-T6	Solution heat-treated and artificially aged
-T62	Solution heat-treated and aged by user regardless of prior temper (applicable only to 2014 and 2024 alloys)
-T351, -T451, -T3510, -T3511, -T4510, -T4511	Solution heat-treated and stress relieved by stretching to produce a permanent set of 1 to 3 percent, depending on the product
-T651, -T851, -T6510, -T8510, -T6511, -T8511	Solution heat-treated, stress relieved by stretching to produce a permanent set of 1 to 3 percent, and artificially aged
-T652	Solution heat-treated, compressed to produce a permanent set and then artificially aged
-T8	Solution heat-treated, cold-worked and then artificially aged
-T4	Solution heat-treated, cold-worked by the flattening or straightening operation, and then artificially aged
-T86	Solution heat-treated, cold-worked by reduction of 6 percent, and then artificially aged
-T9	Solution heat-treated, artificially aged and then cold-worked

4.4 Temper Designations for Aluminum Alloys (cont'd)

Heat-treatable Alloys

Temper	Definition
-T10	Cooled from an elevated temperature shaping process artificially aged and then cold-worked
-F	For wrought alloys as fabricated; no mechanical properties limits; for cast alloys; as cast
-H1	Strain-hardened only. Applies to products which are strain-hardened to obtain the desired strength without supplementary thermal treatment
-H12	Strain-hardened one-quarter-hard temper
-H14	Strain-hardened half-hard temper
-H16	Strain-hardened three-quarters-hard temper
-H18	Strain-hardened full-hard temper
-H2	Strain-hardened and then partially annealed. Applies to products which are strain-hardened more than the desired final amount and then reduced in strength to the desired level by partial annealing
-H22	Strain-hardened and partially annealed to one-quarter-hard temper
-H24	Strain-hardened and partially annealed to half-hard temper
-H26	Strain-hardened and partially annealed to three-quarters-hard temper
-H28	Strain-hardened and partially annealed to full-hard temper
-H30	Strain-hardened and then stabilized. Applies to products which are strain-hardened and then stabilized by a low temperature heating to slightly lower their strength and increase ductility
-H32	Strain-hardened and then stabilized; final temper is one-quarter hard
-H34	Strain-hardened and then stabilized; final temper is one-half hard
-H36	Strain-hardened and then stabilized; final temper is three-quarters hard
-H38	Strain-hardened and then stabilized; final temper is full-hard
-H112	As fabricated; with specified mechanical property limits

4.5 Temperatures for Aluminum Heat Treatment

Alloy	Annealing Temp. (°F)	Annealing Time (hrs.)	Solution (°F)	Heat Treat. Temper	Precip. (°F)	Heat Treatment Time (hrs.)	Heat Treatment Temper
1100	650	2-3	–	–	–	–	–
2017	775	2-3	940	-T4	–	–	–
2024	775	2-3	920	-T4	375	7-9	-T86
2117	775	2-3	940	-T4	–	–	–
3003	775	2-3	–	–	–	–	–
5052	650	2-3	–	–	–	–	–
6061	775	2-3	970	-T4	320	16-20	-T6
7075	775	2-3	870	-W	250	24-28	-T6

4.6 Mechanical Properties of Wrought Aluminum

Alloy and Temper	Tensile Strength, p.s.i. Ultimate	Tensile Strength, p.s.i. Yield	Brinell Hardness 500 kg Load, 10 mm Ball
1100-O	13,000	5,000	23
1100-H18	24,000	22,000	44
2017-O	26,000	10,000	45
2017-T4	62,000	40,000	105
2024-O	27,000	11,000	47
2024-T36	72,000	57,000	130
2024-T4	68,000	47,000	120
Alclad 2024-O	26,000	11,000	N/A
Alclad 2024-T36	67,000	53,000	N/A
3003-O	16,000	6,000	40
3003-H18	29,000	27,000	10
5052-O	28,000	13,000	47
5052-H38	42,000	37,000	77
6061-O	18,000	8,000	30
6061-T6	45,000	40,000	95
7075-O	33,000	15,000	60
7075-T6	83,000	73,000	150
Alclad 7075-O	32,000	14,000	N/A
Alclad 7075-T6	76,000	67,000	N/A

4.7 Single-Shear Strength: Aluminum-Alloy Rivets

Composition of Rivet (Alloy)	Ultimate Strength of Rivet Metal (lbs/in²)	Diameter of Rivet							
		1/16	3/32	1/8	5/32	3/16	1/4	5/16	3/8
2117 T	27,000	83	186	331	518	745	1,325	2,071	2,981
2017 T	30,000	92	206	368	573	828	1,472	2,300	3,313
2024 T	35,000	107	241	429	670	966	1,718	2,684	3,865

NOTE: Double-shear strength is found by multiplying the above values by 2.
All dimensions are in inches

4.8 Bearing Strength: Sheet Aluminum

Thickness	Diameter of Rivet							
	1/16	3/32	1/8	5/32	3/16	1/4	5/16	3/8
0.014	71	107	143	179	215	287	358	430
0.016	82	123	164	204	246	328	410	492
0.018	92	138	184	230	276	369	461	553
0.020	102	153	205	256	307	410	412	615
0.025	128	192	256	320	284	512	640	768
0.032	164	245	328	409	492	656	820	984
0.036	184	276	369	461	553	738	922	1,107
0.040	205	307	410	512	615	820	1,025	1,230
0.045	230	345	461	576	691	922	1,153	1,383
0.051	261	391	522	653	784	1,045	1,306	1,568
0.064	–	492	656	820	984	1,312	1,640	1,968
0.072	–	553	738	922	1,107	1,476	1,845	2,214
0.081	–	622	830	1,037	1,245	1,660	2,075	2,490
0.091	–	699	932	1,167	1,398	1,864	2,330	2,796
0.102	–	784	1,046	1,307	1,569	2,092	2,615	3,138
0.125	–	961	1,281	1,602	1,922	2,563	3,203	3,844
0.156	–	1,198	1,598	1,997	2,397	3,196	3,995	4,794
0.188	–	1,445	1,927	2,409	2,891	3,854	4,818	5,781
0.250	–	1,921	2,562	3,202	3,843	5,125	6,405	7,686
0.313	–	2,405	3,208	4,009	4,811	6,417	7,568	9,623
0.375	–	2,882	3,843	4,803	5,765	7,688	9,068	11,529
0.500	–	3,842	5,124	6,404	7,686	10,250	12,090	15,372

NOTE: All dimensions are in inches

To determine the number of rivets used on each side of a break:

$$\frac{\text{Length} \times \text{Thickness of Material} \times 75{,}000}{\text{Shear or Bearing (whichever is smaller)}}$$

4.9 SAE Classification of Steels

Series Designation	Types of Steel
10xx	Non-sulphurized carbon steels
11xx	Re-sulphurized carbon steels (free machining)
12xx	Re-phosphorized and re-sulphurized carbon steels (free machining)
13xx	Manganese (1.75%)
*23xx	Nickel (3.50%)
*25xx	Nickel (5.00%)
31xx	Nickel (1.25%); Chromium (0.65%)
33xx	Nickel (3.50%); Chromium (1.55%)
40xx	Molybdenum (0.20 or 0.25%)
41xx	Chromium (0.50 or 0.95%); Molybdenum (0.12 or 0.20%)
43xx	Nickel (1.80%); Chromium (0.50 or 0.80%); Molybdenum (0.25%)
44xx	Molybdenum (0.40%)
45xx	Molybdenum (0.52%)
46xx	Nickel (1.80%); Molybdenum (0.25%)
47xx	Nickel (1.05%); Chromium (0.45%); Molybdenum (0.20 or 0.35%)
48xx	Nickel (3.50%); Molybdenum (0.25%)
50xx	Chromium (0.25, 0.45 or 0.50%)
50xxx	Carbon (1.00%); Chromium (0.50%)
51xx	Chromium (0.80, 0.90, 0.95 or 1.00%)
51xxx	Carbon (1.00%); Chromium (1.05%)
52xxx	Carbon (1.00%); Chromium (1.45%)
61xx	Chromium (0.60, 0.80 or 0.95%); Vanadium (0.12%, 0.10% min. or 0.15% min.)
81xx	Nickel (0.30%); Chromium (0.40%); Molybdenum (0.12%)
86xx	Nickel (0.55%); Chromium (0.50%); Molybdenum (0.20%)
87xx	Nickel (0.55%); Chromium (0.05%); Molybdenum (0.25%)
88xx	Nickel (0.55%); Chromium (0.05%); Molybdenum (0.35%)
92xx	Manganese (0.85%); Silicon (2.00%); Chromium (0 or 0.35%)
93xx	Nickel (3.25%); Chromium (1.20%); Molybdenum (0.12%)
94xx	Nickel (0.45%); Chromium (0.40%); Molybdenum (0.12%)
98xx	Nickel (1.00%); Chromium (0.80%); Molybdenum (0.25%)

NOTE: *Not included in the current list of standard steels

4.10 Strength Properties of Steels

Steel Designation Number	Temperatures			Quenching Medium (n)	Tempering (Drawing) Temperature for Tensile Strength (p.s.i.)				
	Normalizing Air Cool (°F)	Annealing (°F)	Hardening (°F)		100,000 (p.s.i.)	125,000 (p.s.i.)	150,000 (p.s.i.)	180,000 (p.s.i.)	200,000 (p.s.i.)
1020	1,650-1,750	1,600-1,700	1,575-1,675	H_2O	-	-	-	-	-
1022 (x1022)	1,650-1,750	1,600-1,700	1,575-1,675	H_2O	-	-	-	-	-
1025	1,600-1,700	1,575-1,650	1,575-1,675	H_2O	(a)	-	-	-	-
1035	1,575-1,650	1,575-1,625	1,525-1,625	H_2O	875	-	-	-	-
1045	1,550-1,600	1,550-1,600	1,475-1,550	Oil/H_2O	1,150	-	-	(n)	-
1095	1,475-1,550	1,450-1,500	1,425-1,500	Oil	(b)	-	1,100	850	750
2330	1,475-1,525	1,425-1,475	1,450-1,500	Oil/H_2O	1,100	950	800	-	-
3135	1,600-1,650	1,500-1,550	1,475-1,525	Oil	1,250	1,050	900	750	650
3140	1,600-1,650	1,500-1,550	1,475-1,525	Oil	1,325	1,075	925	775	700
4037	1,600	1,525-1,575	1,525-1,575	Oil/H_2O	1,225	1,100	975	-	-
4130 (x4130)	1,600-1,700	1,525-1,575	1,575-1,625	Oil (c)	(d)	1,050	900	700	575
4140	1,600-1,650	1,525-1,575	1,525-1,575	Oil	1,350	1,100	1,025	825	675
4150	1,550-1,600	1,475-1,525	1,500-1,550	Oil	-	1,275	1,175	1,050	950
4340 (x4340)	1,550-1,625	1,525-1,575	1,475-1,550	Oil	-	1,200	1,050	950	850
4640	1,675-1,700	1,525-1,575	1,500-1,550	Oil	-	1,200	1,050	750	625
6135	1,600-1,700	1,550-1,600	1,575-1,625	Oil	1,300	1,075	950	800	750
6150	1,600-1,650	1,525-1,575	1,550-1,625	Oil	(d) (e)	1,200	1,000	900	800
6195	1,600-1,650	1,525-1,575	1,500-1,550	Oil	(f)	-	-	-	-

4.10 Strength Properties of Steels (cont'd)

Steel Designation Number	Temperatures			Quenching Medium (n)	Tempering (Drawing) Temperature for Tensile Strength (p.s.i.)				
	Normalizing Air Cool (°F)	Annealing (°F)	Hardening (°F)		100,000 (p.s.i.)	125,000 (p.s.i.)	150,000 (p.s.i.)	180,000 (p.s.i.)	200,000 (p.s.i.)
NE8620	-	-	1,525-1,575	Oil	-	1,000	-	-	-
NE8630	1,650	1,525-1,575	1,525-1,575	Oil	-	1,125	975	775	675
NE8735	1,650	1,525-1,575	1,525-1,575	Oil	-	1,175	1,025	875	775
NE8735	1,625	1,500-1,550	1,500-1,550	Oil	-	1,200	1,075	925	850
30905	-	(g) (h)	(i)	-	-	-	-	-	-
51210	1,525-1,575	1,525-1,575	1,775-1,825 (j)	Oil	1,200	1,100	(k)	750	-
51335	-	1,525-1,575	1,775-1,850	Oil	-	-	-	-	-
52100	1,625-1,700	1,400-1,450	1,525-1,550	Oil	(f)	-	-	-	-
Corrosion resisting (16-2) (l)	-	-	-	-	(m)	-	-	-	-
Silicon chromium (for springs)	-	-	1,700-1,725	Oil	-	-	-	-	-

(a) Draw at 1,150°F for tensile strength of 70,000 p.s.i.
(b) For spring temper draw at 800-900°F. Rockwell hardness C-40-45
(c) Bars and forgings may be quenched in water from 1,500-1,600°F.
(d) Air-cooling from the normalizing temperature will produce a tensile strength of approx. 90,000 p.s.i.
(e) For spring temper draw at 858-950°F. Rockwell hardness C-40-45.
(f) Draw at 350-450°F to remove quenching strains. Rockwell hardness C-60-65.
(g) Anneal at 1,600-1,700°F to remove residual stresses due to welding or cold-work. May be applied to steel containing titanium or columbium.
(h) Anneal at 1,900-2,100°F to produce maximum softness and corrosion resistance. Cool in air or quench in water.
(i) Harden by cold-work only.
(j) Lower side of range for sheet 0.06 inch and under. Middle of range for sheet and wire 0.125 inch. Upper side of range for forgings.
(k) Not recommended for intermediate strengths because of low impact.
(l) AN-QQ-S-770. It is recommended that, prior to tempering, corrosion-resisting (16 Cr2Ni) steel be quenched in oil from a temperature of 1,875-1,900°F, after a soaking period of 1/2 hour at this temperature. To obtain a tensile strength of 115,000 p.s.i., the tempering temperature should be approximately 525°F. A holding time at these temperatures of 2 hours is recommended. Tempering temperatures from 700-1,100°F will not be approved.
(m) Draw at approximately 800°F and cool in air for Rockwell hardness of C-50.
(n) Water used for quenching shall not exceed 65°F. Oil used for quenching shall be within a range of 80-150°F.

4.11 Classification of Stainless Steels

Examples of Stainless and Heat-resistant Steels
Nominal Composition (Percent)

Alloy Designation	Carbon	Chromium	Nickel	Other	General Class of Steel
302	0.15	18	9	–	Austenitic
310	0.25	25	20	–	Austenitic
321	0.08	18	11	Titanium	Austenitic
347	0.08	18	11	Columbium or Tantalum	Austenitic
410	0.15	12.5	–	–	Martensitic, Magnetic
430	0.12	17	–	–	Ferritic, Magnetic
446	0.20	25	–	Nitrogen	Ferritic, Magnetic
PH15–7 Mo	0.09	15	7	Molybdenum, Aluminum	Precipitation Hardening
17–4 PH	0.07	16.5	4	Copper, Columbium or Tantalum	Precipitation Hardening

4.12 Rockwell Hardness

Scale Symbol	Penetrator	Major Load (kg)	Dial Number
A	Diamond	60	Black
B	1/16 ball	100	Red
C	Diamond	150	Black
D	Diamond	100	Black
E	1/8 ball	100	Red
F	1/16 ball	60	Red
G	1/16 ball	150	Red
H	1/8 ball	60	Red
K	1/8 ball	150	Red

NOTE: All dimensions are in inches

4.13 Strength of Steel Related to its Hardness

Hardness Number		Tensile Strength 1,000 psi	Hardness Number		Tensile Strength 1,000 psi
Rockwell C-Scale	Brinell		Rockwell C-Scale	Brinell	
52	500	262	29	279	138
51	487	253	28	271	134
50	475	245	27	264	131
49	464	239	26	258	127
48	451	232	25	253	124
47	442	225	24	247	121
46	432	219	23	243	118
45	421	212	22	237	115
44	409	206	21	231	113
43	400	201	20	226	110
42	390	196	(18)	219	106
41	381	191	(16)	212	102
40	371	186	(14)	203	98
39	362	181	(12)	194	94
38	353	176	(10)	187	90
37	344	172	(8)	179	87
36	336	168	(6)	171	84
35	327	163	(4)	165	80
34	319	159	(2)	158	77
33	311	154	(0)	152	75
32	301	150	-	-	-
31	294	146			
30	286	142			

NOTE: Numbers in parentheses ( ) are beyond the normal range of the Rockwell C-Scale.

4.14 Classification of Titanium Alloys

Weighing 0.63 lbs. per cubic inch, titanium has a very high strength, particularly in an alloyed form. In addition, it has excellent corrosion-resistant characteristics. Certain forms of titanium alloys are used extensively in many aerospace applications. Sensitive to both nitrogen and oxygen, titanium has to be converted to titanium dioxide with chlorine gas and a reducing agent, usually carbon, to be used effectively as a strong metal. Not as lustrous as chromium or stainless steel, pure titanium is soft and ductile, and its weight is between that of aluminum and iron.

Titanium alloys are classified as alpha, alpha-beta, and beta alloys. These classifications are based on the specific chemical bonding within the alloy itself.

Alloy	Description
Alpha Titanium	Alpha alloys have medium strength, and good elevated-temperature strength. They can be welded, and are used mostly for forgings.
Alpha-Beta Titanium	Alpha-beta alloys are the most versatile of the titanium alloys. In the annealed condition they have medium strength, but when heat-treated their strength greatly increases. This form of titanium is generally not weldable, but it has good forming characteristics.
Beta Titanium	Beta alloys have medium strength, and excellent forming characteristics. Beta titanium can be heat treated to a very high strength.

4.15 Minimum Inner Bend Radii 90° Bends in Aluminum

Gauge	2024-O 5052-H34	2024-T3 2024-T4	5052-O	7178-O 7075-O	7178-T6 7075-T6
0.016	0.030	0.060	0.030	0.030	0.090
0.018	0.030	0.060	0.030	0.030	0.120
0.020	0.030	0.060	0.030	0.030	0.120
0.022	0.060	0.090	0.030	0.060	0.120
0.025	0.060	0.090	0.030	0.060	0.120
0.028	0.060	0.090	0.030	0.060	0.160
0.032	0.060	0.120	0.030	0.060	0.160
0.036	0.060	0.160	0.060	0.060	0.190
0.040	0.060	0.160	0.060	0.060	0.190
0.045	0.090	0.190	0.060	0.090	0.250
0.050	0.090	0.190	0.060	0.090	0.250
0.056	0.120	0.220	0.060	0.120	0.280
0.063	0.120	0.220	0.060	0.120	0.310
0.071	0.120	0.280	0.090	0.120	0.380
0.080	0.160	0.340	0.090	0.190	0.440
0.090	0.190	0.380	0.090	0.190	0.500
0.100	0.220	0.440	0.120	0.220	0.620
0.112	0.250	0.500	0.120	0.280	0.750
0.125	0.250	0.560	0.120	0.280	0.880
0.140	0.340	0.620	0.120	0.380	1.000
0.160	0.380	0.750	0.160	0.440	1.120
0.180	0.440	0.880	0.190	0.500	1.250
0.190	0.500	0.880	0.190	0.560	1.250

NOTE: All dimensions are in inches

Degree	K	Degree	K	Degree	K
1°	0.00873	31°	0.27732	61°	0.58904
2°	0.01745	32°	0.28674	62°	0.60086
3°	0.02618	33°	0.29621	63°	0.61280
4°	0.03492	34°	0.30573	64°	0.62487
5°	0.04366	35°	0.31530	65°	0.63707
6°	0.05241	36°	0.32492	66°	0.64941
7°	0.06116	37°	0.33459	67°	0.66188
8°	0.06993	38°	0.34433	68°	0.67451
9°	0.07870	39°	0.35412	69°	0.68728
10°	0.08749	40°	0.36397	70°	0.70021
11°	0.09629	41°	0.37388	71°	0.71329
12°	0.10510	42°	0.38386	72°	0.72654
13°	0.11393	43°	0.39391	73°	0.73996
14°	0.12278	44°	0.40403	74°	0.75355
15°	0.13165	45°	0.41421	75°	0.76733
16°	0.14054	46°	0.42447	76°	0.78128
17°	0.14945	47°	0.43481	77°	0.79546
18°	0.15838	48°	0.44523	78°	0.80978
19°	0.16734	49°	0.45573	79°	0.82434
20°	0.17633	50°	0.46631	80°	0.83910
21°	0.18534	51°	0.47697	81°	0.85408
22°	0.19438	52°	0.48773	82°	0.86929
23°	0.20345	53°	0.49858	83°	0.88472
24°	0.21256	54°	0.50952	84°	0.90040
25°	0.22169	55°	0.52057	85°	0.91633
26°	0.23087	56°	0.53171	86°	0.93251
27°	0.24008	57°	0.54295	87°	0.94896
28°	0.24933	58°	0.55431	88°	0.96569
29°	0.25862	59°	0.56577	89°	0.98270
30°	0.26795	60°	0.57735	90°	1.00000

Degree	K	Degree	K	Degree	K
91°	1.0176	121°	1.7675	151°	3.8667
92°	1.0355	122°	1.8040	152°	4.0108
93°	1.0538	123°	1.8418	153°	4.1653
94°	1.0724	124°	1.8807	154°	4.3315
95°	1.0913	125°	1.9210	155°	4.5107
96°	1.1106	126°	1.9626	156°	4.7046
97°	1.1303	127°	2.0057	157°	4.9151
98°	1.1504	128°	2.0503	158°	5.1455
99°	1.1708	129°	2.0965	159°	5.3995
100°	1.1917	130°	2.1445	160°	5.6713
101°	1.2131	131°	2.1943	161°	5.9758
102°	1.2349	132°	2.2460	162°	6.3137
103°	1.2572	133°	2.2998	163°	6.6911
104°	1.2799	134°	2.3558	164°	7.1154
105°	1.3032	135°	2.4142	165°	7.5957
106°	1.3270	136°	2.4751	166°	8.1443
107°	1.3514	137°	2.5386	167°	8.7769
108°	1.3764	138°	2.6051	168°	9.5144
109°	1.4019	139°	2.6746	169°	10.385
110°	1.4281	140°	2.7475	170°	11.430
111°	1.4550	141°	2.8239	171°	12.706
112°	1.4826	142°	2.9042	172°	14.301
113°	1.5108	143°	2.9887	173°	16.350
114°	1.5399	144°	3.0777	174°	19.081
115°	1.5697	145°	3.1716	175°	22.904
116°	1.6003	146°	3.2708	176°	26.636
117°	1.6318	147°	3.3759	177°	38.188
118°	1.6643	148°	3.4874	178°	57.290
119°	1.6977	149°	3.6059	179°	114.590
120°	1.7320	150°	3.7320	180°	Infinite

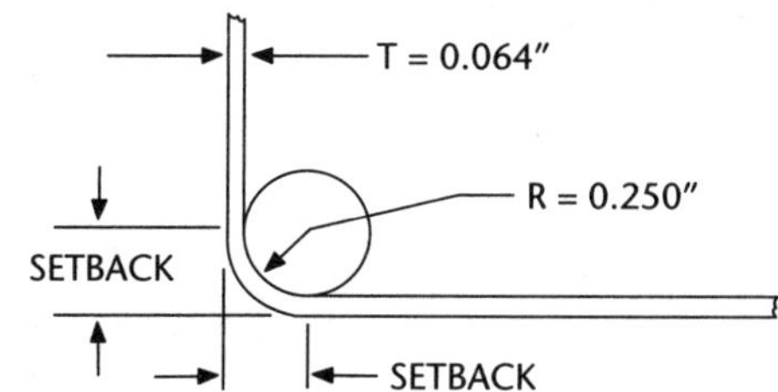

This is a 90° angle.
Setback = BR + MT
       = 0.250" + 0.064"
       = 0.314"

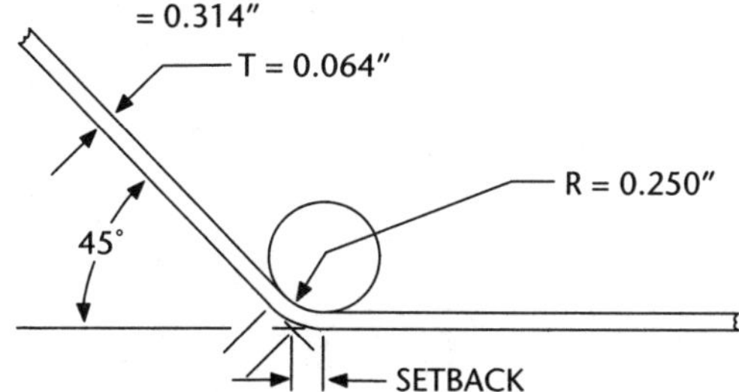

This is a 135° open angle. The metal has only been bent 45°.
Setback = (BR + MT)K
       = (0.250" + 0.064") 0.41421"
       = 0.130"

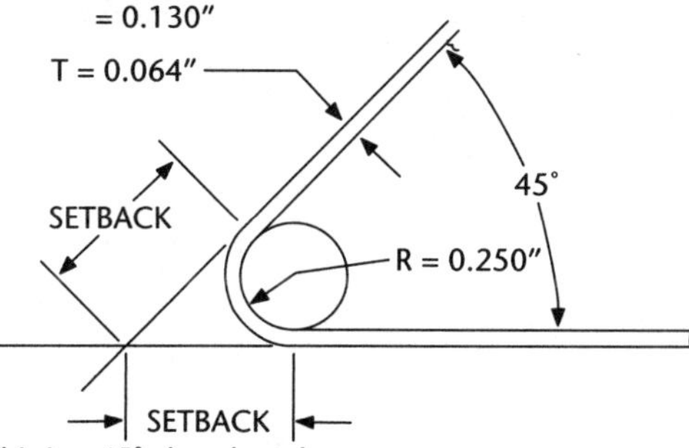

This is a 45° closed angle.
Setback = (BR + MT)K
       = (0.250" + 0.064") 2.4142"
       = 0.758"

Where: BR = Bend Radius
       MT = Material Thickness
        K = Setback Factor

Radius Gauge

Metal Thickness	0.031 (1/32)	0.063 (1/16)	0.125 (1/8)	0.156 (5/32)	0.188 (3/16)	0.250 (1/4)	0.313 (5/16)	0.344 (11/32)	0.500 (1/2)
0.020"	0.062 / 0.000693	0.113 / 0.001251	0.210 / 0.002333	0.259 / 0.002874	0.309 / 0.003433	0.406 / 0.004515	0.505 / 0.005614	0.554 / 0.006695	0.799 / 0.008877
0.025"	0.066 / 0.000736	0.116 / 0.001294	0.214 / 0.002376	0.263 / 0.002917	0.313 / 0.003476	0.410 / 0.004558	0.509 / 0.005657	0.558 / 0.006198	0.803 / 0.008920
0.032"	0.071 / 0.000787	0.121 / 0.001345	0.218 / 0.002427	0.267 / 0.002968	0.317 / 0.003526	0.415 / 0.004608	0.514 / 0.005149	0.562 / 0.006249	0.807 / 0.008971
0.040"	0.007 / 0.000853	0.127 / 0.001411	0.224 / 0.002493	0.273 / 0.003034	0.323 / 0.003593	0.421 / 0.004675	0.520 / 0.006315	0.568 / 0.006856	0.813 / 0.009037
0.051"	–	0.134 / 0.001413	0.232 / 0.002575	0.280 / 0.003116	0.331 / 0.003675	0.428 / 0.004756	0.527 / 0.005855	0.576 / 0.006397	0.821 / 0.00919
0.064"	–	0.144 / 0.00595	0.241 / 0.002680	0.290 / 0.003218	0.340 / 0.003776	0.437 / 0.004858	0.536 / 0.005957	0.585 / 0.006498	0.830 / 0.009220
0.072"	–	–	0.247 / 0.002743	0.296 / 0.003284	0.346 / 0.003842	0.443 / 0.004924	0.542 / 0.006023	0.591 / 0.006564	0.836 / 0.009287
0.091"	–	–	0.260 / 0.002891	0.309 / 0.003432	0.359 / 0.003990	0.456 / 0.005072	0.555 / 0.006172	0.604 / 0.006713	0.849 / 0.009435
0.102"	–	–	0.268 / 0.002977	0.317 / 0.003518	0.367 / 0.004076	0.464 / 0.005158	0.563 / 0.006257	0.612 / 0.006798	0.857 / 0.009521
0.109"	–	–	0.273 / 0.003031	0.321 / 0.003572	0.372 / 0.004131	0.469 / 0.005213	0.568 / 0.006312	0.617 / 0.006853	0.862 / 0.009575
0.125"	–	–	0.284 / 0.003156	0.333 / 0.003697	0.383 / 0.004256	0.480 / 0.005338	0.579 / 0.006437	0.628 / 0.006978	0.873 / 0.009700
0.250"	–	–	–	–	–	0.568 / 0.006313	0.667 / 0.007412	0.716 / 0.007953	0.961 / 0.010675

NOTE: The top numbers in each box are for a 90° bend. The bottom numbers are the bend allowance for 1 degree of bend.

4.19 Sheet Metal Development and Layout

By definition, sheet metal development means the flat layout of a formed part. This flat layout when fabricated (trimmed, drilled and formed), will conform to the dimensions required on the finished part within the allowable tolerances. Figure 1 shows the flat development of a part, and Figure 2 shows the finished part.

By using this flat development, the trimming and drilling of the part is simplified and at the same time material is conserved.

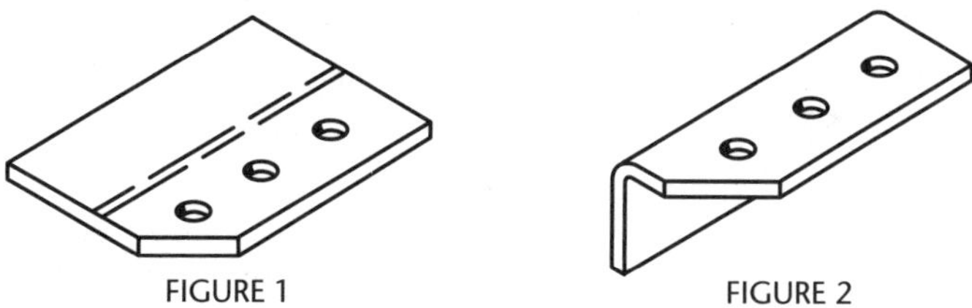

FIGURE 1   FIGURE 2

Flat pattern layout by bend allowance (BA) is most universally accepted. By the use of the bend allowance chart and equations, any straight bend may be accurately developed.

4.20 **Bend Allowance**

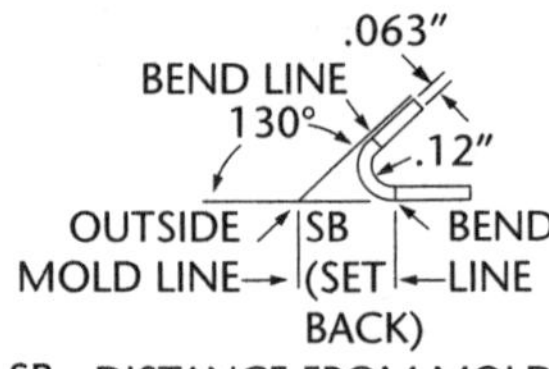

SB = DISTANCE FROM MOLD LINE TO BEND LINE
BA = BEND ANGLE
R = BEND RADIUS
T = THICKNESS

1. ENTER CHART AT BOTTOM ON APPROPRIATE SCALE USING SUM OF T + R
2. READ UP TO BEND ANGLE
3. DETERMINE SET BACK FROM CORRESPONDING SCALE ON LEFT

EXAMPLE:

T (0.063) + R (0.12)	= 0.183
BA	= 135°
SET BACK	= 0.453

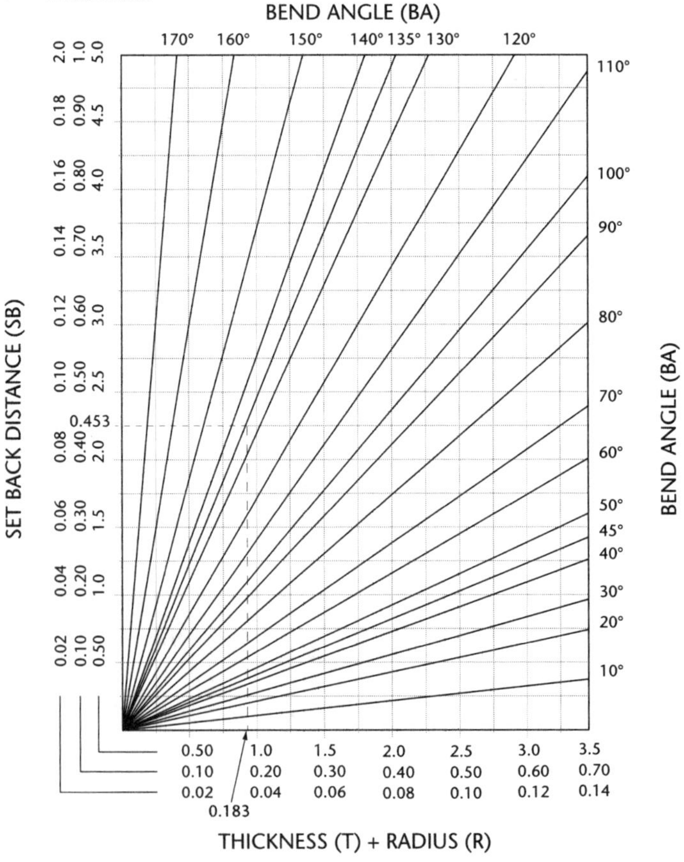

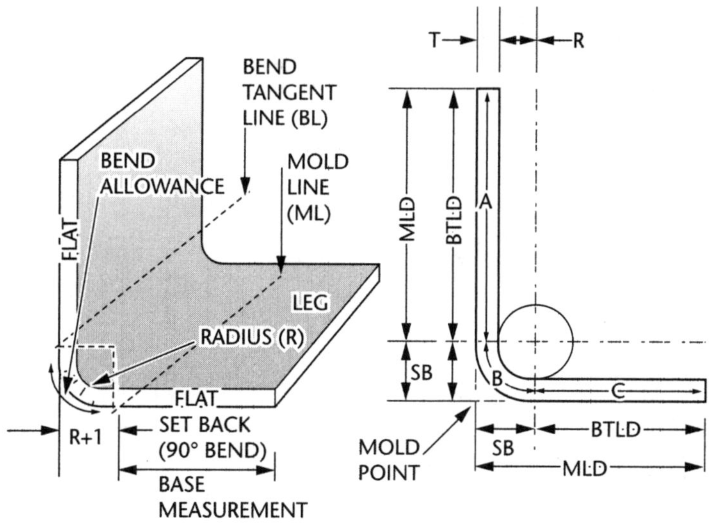
BEND
TANGENT
LINE (BL)
BEND
ALLOWANCE
MOLD
LINE
(ML)
FLAT
LEG
RADIUS (R)
FLAT
R+1
SET BACK
(90° BEND)
BASE
MEASUREMENT
T
R
MLD
BTLD
A
SB
B
C
MOLD
POINT
BTLD
SB
MLD

4.22 Rivet Dimensions

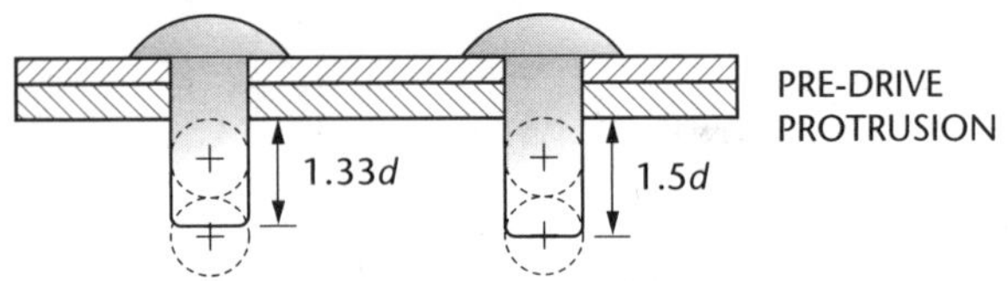

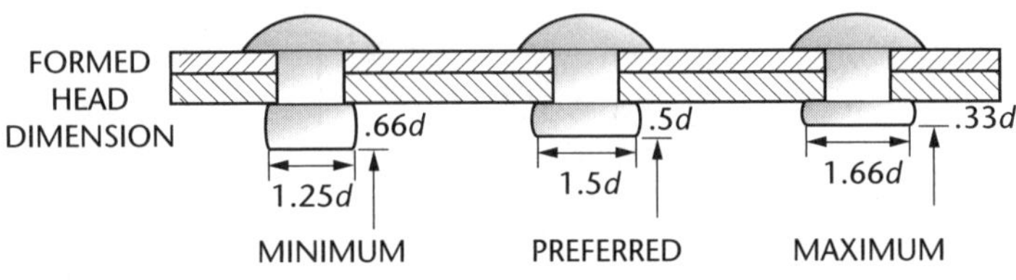

D, E, (KE), M Rivets

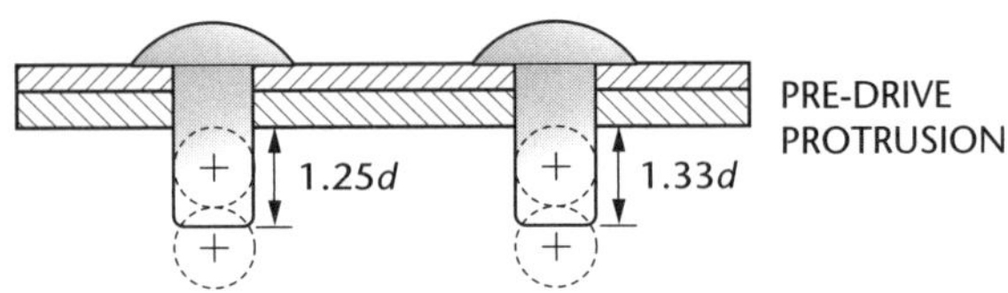

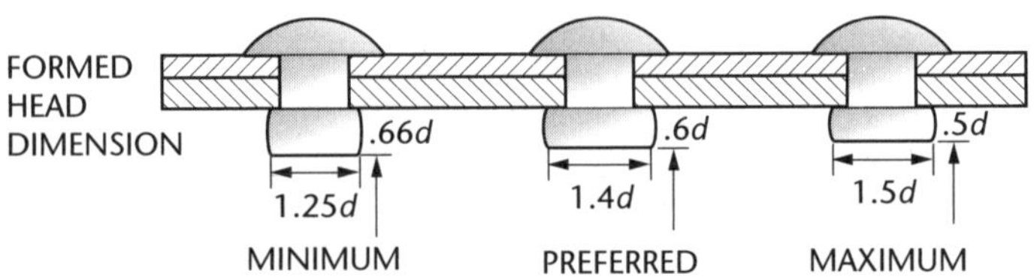

A, AD, B, DD Rivets

d = RIVET DIAMETER

4.23 Rivet Imperfections

(A) Dimensions for Formed Rivet Heads

(B) Riveting Tools

(C) Rivet Imperfections

RIVET DRIVEN AT SLANT

RIVET DRIVEN CORRECTLY, DOLLY HEAD AT SLANT

RIVET FLAT ON ONE SIDE OR DOLLY HELD FLAT

BODY OF RIVET TOO SHORT. CLOSING HEAD SHAPED TOO MUCH WITH SNAP DIE

RIVET NOT PULLED TIGHT, CLINCHES BETWEEN PLATES, CLOSING HEAD TOO FLAT

RIVET TIGHT, PLATES BULGED ON ACCOUNT OF POOR FIT

RIVETED TOO MUCH. RIVET BODY CLINCHED TOO MUCH, PLATES CLINCHED AT RIVET AND DRIVEN APART

RIVETING TOOL DAMAGED PLATE

HEAD CRACKED. MATERIAL TOO HARD WHEN FORMED

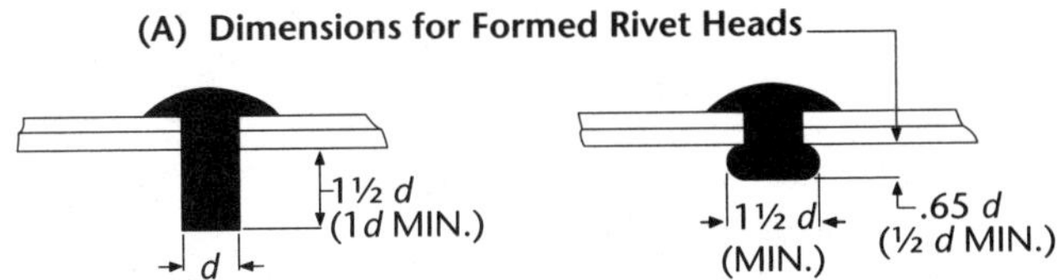

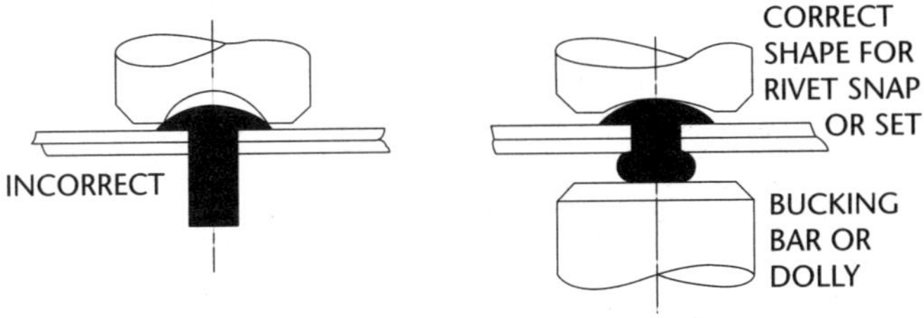

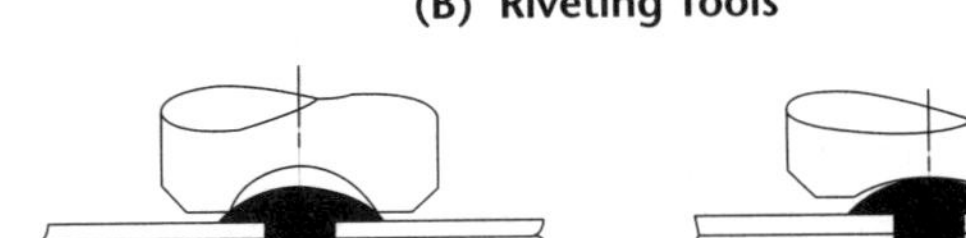

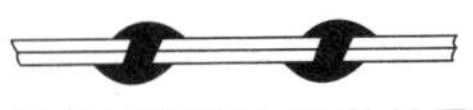

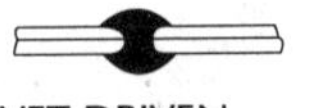

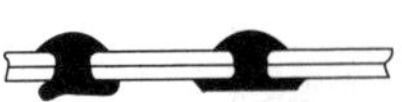

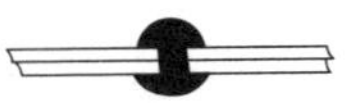

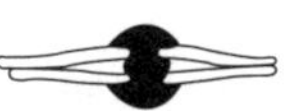

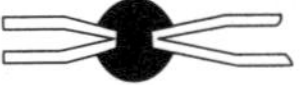

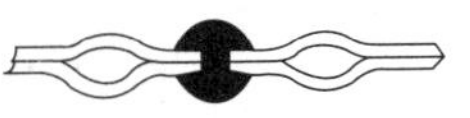

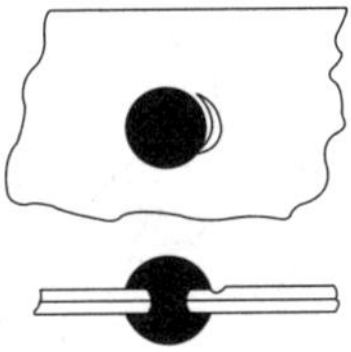

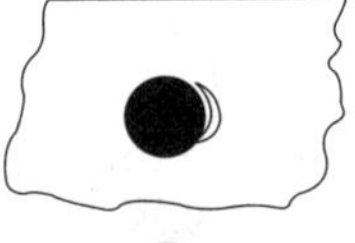

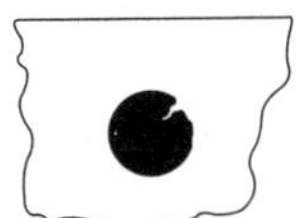

4.24 Driven Rivet Defects

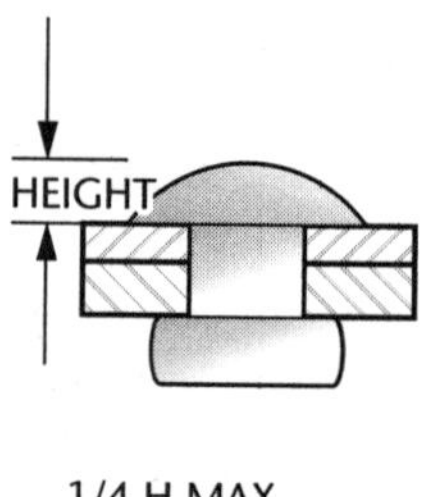

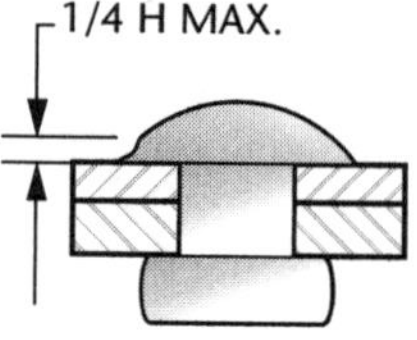

Marred

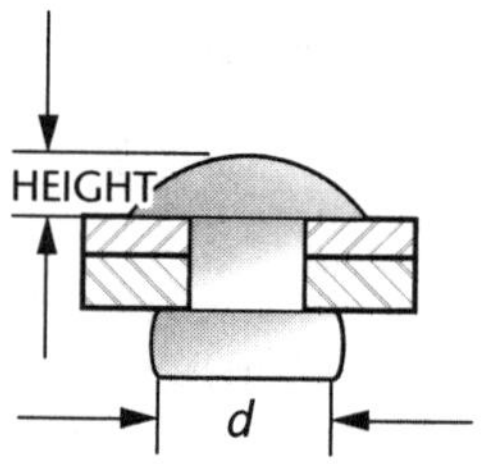

Flattened

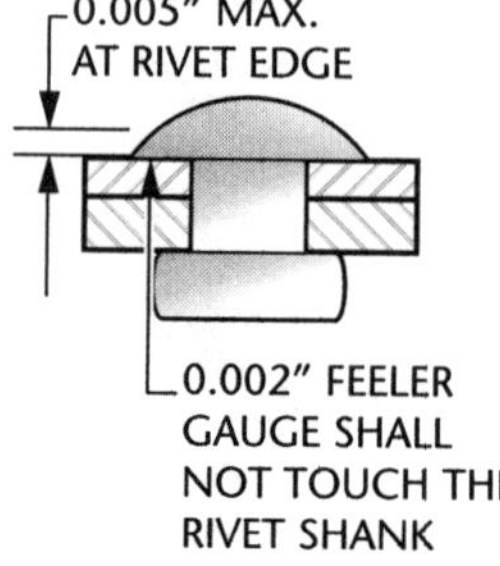

Open-head

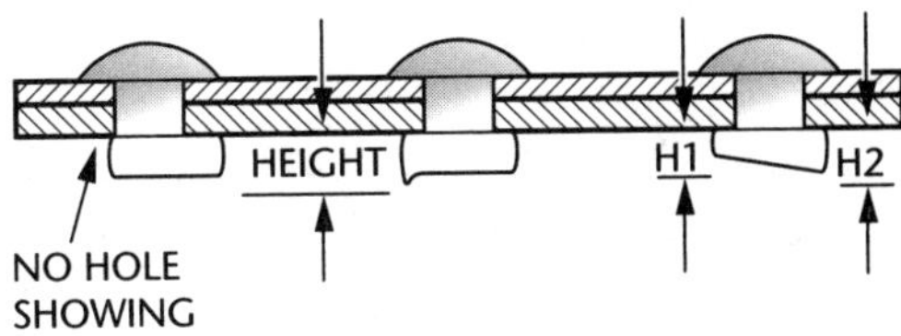

NO TRANSVERSE, CIRCUMFERENTIAL
OR TANGENTIAL CRACKS

4.26 **Rivet Countersinking**

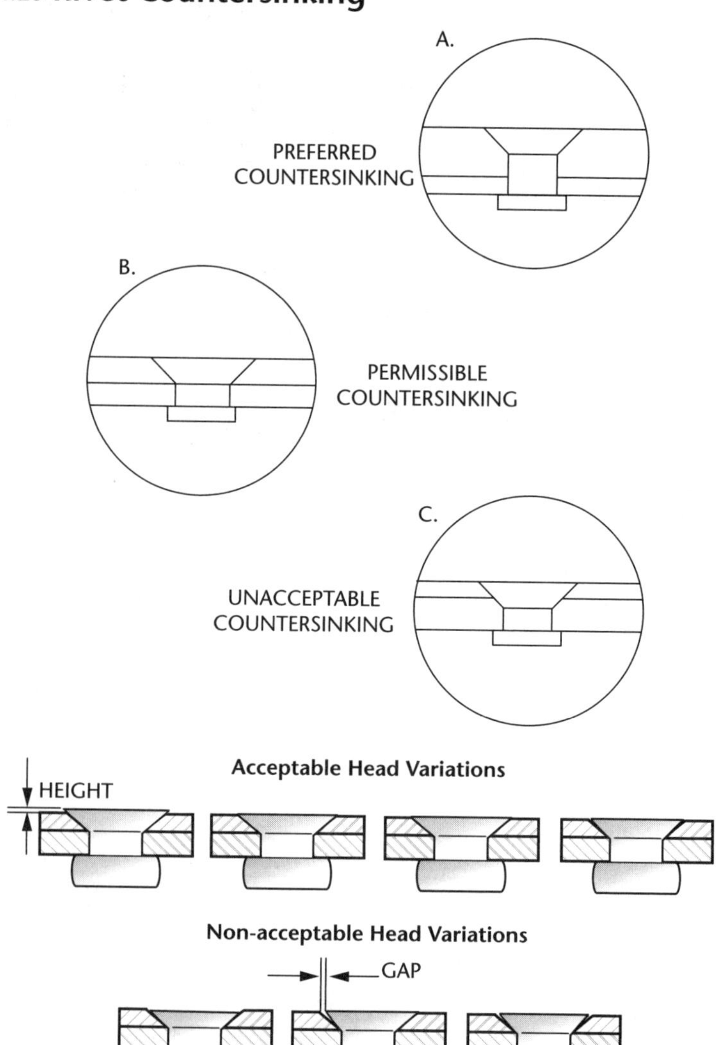

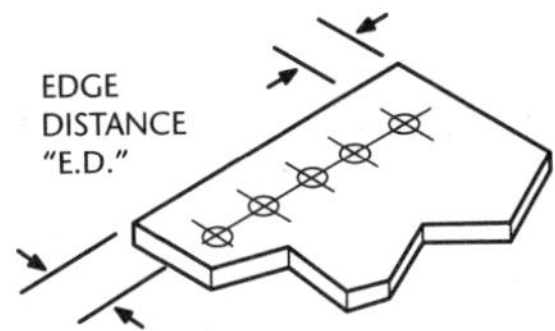

1. "E.D." is the distance from the edge of the material to the center of the nearest rivet hole.

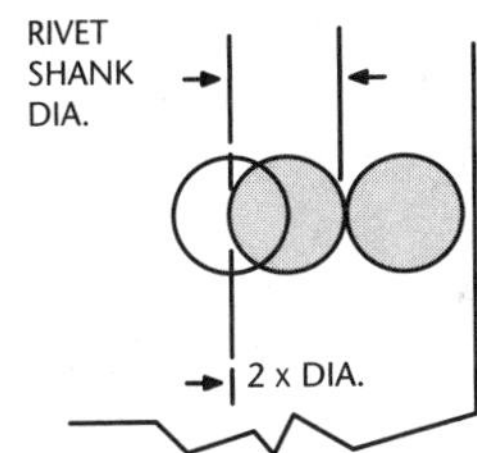

2. If the blueprint does not specify a minimum edge distance, the preferred edge distance is two times the diameter of the rivet shank.

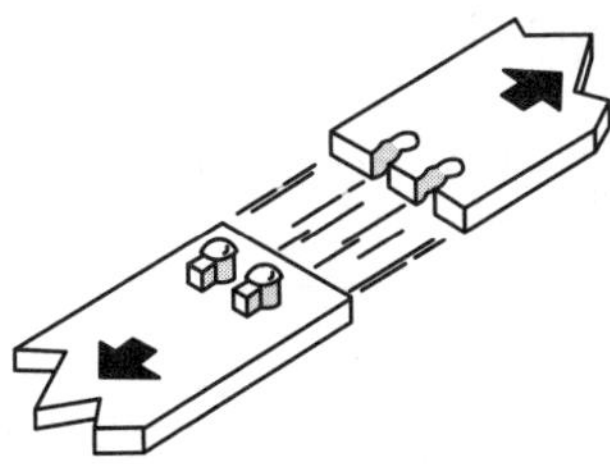

3. If E.D. is not adequate material may tear out under stress.

4.28 Rivet Spacing

Rivet spacing is the distance between the center of one rivet and the center of the next rivet.

A sufficient number of rivets must be spaced properly to withstand the load requirements determined by the stress engineers, or the rivets will shear under stress.

The spacing of rivets is determined by engineers and following are examples of how rivet spacing is shown on a blueprint.

  The spacing is 0.50" center to center between flagged rivets

14 = Spaces The area between located rivets is to be divided into 14 equal spaces.

24 = Spaces @ 0.75 C.C. The spacing is 0.75" center to center for 24 spaces from located rivet or rivets.

4.29 Removing Rivets: Two Thicknesses of Material

When removing rivets from two thicknesses of material, use standard size drills. Select the correct size drill and pin punch:

Punch and Rivet Diameter	Drill to be Used
3/32	#41
1/8	#30
5/32	#21
3/16	#11
1/4	F

NOTE: All dimensions are in inches

1. Centerpunch "A" and "DD" rivets. "AD" rivets need no centerpunching since they are dimpled. Start the drill at the center of the head in a straight line with the rivet shank.

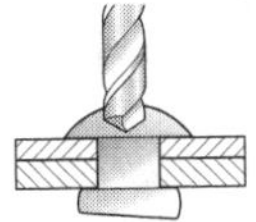

2. Drill through the rivet head and into the shank as shown.

3. Use a pin punch to snap the head from the shank.

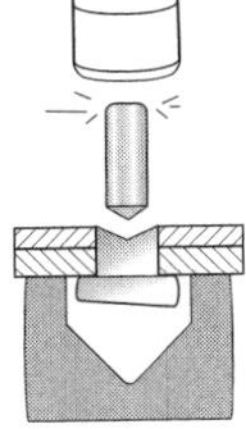

4. Use a fiber block to support the material and drive out the rivet shank with a pin punch and light hammer.

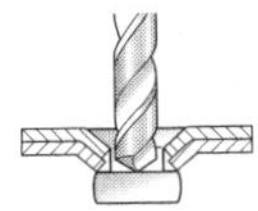

5. When removing flush rivets from dimpled sheets, drill as shown.

4.30 Removing Rivets from Multiple Sheets

The steps for removing rivets from multiple thicknesses of material, forgings,or castings are similar to those used for two thicknesses. However, use undersize rather than standard size drills to avoid enlarging the hole.
Select the correct size drill:

Rivet Diameter	Drill to be Used
1/8	#41
5/32	#30
3/16	#21
1/4	F

NOTE: All dimensions are in inches

1. Centerpunch "A" and "DD" rivets. "AD" Rivets need no centerpunching since they are dimpled. Start the drill at the center of the head in a straight line with the rivet shank.

2. Drill through the rivet head and into the shank as shown.

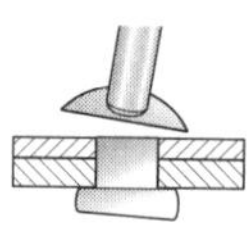

3. Use a pin punch to snap the head from the shank.

4. Use a fiber block to support the material and drive out the shank with a pin punch and light hammer.

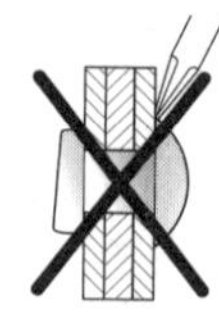

5. Never use a chisel or a screw driver to remove a rivet or the material may be cut or the hole elongated.

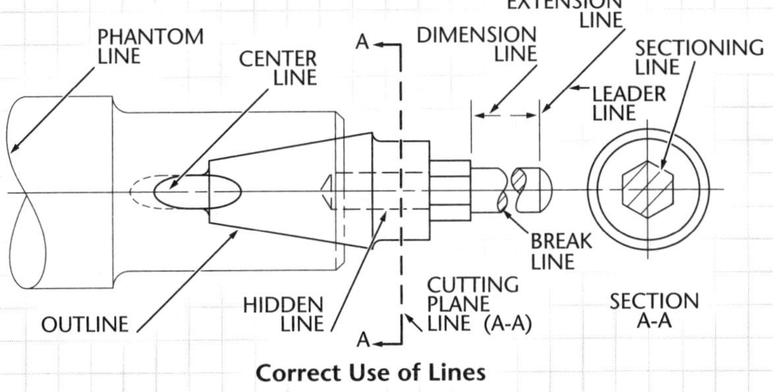

Correct Use of Lines

5

Aircraft Drawings

5.1 **Types of Drawings**

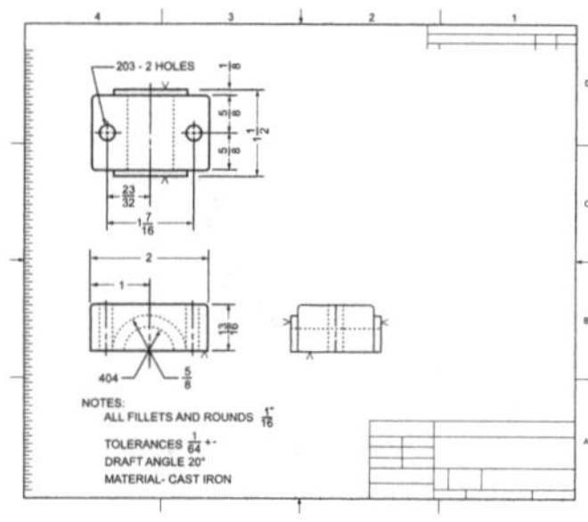

Single Detail Drawing

Assembly Drawing

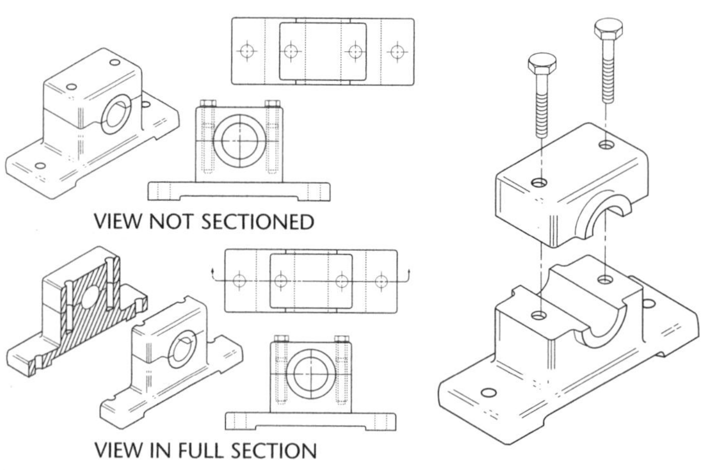

Sectional Drawings

Exploded View

5.1 **Types of Drawings (cont'd)**

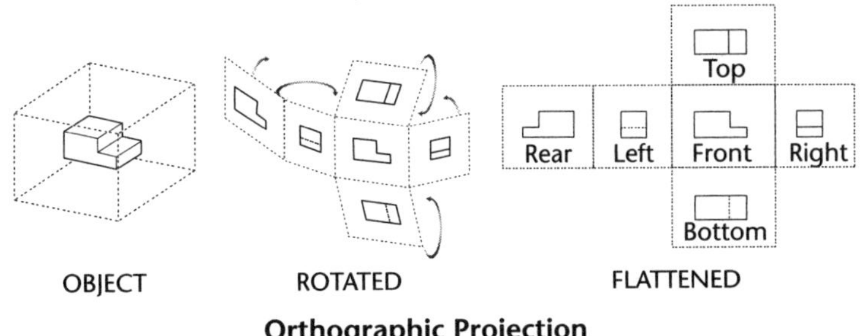

Orthographic Projection

5.2 **Meaning of Lines**

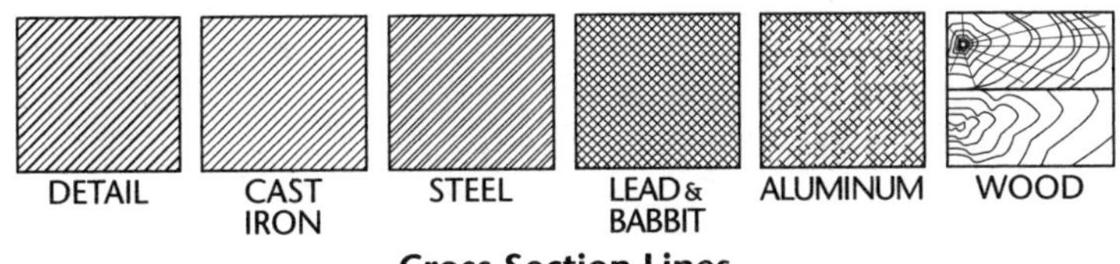

Cross Section Lines

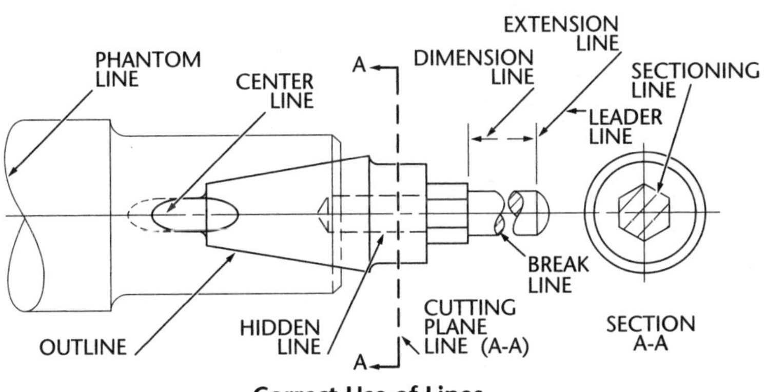

Correct Use of Lines

5.2 **Meaning of Lines (cont'd)**

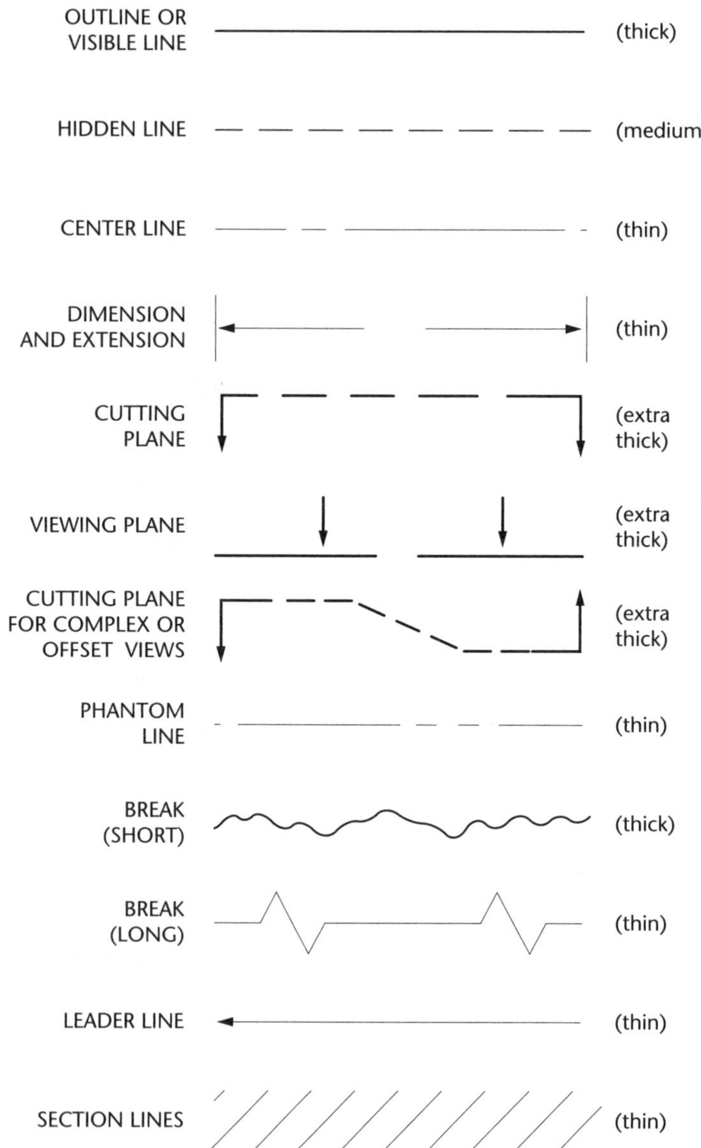

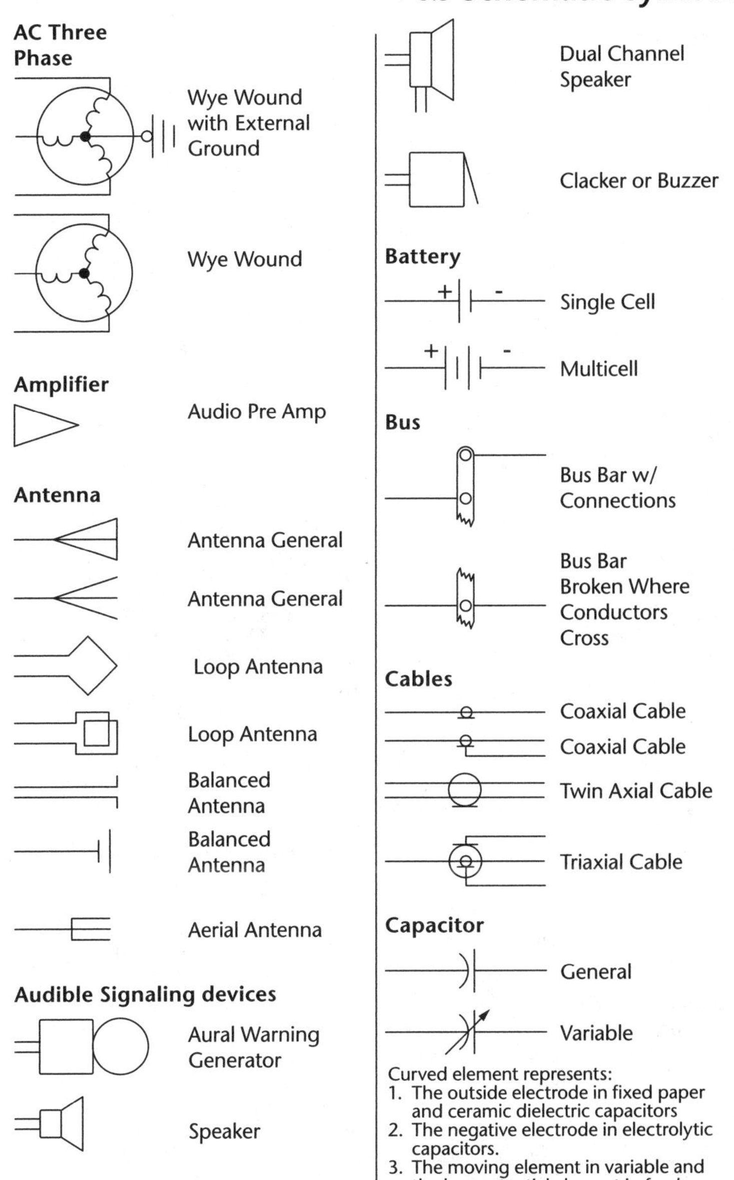

Curved element represents:
1. The outside electrode in fixed paper and ceramic dielectric capacitors
2. The negative electrode in electrolytic capacitors.
3. The moving element in variable and the low potential element in feed through capacitors.

5.3 **Schematic Symbols (cont'd)**

Circuit Breaker

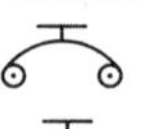

Single-Phased

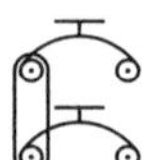

Single
Phase-Bussed

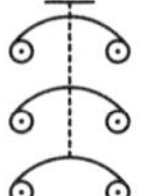

Three Phase

Connector

Quick
Disconnect

○

Terminal

•

Solder Point

Separate
Connectors
Engaged[1]

[1] One connector shown.

Coaxial-Outside Conductor

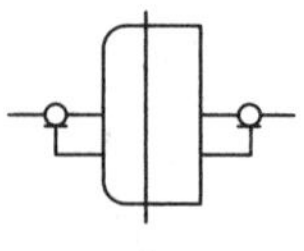

Carried Through

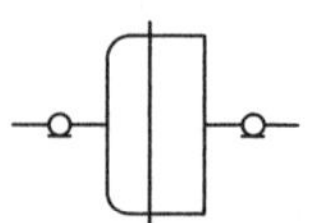

Not Carried
Through

Convenience Outlet
(Receptacle)

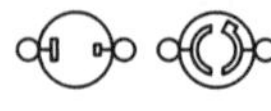

2 Conductor
Polarized

3 Conductor
Polarized

Critical Ground

▲ 1

Symbol

Data Bus

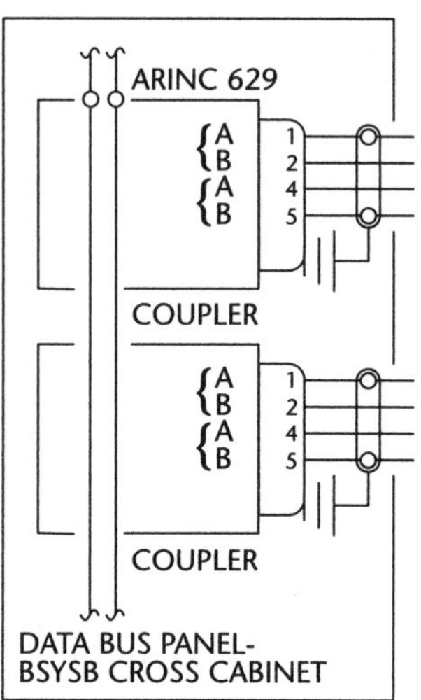

Diode

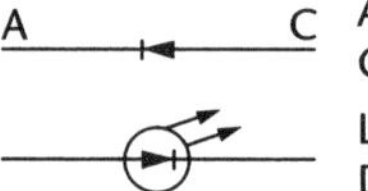

A (Anode)
C (Cathode)

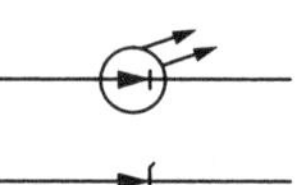

Light Emitting
Diode (LED

Zener Diode

Fire Detector

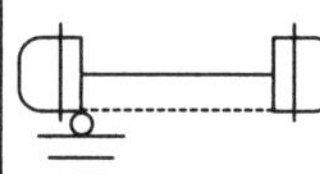

Continuous
Loop Fire
Detector

Fire Extinguisher Actuator Head

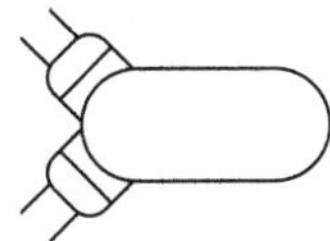

Fluorescent

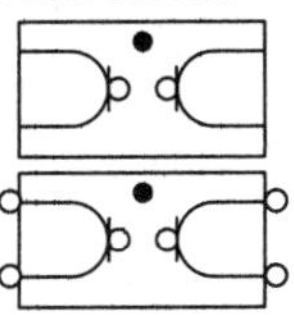

Lamp Color:	Symbol:
Amber	A
Blue	B
Green	G
Red	R
White	W
Yellow	Y
Violet	V

Flag Notes

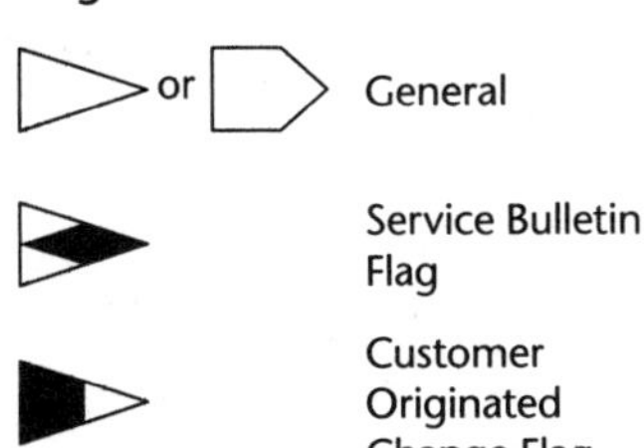

General

Service Bulletin Flag

Customer Originated Change Flag

Fuse

Generator

Standard

General Symbols

Frequency

Ω Ohm or Resistance

— Negative Polarity

+ Positive Polarity

Governor

Speed Regulator

Ground

Standard

Chassis

Internal

Burundy Block

Burundy Track

5.3 Schematic Symbols (cont'd)

Gyro

Gyrosope or Gyrocompass

Handset

Press to Talk

Head Set

Standard

Boom Mic

Heater

Standard

Ignitor Plug

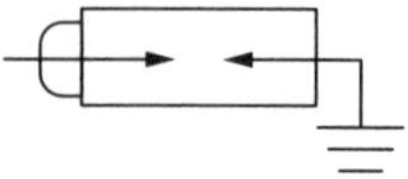

Indicator or Warning

Alternating Current Type

Indicator or Warning

Press to Test

Lamp

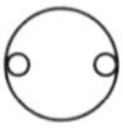

Basic

Ballast Lamp

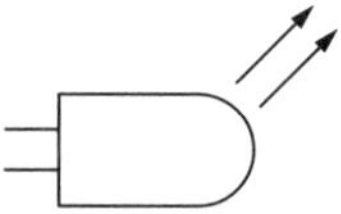

Light Emitting Diode

Incandescent

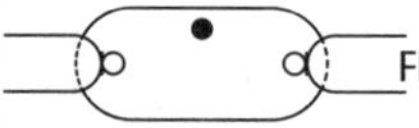

Fluorescent

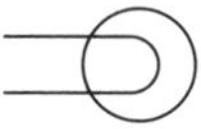

Incandescent

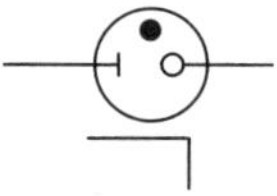

Press to Test

Logic Devices

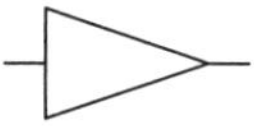

Buffer or Amplifier

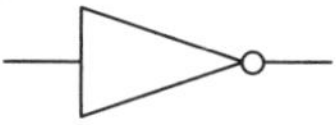

Inverter

AND Gate

NAND Gate

AND Gate with one input having an active low

OR Gate

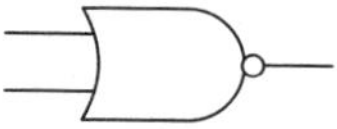

NOR Gate

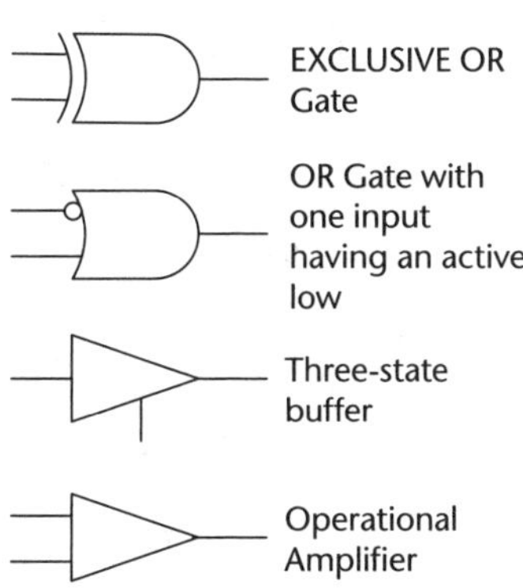

EXCLUSIVE OR Gate

OR Gate with one input having an active low

Three-state buffer

Operational Amplifier

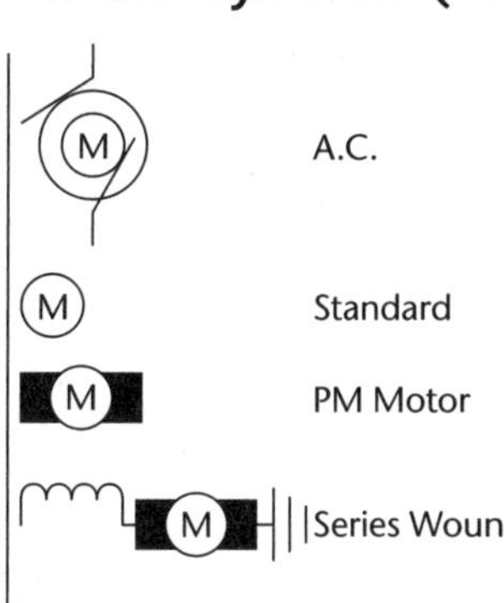

A.C.

Standard

PM Motor

Series Wound

Phone Jack

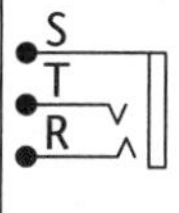

Phone Plug

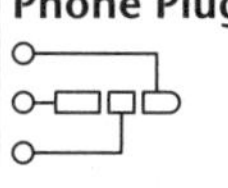

Photocell

Plug and Receptacle

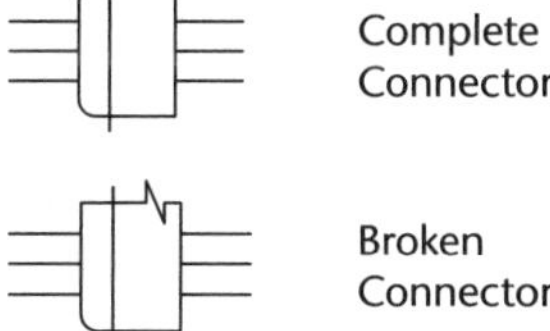

Complete Connector

Broken Connector

Loud Speaker

Horn

Magnetic Blowout Coil

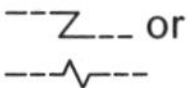 or

Microphone

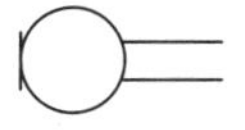

Motor

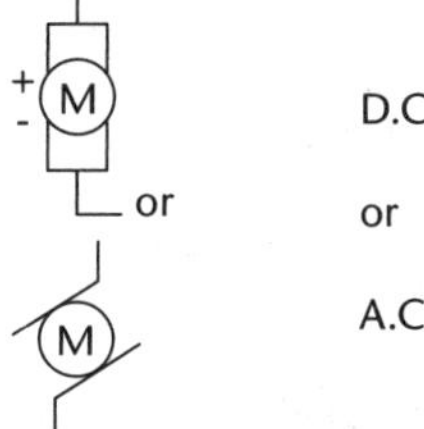

D.C.

or

A.C.

5.3 **Schematic Symbols (cont'd)**

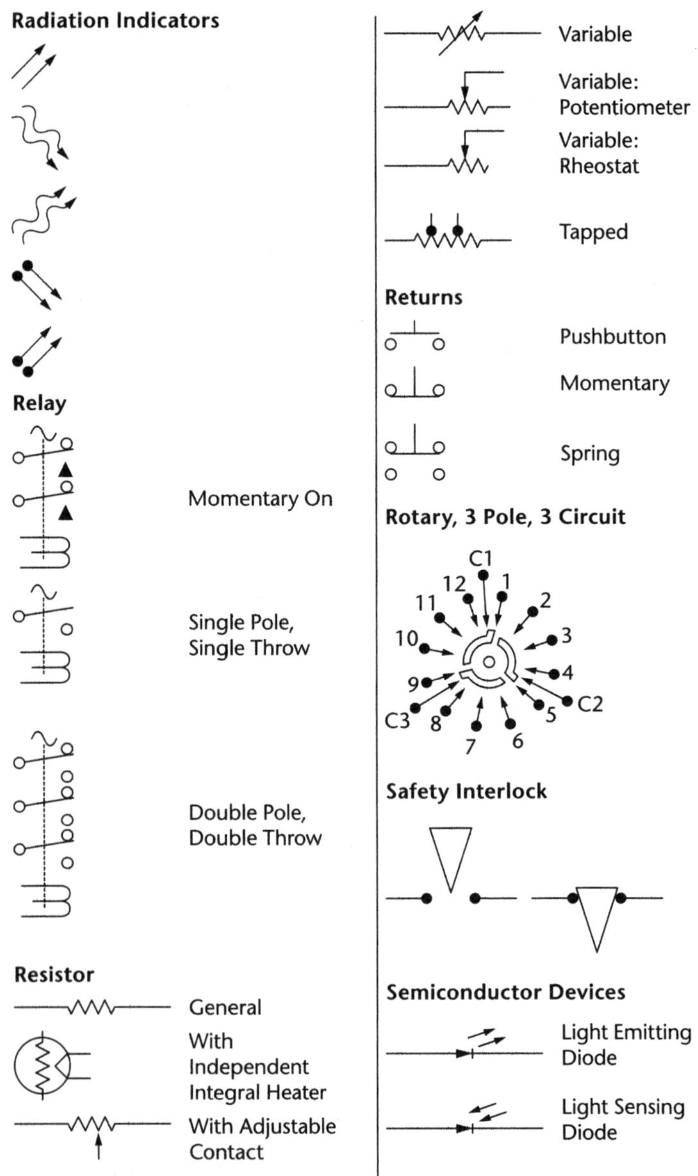

5.3 Schematic Symbols (cont'd)

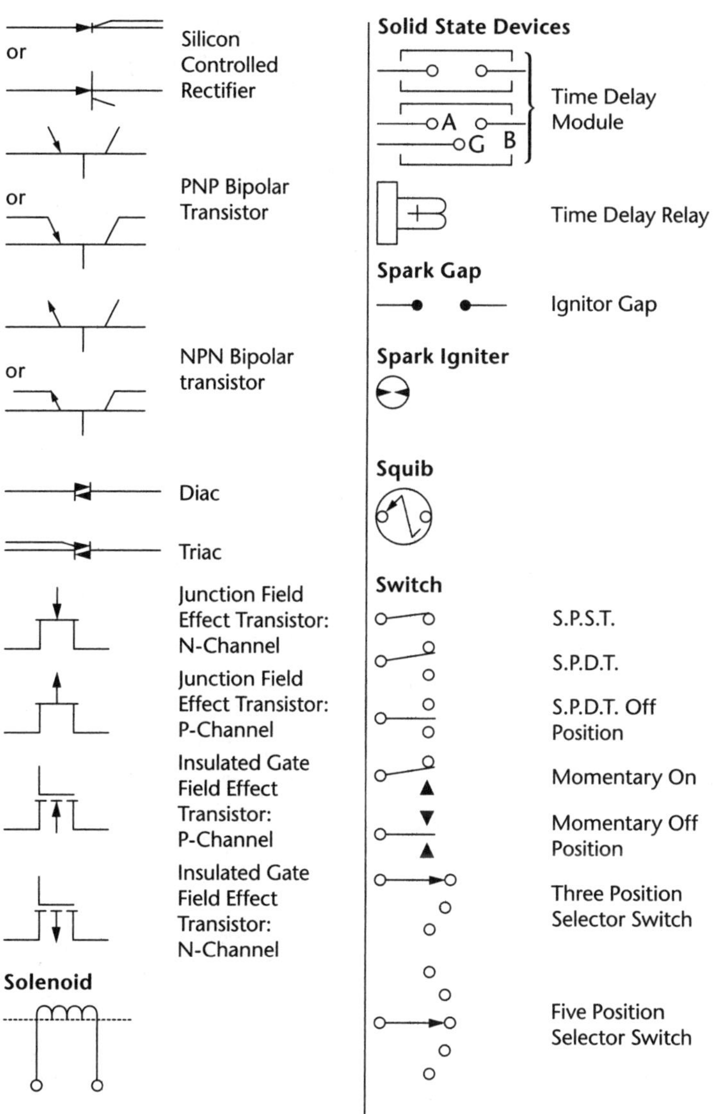

5.3 Schematic Symbols (cont'd)

Switch/Relay Actuators

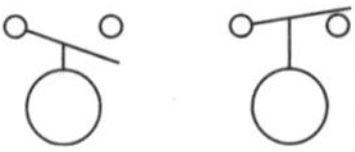

Liquid Level Actuated

Pressure or Vacuum Actuated

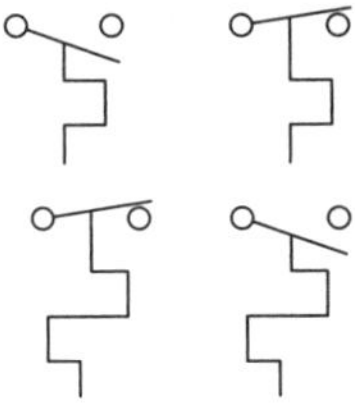

Temperature Actuated

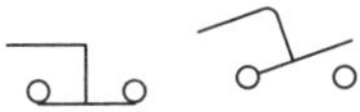

Foot Operated

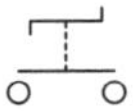

Operate by Turning

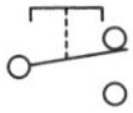

Operate by Pushing

Operate by Pulling

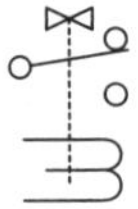

Valve Controlled

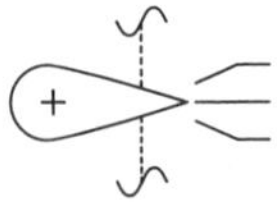

Three Position Toggle

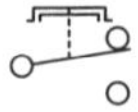

Shielded Push Operated

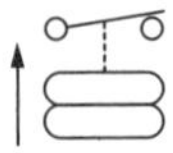

Pressure Operated (Arrow indicates Direction of Bar Movement)

Terminal Block Symbols

Terminal Block Diode

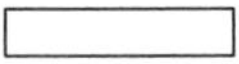

Intended for 24-20 Gauge Wire

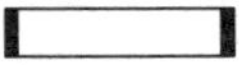

Intended for 18-16 Gauge Wire

Terminal Block Resistor

Terminal Strip and Bus

•   Solder Point

Terminals and Sizes

Symbol	Stud Sizes
	2
	4
	6
	8
	10
	3/4
	5/16
	3/8
	1/2

Test Point Recognition

Thermal Element

Thermomechanical Transducer

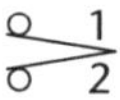

Thermocouple Temp Sensor

Thermal Switch

Opens on Rising Temperature

Closes on Rising Temperature

Transformer

Auto Transformer

Basic Air Core

Current

or

Iron Core

Transmission Patch

Conductor Cable Wiring

Wires

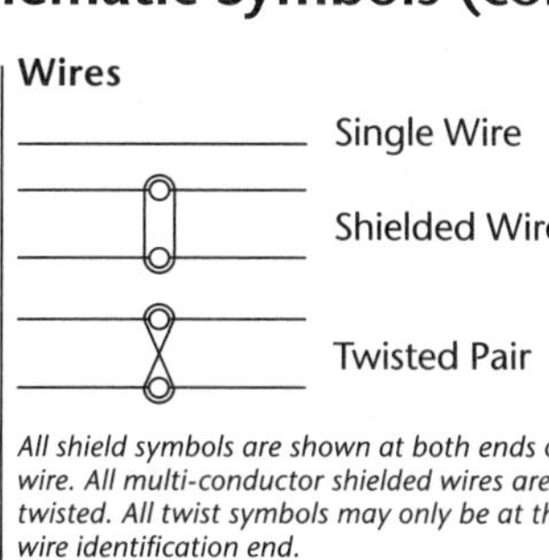

Single Wire

Shielded Wire

Twisted Pair

All shield symbols are shown at both ends of wire. All multi-conductor shielded wires are twisted. All twist symbols may only be at the wire identification end.

Stowed Wire

Capped Wire

Cap & Stow Near DXXXXXXX

Taped Terminal

Contact

Size 4 Lug

Size 5 Lug

Size 8 Lug

Size 10 Lug

Tape and Stow Near DXXXXXX

Shielded Wire

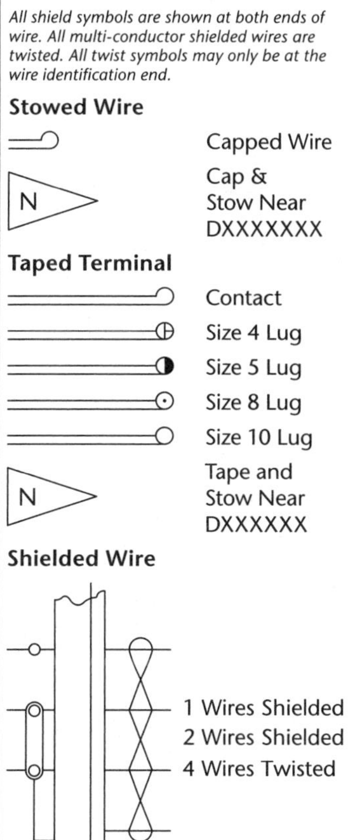

1 Wires Shielded
2 Wires Shielded
4 Wires Twisted

 Schematic Symbols (cont'd)

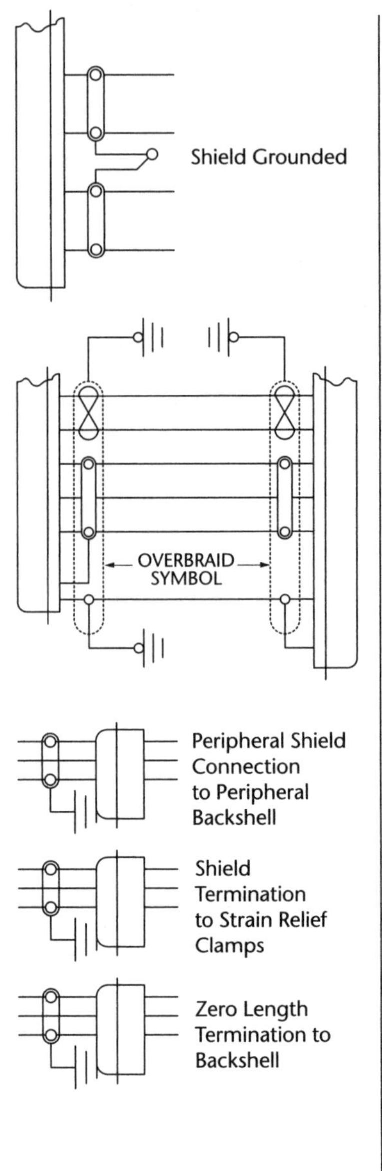

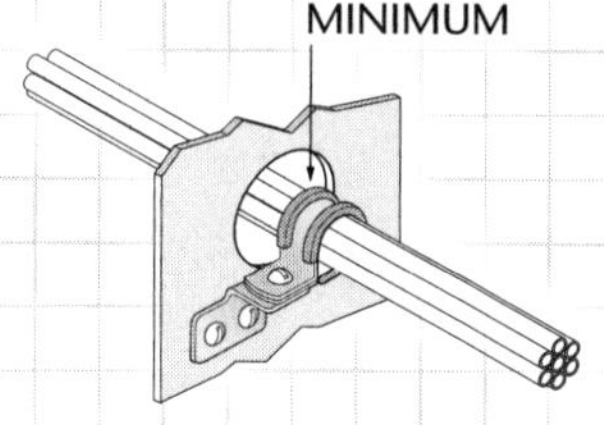

6

Electrical Systems

6.1 **Alternating Current Terms and Values**

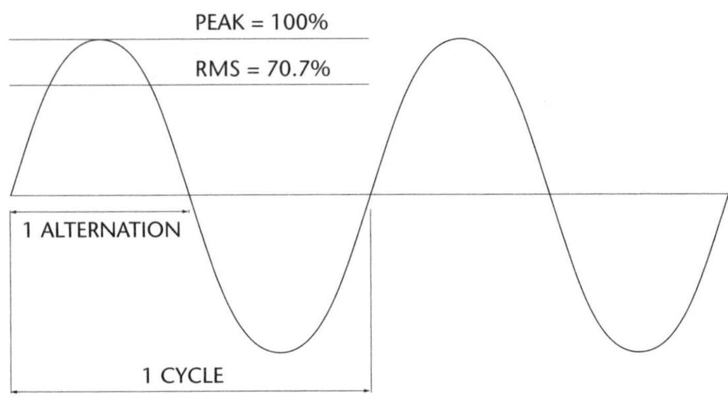

Alternation	One half cycle of alternating current
Cycle	One complete series of values of alternating current in which the voltage or current starts from zero and then returns to zero represented by the tilde symbol (~)
Frequency	The number of cycles of alternating current that occur in one second
Peak Value	The maximum amplitude of current or voltage in one alternation
Peak-to-Peak Value	The voltage or current measured from a positive peak to a negative peak
Period	The time required for one cycle of alternating current
Phase	The angular relationship between the current and voltage in an AC circuit.
Power	Power in an AC circuit is determined by the voltage and the amount of current that is in phase with the voltage
Power Factor	The percentage of current in an AC circuit that is in phase with the voltage.
RMS Value	Root mean square, or effective value. This is 70.7 percent of peak value.

Terms

R = Value of a Single Resistor
R_T = Total Resistance
R_1, R_2, R_3 = Value of Individual Resistors
n = Number of Resistors or Capacitors
X_C = Capacitive Reactance in Ohms
K = Dielectric Constant
A = Area of plates in square inches
D = Thickness of dielectric in inches
N = Number of plates
C = Capacity in picofarads
C_T = Total Capacitance
C_1, C_2, C_3 = Value of Individual Capacitors

Formulas Involving Resistors

Resistors in series:

$$R_T = R_1 + R_2 + R_3 + \ldots$$

Resistors of the same value in parallel:

$$R_T = \frac{R}{n}$$

Resistors of a different value in parallel:

$$R_T = \frac{R_1 \times R_2}{R_1 + R_2}$$

More than two resistors of a different value in parallel:

$$R_T = \frac{1}{1/R_1 + 1/R_2 + 1/R_3 + 1/R_4}$$

Formulas Involving Capacitance

Capacitors in parallel:

$$C_T = C_1 + C_2 + C_3 + \ldots$$

Capacitors of the same value in series:

$$C_T = \frac{C}{n}$$

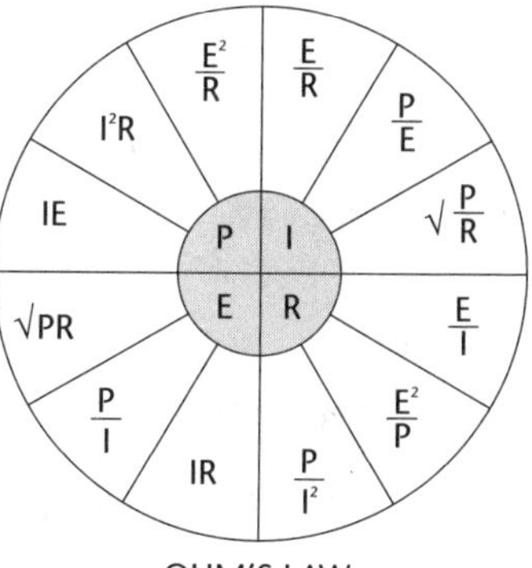

OHM'S LAW

6.2 **Electrical Formulas (cont'd)**

Two capacitors of different values in series:

$$C_T = \frac{C_1 \times C_2}{C_1 + C_2}$$

More than two capacitors of different values in series:

$$C_T = \frac{1}{1/C_1 + 1/C_2 + 1/C_3 + 1/C_4}$$

Capacitive Reactance:

$$X_C = \frac{1}{2\pi FC}$$

Formulas Involving Inductance
Inductors in series with no mutual inductance:

$$L_T = L_1 + L_2 + L_3 + \ldots$$

Two inductors of different size in parallel with no mutual inductance:

$$L_T = \frac{L_1 \times L_2}{L_1 + L_2}$$

More than two inductors of different size in parallel with no mutual inductance:

$$L_T = \frac{1}{1/L_1 + 1/L_2 + 1/L_3 + 1/L_4}$$

Formulas Involving Inductance and Capacitance
Inductive Reactance:

$$X_L = 2\pi FL$$

Resonant Frequency:

$$F_R = \frac{1}{2\pi\sqrt{LC}}$$

The *resonant frequency* of an AC circuit is that frequency which causes the capacitive reactance and the inductive reactance to be the same.
Total Reactance:

$$X_T = X_C - X_L \quad \text{or} \quad X_T = X_L - X_C$$

Current in a purely capacitive circuit leads the voltage by 90 degrees, and current in a purely inductive circuit lags 90 degrees behind the voltage.
Capacitive reactance and inductive reactance are 180 degrees out of phase with each other, and they cancel.

Gauge	Diam. (mm)	Circular (mm)	Area (sq. in.)
			(Nominal Cross Section)
0000	460.0	211,600	0.460000
000	409.6	167,800	0.409642
00	364.8	133,100	0.364796
0	324.9	105,600	0.324861
1	289.3	83,690	0.289297
2	257.6	66,360	0.257627
3	229.4	52,620	0.229423
4	204.3	41,740	0.2043
5	181.9	33,090	0.1819
6	162.0	26,240	0.1620
7	144.3	20,820	0.1443
8	128.5	16,510	0.1285
9	114.4	13,090	0.1144
10	101.9	10,380	0.1019
11	90.7	8,230	0.0907
12	80.8	6,530	0.0808
13	72.0	5,180	0.0720
14	64.1	4,110	0.0641
15	57.1	3,260	0.0571
16	50.8	2,580	0.0508
17	45.3	2,050	0.0453
18	40.3	1,620	0.0403
19	35.9	1,200	0.0359
20	32.0	1,020	0.0320
21	28.5	812	0.0285
22	25.3	640	0.0253
23	22.6	511	0.0226
24	20.1	404	0.0201
25	17.9	320	0.0179
26	15.9	253	0.0159
27	14.2	202	0.0142
28	12.6	159	0.0126
29	11.3	128	0.0113
30	10.0	100	0.0100

Gauge	Diam. (mm)	Circular (mm)	Area (sq. in.)
			(Nominal Cross Section)
31	8.9	79.2	0.0089
32	8.0	64.0	0.0080
33	7.1	50.4	0.0071
34	6.3	39.7	0.0063
35	5.6	31.4	0.0056
36	5.0	25.0	0.0050
37	4.5	20.2	0.0045
38	4.0	16.0	0.0040
39	3.5	12.2	0.0035
40	3.1	9.61	0.0031
41	2.8	7.84	0.0028
42	2.5	6.25	0.0025
43	2.2	4.84	0.0022
44	2.0	4.00	0.0020
45	1.76	3.10	0.0018
46	1.57	2.46	0.0016
47	1.40	1.96	0.0014
48	1.24	1.54	0.0012
49	1.11	1.23	0.0011
50	0.99	0.980	0.0010

6.4 Current Carrying Capacity

Current Carrying Capacity of Aluminum Wire

Wire Size	Single Wire Maximum Amps	Wire Bundle Or Conduit Maximum Amps
6	83	50
4	108	66
2	152	90
0	202	123
00	235	145
000	266	162
0000	303	190

Current Carrying Capacity of Copper Wire

Wire Size	Single Wire Maximum Amps	Wire Bundle Or Conduit Maximum Amps
20	11	7.5
18	16	10.0
16	22	13.0
14	32	17.0
12	41	23.0
10	55	33.0
8	73	46.0
6	101	60.0
4	135	80.0
2	181	100.0
1	211	125.0
0	245	150.0
00	283	175.0
000	328	200.0
0000	380	225.0

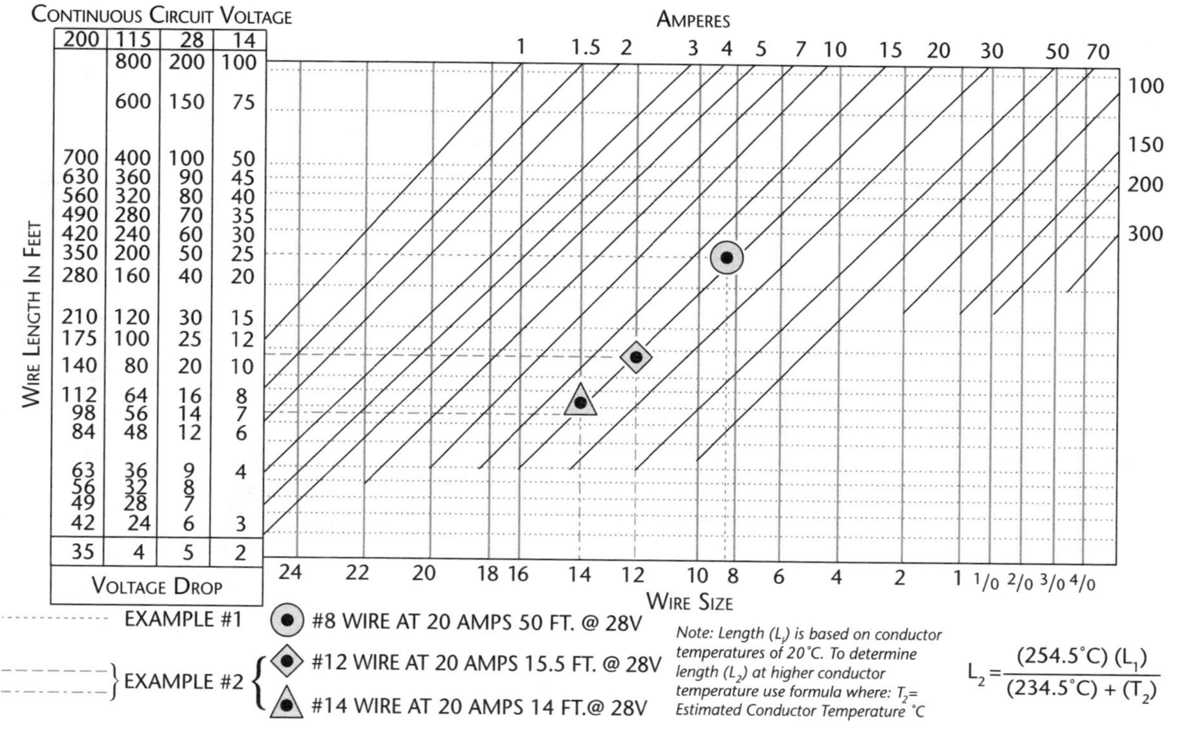

$$L_2 = \frac{(254.5°C)\,(L_1)}{(234.5°C)+(T_2)}$$

Continuous Circuit Voltage			
200	115	28	14
	800	200	100
	600	150	75
700	400	100	50
630	360	90	45
560	320	80	40
490	280	70	35
420	240	60	30
350	200	50	25
280	160	40	20
210	120	30	15
175	100	25	12
140	80	20	10
112	64	16	8
98	56	14	7
84	48	12	6
63	36	9	4
56	32	8	
49	28	7	
42	24	6	3
35	4	5	2

6.5 Electrical Installation Practices: Clamps

Correct

Incorrect

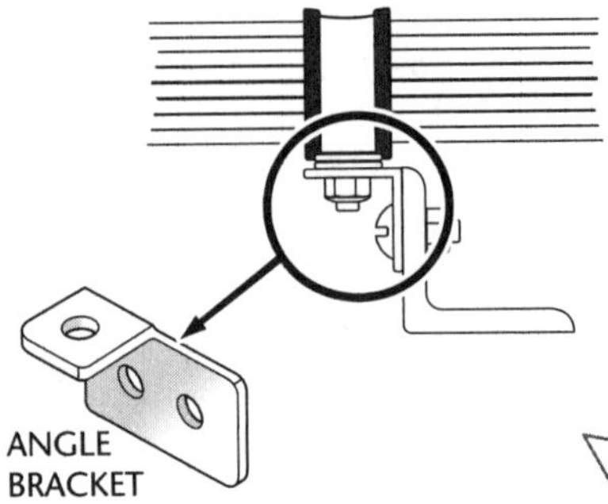

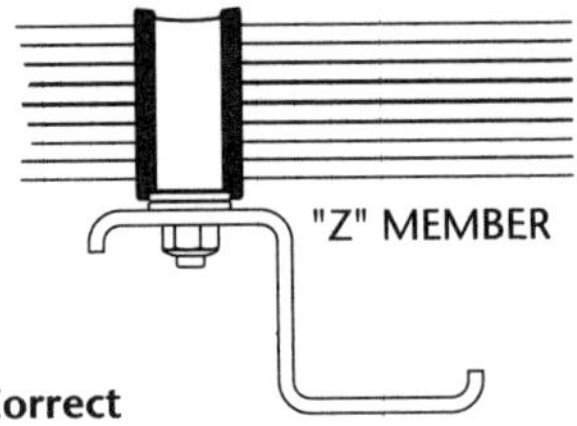

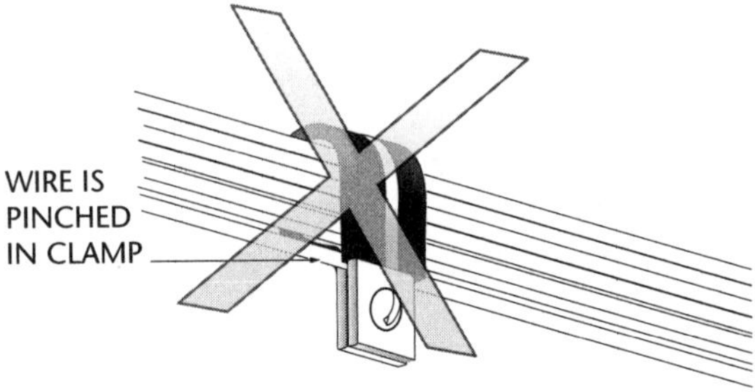

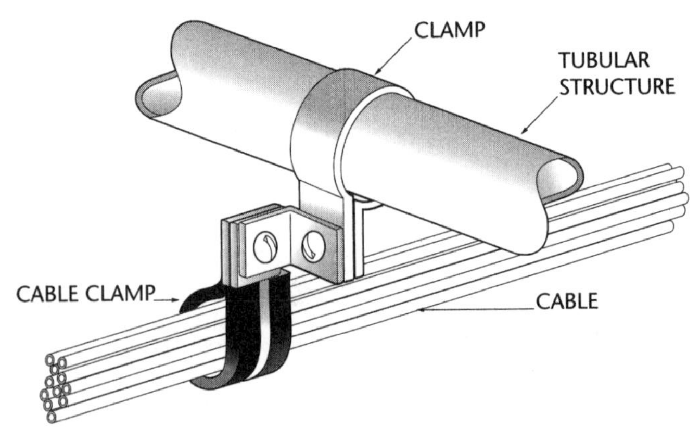

Adel Clamps and Acceptable Hardware

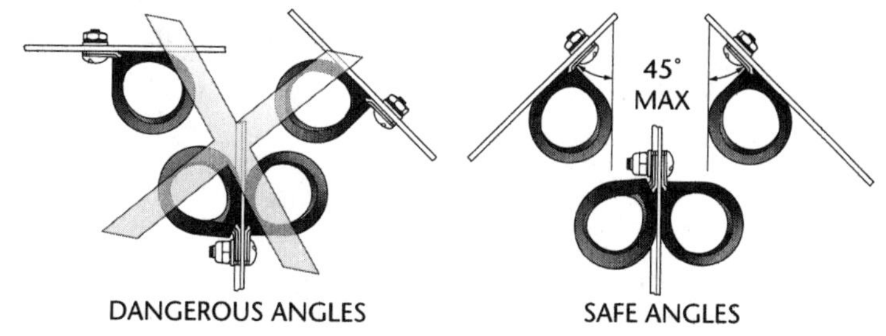

Acceptable Mounting Angles for Adel Clamps

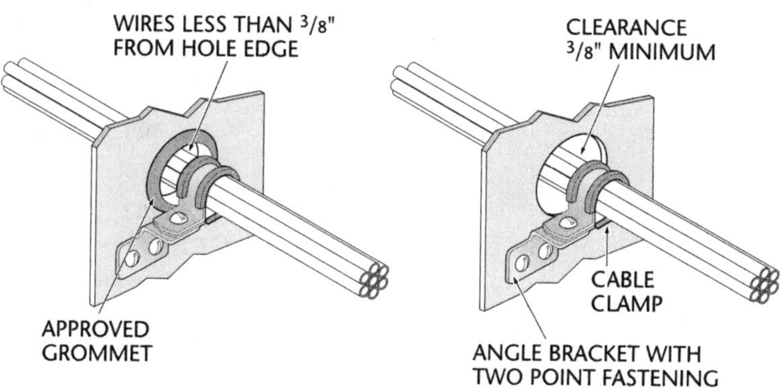

**Acceptable Methods for Routing Wire through a
Former Lightening Hole**

6.6 Circuit Breaker and Fuse Selections

Wire AN gauge copper	Circuit breaker amp	Fuse amp
22	5.0	5
20	7.5	5
18	10.0	10
16	15.0	10
14	20.0	15
12	30.0	20
10	40.0	30
8	50.0	50
6	80.0	70
4	100.0	70
2	125.0	100
1		150
0		150

Basis of Chart
- Wire bundles in 135°F ambient and altitudes up to 30,000 feet
- Wire bundles of 15 or more wires, with wires carrying no more than 20 percent of the total current carrying capacity of the bundle as given in specification MIL-W-5088 (ASG)
- Protectors in 75 to 85°F ambient
- Copper wire specification MIL-W-5088
- Circuit breakers to specification MIL-C-5809 or equivalent
- Fuses to specification MIL-F-1 5160 or equivalent

6.7 Switch Derating Factors

Nominal System Voltage	Type of Load	Derating Factor
28VDC	Lamp	8
28VDC	Inductive (relay solenoid)	4
28VDC	Resistive (Heater)	2
28VDC	Motor	3
12VDC	Lamp	5
12VDC	Inductive (relay-solenoid)	2
12VDC	Resistive (Heater)	1
12VDC	Motor	2

NOTES: To find the nominal rating of a switch required to operate a given device multiply the continuous current rating of the device by the derating factor corresponding to the voltage and type of load.

To find the continuous rating that a switch of a given nominal rating will handle efficiently, divide the switch nominal rating by the derating factor corresponding to the voltage and type of load.

6.8 Electrical Installation Practices: Bolted

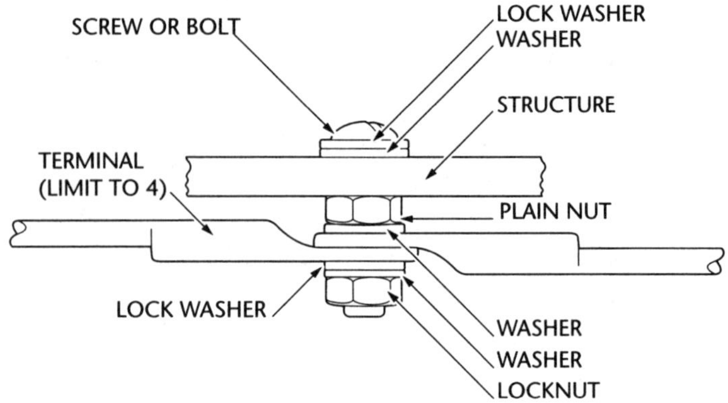

Grounding a Stud to a Flat Surface

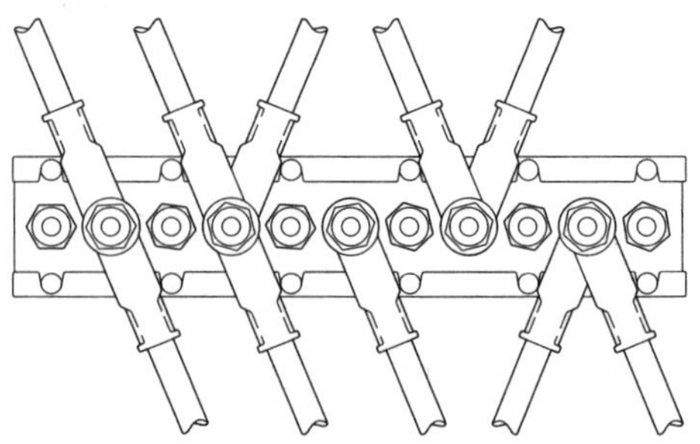

NOTE: All terminals should be placed so that
movement will tighten nut

**Appropriate Method for Connecting Terminals
to Terminal Board**

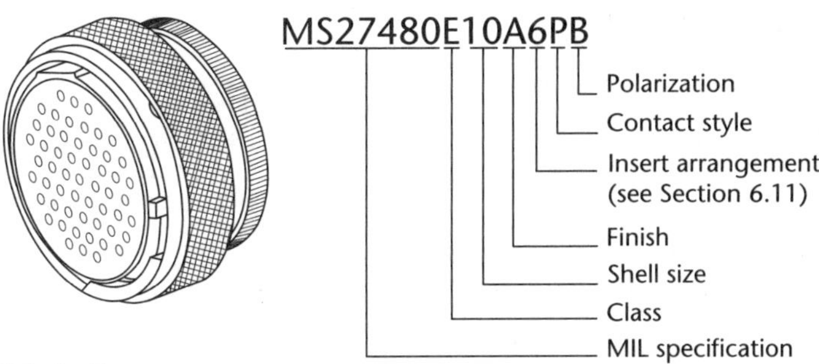

Polarization

A Normal-No Letter required
B Normal-No Letter required
C Normal-No Letter required
D Normal-No Letter required

Contact Style

A Without pin contacts
B Without socket contacts
C Feed through
P Pin contacts-including hermetic with solder cups
X Pin contacts with eyelet (hermetic)
Z Socket contacts with eyelet (hermetic)

Finish

A Silver to light iridescent yellow color cadmium plate over nickel
  (conductive), -65°C to +150°C (inactive for new design)
B Olive drab cadmium plate over suitable underplate (conductive), -65°C
  to +175°C
C Anodic (nonconductive), -65°C to+175°C
D Fused Tin, carbon steel (conductive), -65°C to 150°C
E Corrosion resistant steel (CRES), Passivated (conductive),-65°C to
  +200°C
F Electroless nickel coating (conductive), -65°C to +200°C
N Hermetic seal or environment resisting CRES (conductive plating), -65°C
  to +200°C

Class

E Environment resisting box and through bulkhead mounting types only
  (see Class T)
P Potting-includes potting form and short rear grommet
T Environment resisting-wall and jam-nut mounting receptacle and plug
  types: thread and teeth for accessory attachment
Y Hermetically sealed

6.9 Connector Information (cont'd)

MIL Specification

MS27472 Wall Mount Receptacle
MS27484 Straight Plug EMI Grounding
MS27473 Straight Plug
MS27497 Wall Receptacle, Back Panel Mounting
MS27474 Jam Nut Receptacle
MS27499 Box Mounting Receptacle
MS27475 Hermitic Wall Mount Receptacle
MS27500 90° Plug
MS27476 Hermetic Box Mount Receptacle
MS27503 Hermetic Solder Mount Receptacle
MS27477 Hermetic Jam Nut Receptacle

MS27508 Box Mount Receptacle, Back Panel Mounting
MS27480 Straight Plug
MS27481 Jam Nut Receptacle
MS27513 Box Mount Receptacle, Long Grommet
MS27482 Hermetic Wall Mount Receptacle
MS27664 Wall Mount Receptacle, Back Panel Mounting
MS27483 Hermetic Jam Nut Receptacle
MS27667 Thru-bulkhead Receptacle

MS27478 Hermetic Solder Mount Receptacle
MS27504 Box Mount Receptacle
MS27479 Wall Mount Receptacle

Active	Supersedes
MS27472	MS27479
MS27473	MS27480
MS27474	MS27481
MS27475	MS27482
MS27477	MS27483
MS27473 with MS27507 elbow	MS27500
MS27478	MS27503
MS27499	MS27504
MS27497	MS27664

6.10 **Connector/Receptacle Orientation**

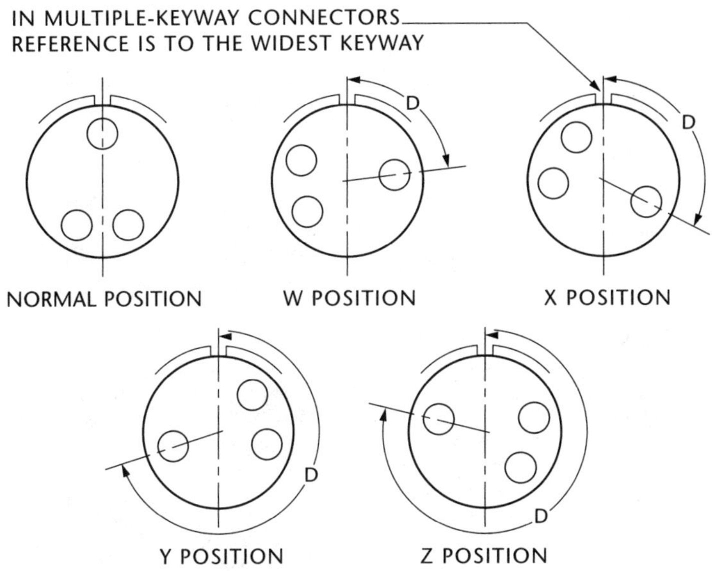

FRONT VIEW SOCKET INSERT (PIN INSERT OPPOSITE)
D EQUALS DEGREES OF ROTATION

6.11 Insert Plug Arrangement

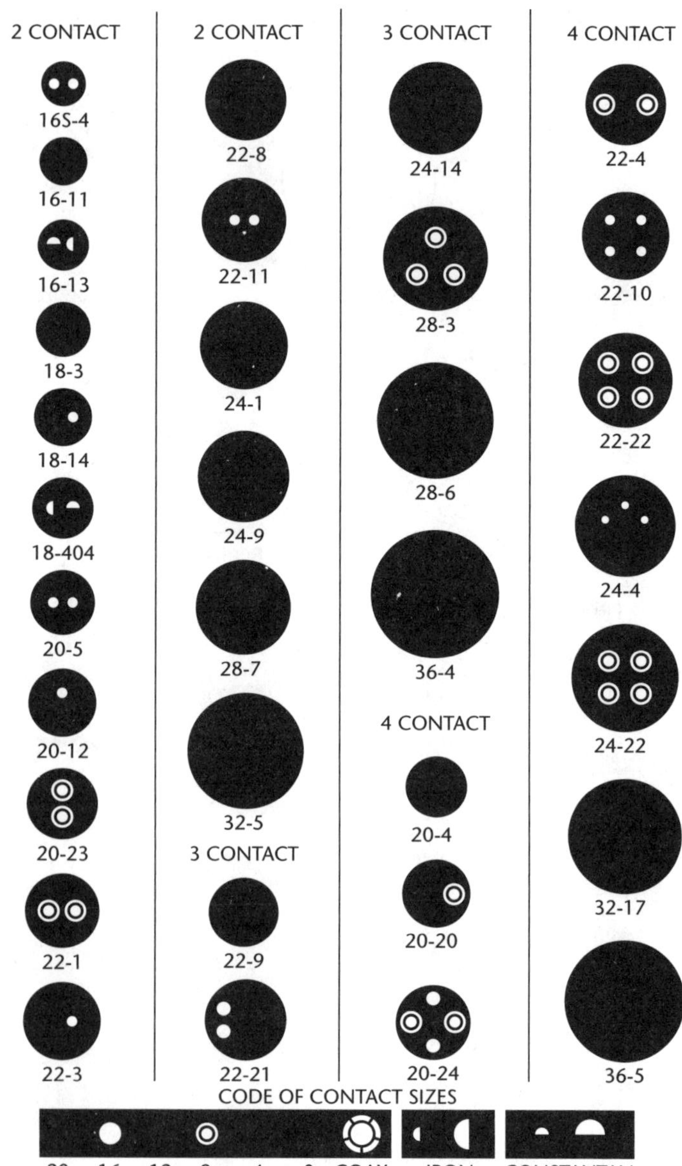

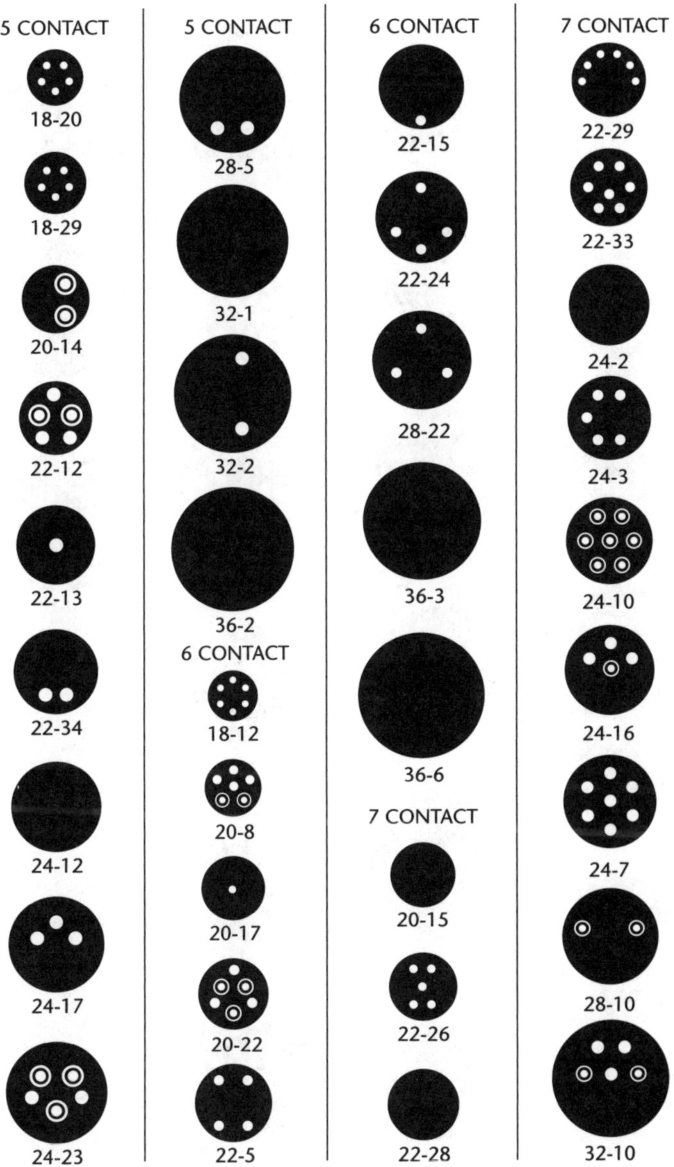

5 CONTACT
18-20
18-29
20-14
22-12
22-13
22-34
24-12
24-17
24-23
5 CONTACT
28-5
32-1
32-2
36-2
6 CONTACT
18-12
20-8
20-17
20-22
22-5
6 CONTACT
22-15
22-24
28-22
36-3
36-6
7 CONTACT
20-15
22-26
22-28
7 CONTACT
22-29
22-33
24-2
24-3
24-10
24-16
24-7
28-10
32-10

6.11 Insert Plug Arrangement (cont'd)

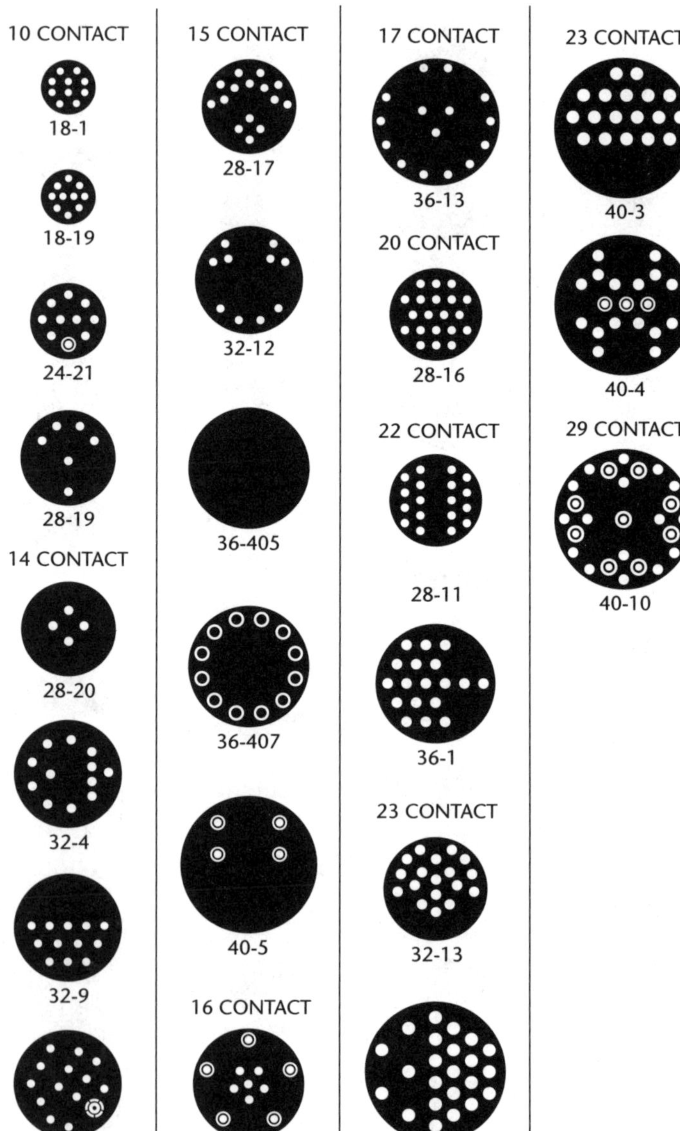

Resistor Color Code

Color Tolerance	Number	Tolerance
Black	0	....
Brown	1	1%
Red	2	2%
Orange	3	3%
Yellow	4	4%
Green	5	5%
Blue	6	6%
Violet	7	7%
Gray	8	8%
White	9	9%
Gold	....	5%
Silver	....	10%

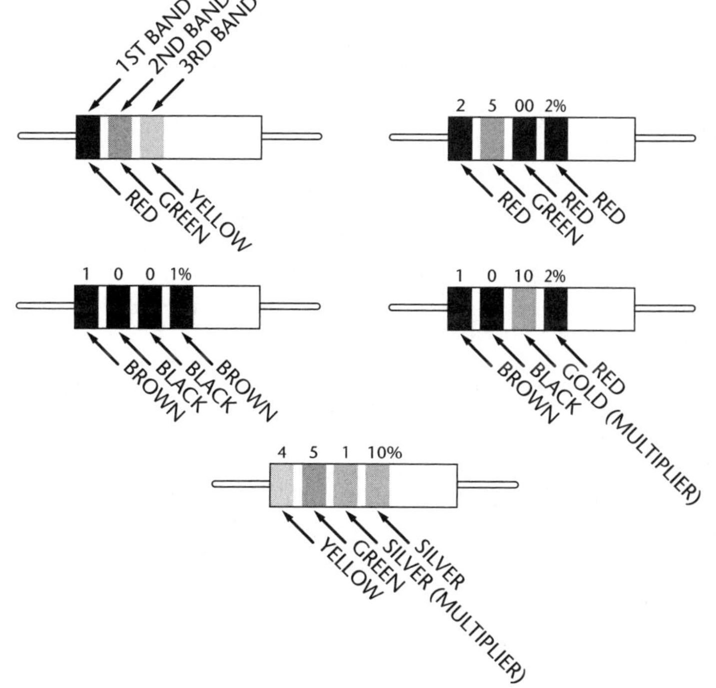

6.13 Lead Acid Batteries

Electrolyte Temperature		Points to be added to or subtracted from specific gravity readings
°C	°F	
60	140	+24
55	130	+20
49	120	+16
43	110	+12
38	100	+8
33	90	+4
27	80	0
23	70	-4
15	60	-8
10	50	-12
5	40	-16
-2	30	-20
-7	20	-24
-13	10	-28
-18	0	-32
-23	-10	-36
-28	-20	-40
-35	-30	-44

Inspect lead acid batteries for:
- Signs of electrolyte leakage
- Loose or missing hold-down fittings or hardware
- Loose of broken terminals
- Loose or missing vent caps
- Proper electrolyte level

Inspect vent lines for:
- Proper attachment
- Cuts or kinks
- Blockage

Clean spilled electrolyte with:
- Bicarbonate of soda and water
- Soft brush
- Restore the acid proof finish

Check the specific gravity of the electrolyte:
- With a hydrometer and temperature correction chart
- Before adding any liquid
- Use only distilled or de-mineralized water

NOTE: Always mix acid into water, NOT water into acid.
Do NOT service lead acid batteries in the same area as nickel-cadmium batteries

Observation	Probable Cause	Corrective Action
High-trickle charge — when charging at constant voltage of 28.5 ($\pm$0.1) volts, current does not drop below 1 amp after a 30-minute charge	Defective cells	While still charging, check individual cells. Those below 0.5 volts are defective and should be replaced. Those between 0.5 and 1.5 volts may be defective or may be unbalanced. Those above 1.5 volts are OK.
High-trickle charge after replacing defective cells, or battery fails to meet amp-hour capacity check	Cell imbalance	Discharge battery and short out individual cells for 8 hours. Charge battery using constant-current method. Check capacity and, if OK, recharge using constant current method.
Battery fails to deliver rated capacity	Cell imbalance or fault cells	Repeat capacity check, discharge and constant-current charge a maximum of 3 times. If capacity does not develop, replace faulty cells.
No potential available	Complete battery failure	Check terminals and all electrical connections. Check for dry cell. Check for high-trickle charge.
Excessive white crystal deposits on cells (There will always be some potassium carbonate present do to normal gassing.)	Excessive spewage	Battery subject to high charge current, high temperature, or high liquid level. Clean battery, constant-current charge and check liquid level. Check charger operation.
Distortion of cell case	Overcharge or high heat	Replace cell
Foreign material in cells — black or gray particles	Impure water, high heat, high concentration of KOH, or improper water level	Adjust specific gravity on electrolyte level. Check battery for cell imbalance or replace defective cell.
Excessive corrosion of hardware	Defective or damaged plating	Replace parts
Heat or blue marks on hardware	Loose connections causing overheating of intercell connector or hardware	Clean hardware and properly torque connectors.
Excessive water consumption — dry cell	Cell imbalance	Proceed as above for cell imbalance.

6.14 **Nickel-Cadmium Batteries (cont'd)**

Inspect nickel-cadmium batteries for:
- Arcing or burning of cell connectors
- Loose cell connectors
- Loose cell caps
- Warped or distorted cell cases
- Functioning battery temperature sensor
- Buildup of potassium carbonate at cell vents
- Loose attaching hardware

Clean spilled electrolyte with:
- Boric acid solution
- Vinegar
- Fresh water
- Soft bristle brush

Check the charge status or the battery:
- With a nickel-cadmium battery analyzer
- All cells must be completely discharged before deep cycle charging
- Check electrolyte levels after charging and add distilled or de-mineralized water

NOTE: Always mix alkali into water NOT water into alkali
Do NOT service nickel-cadmium batteries in the same area as lead acid batteries

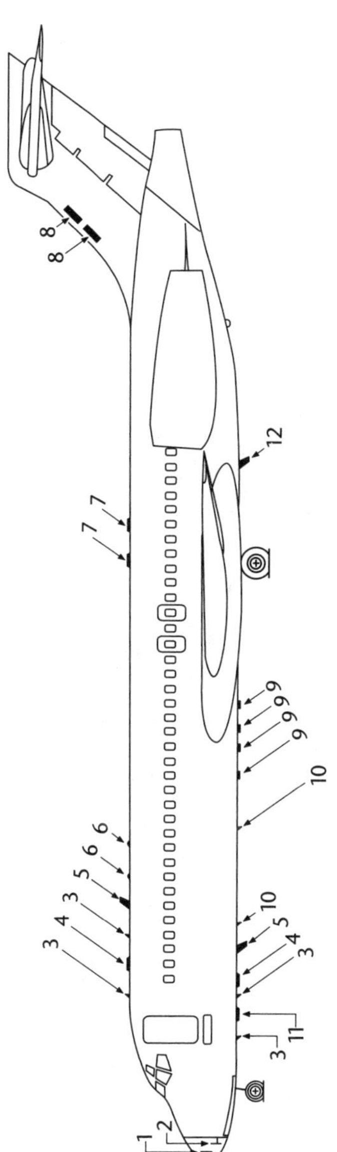

Typical Antenna Locations

1. WEATHER RADAR
2. GLIDESLOPE 1 & 2
3. ATC MODE S TRANSPONDER 1 & 2
4. TCAS
5. VHF COMM 1
6. GPS 1 & 2
7. ADF 1
8. VOR/LOC
9. VHF COMM
10. RADIO ALT RCVR & XMTR
11. DME 1 & 2
12. MARKER BEACON

6.16 Aircraft Antenna Identification

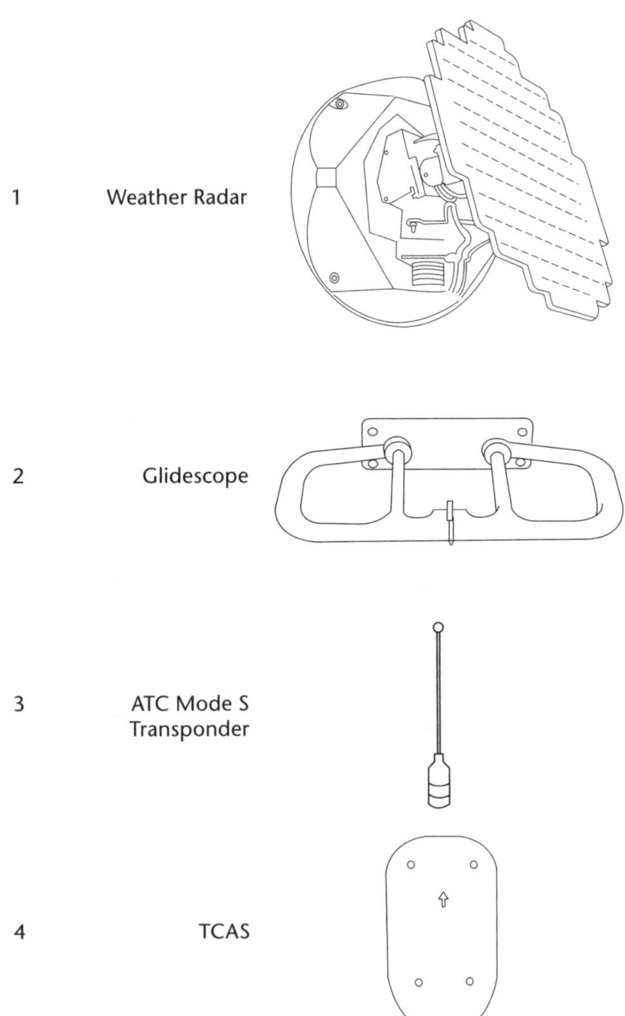

1   Weather Radar

2   Glidescope

3   ATC Mode S
        Transponder

4   TCAS

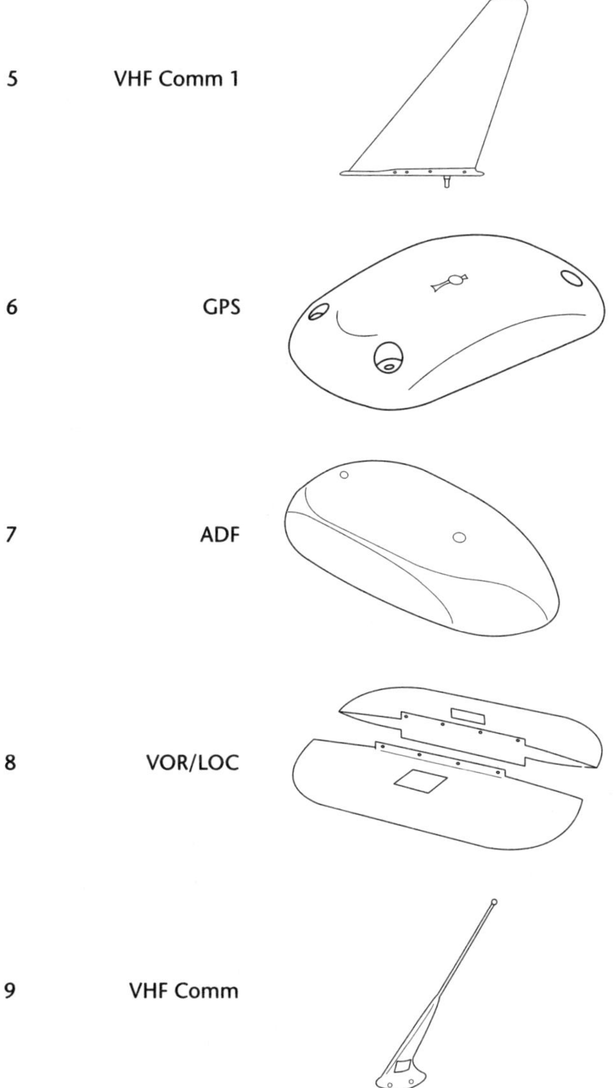

5   VHF Comm 1
6   GPS
7   ADF
8   VOR/LOC
9   VHF Comm

6.16 Aircraft Antenna Identification (cont'd)

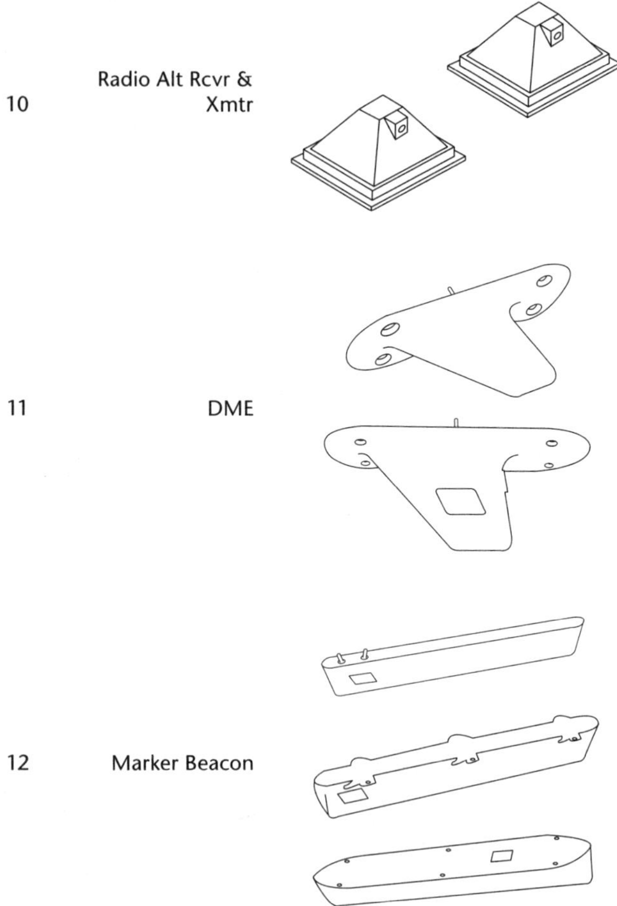

10	Radio Alt Rcvr & Xmtr
11	DME
12	Marker Beacon

7

Fluid Lines

7.1 Lay Lines

A typical lay line consists of:
- MIL SPEC Number
- The dash number (for size)
- The date of manufacture (quarter year/year) also referred to as the cure date
- Hose manufacturer's code
- Manufacturer's name
- Part number assigned to this style of hose
- Operating pressure

These types of hose are normally classified by the amount of pressure they are designed to withstand under normal operating conditions. The hose classifications are:
- Low pressure (with fabric braid reinforcement)
- Medium pressure (with one wire braid reinforcement in smaller sizes)
- High pressure (with multiple reinforcement layers or braid reinforcement)

7.2 Low Pressure Hose

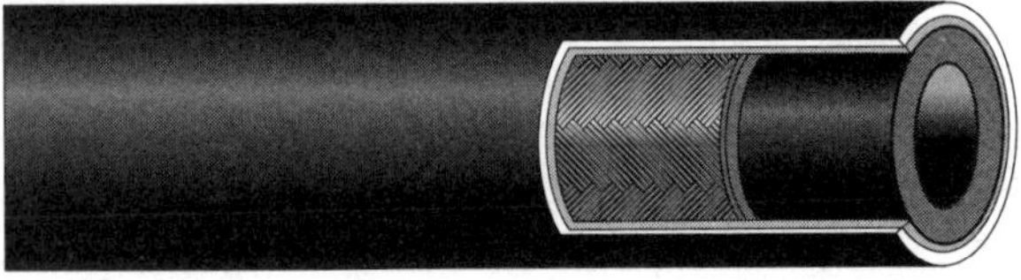

- Low Pressure is generally classified as any pressure below 250 p.s.i..
- Hose is constructed with a seamless synthetic compound rubber inner tube.
- Over the tube is placed a single layer of braided cotton reinforcement.
- The outer cover is synthetic rubber which is compounded to resist abrasion and is oil, moisture, and mildew resistant.
- The hose is black in color with a yellow lay line.
- Hose is available in sizes -2 through -10.

7.3 Medium Pressure Engine/Fuel/Oil Hose

- The hose is identified by its wire braid outer cover. Identification is spaced at regular intervals, showing size, hose manufacturer's code, date of manufacture and operating pressure.
- This hose is available in sizes -4 through -20.

7.4 Medium Pressure Rubber Hose

- Medium pressure hose is generally rated at pressures of 1,500 p.s.i.
- This hose is designed to operate with pressures up to 3,000 p.s.i. in sizes -3, -4 and -5.
- The larger the hose the lower the recommended operating pressure, and the smaller the size, the greater the pressures.
- Medium pressure hose is constructed with a seamless synthetic rubber inner tube.
- Over this is placed a synthetic rubber impregnated oil resistant fabric braid.
- The outer cover is designed to be oil, mildew and abrasion resistant.
- The cover is grey black in color with a yellow lay line consisting of MIL SPEC, size, date of manufacture, hose manufacturer's code and operating pressure.
- This hose is available in sizes -3 through -12.
- This type of hose is used for aircraft hydraulic, pneumatic, fuel, oil and coolant systems specified in MS33620.

7.5 Medium Pressure Engine Oil Hose

- This hose is constructed with a seamless, specially formulated, synthetic rubber compound inner tube.
- Over the inner tube is a partial inner braid of stainless steel wire and a full coverage outer braid of the same material.
- The hose is identified by its bright wire braid outer cover and a tape, spaced at regular intervals, showing size, hose manufacturer's code, hose cure date, date of manufacture and operating pressure.
- This hose is available in sizes -3 through -32.
- The hose is used for aircraft powerplant and airframe oil lines.

7.6 Medium Pressure Teflon Hose

- Teflon hose is constructed with a seamless extruded Teflon resin inner tube.
- The tube is covered with a single layer of stainless steel wire braid.
- The hose is identified by a white tape showing size, manufacturer's code, MIL SPEC, operating pressure and lot number.
- Teflon hose is unaffected by fuels, lube oils, coolants or solvents commonly used in aircraft service.
- Available in sizes -4 through -12 and sizes -16 through -24.

7.7 **High Pressure Rubber Hose**

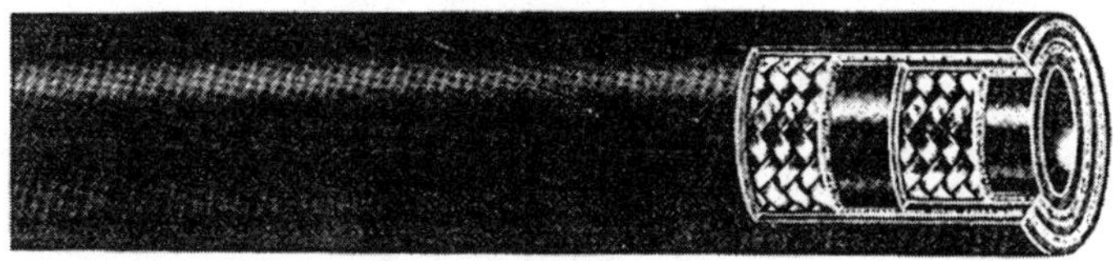

- Constructed with a seamless synthetic rubber compound inner tube.
- Over the tube is a double layer of high tensile carbon steel wire braid (three layers on -16 size).
- The outer cover is a synthetic rubber compound over one layer of fabric braid.
- It is compounded to resist abrasion and is oil, moisture and mildew resistant.
- The hose is black in color with a linear yellow marking consisting of MIL SPEC, size, date of manufacture and manufacturer's code.
- Hose is available in sizes -4 through -16 and all sizes have a hydraulic operating pressure of 3,000 p.s.i. in hydraulic systems specified MS33620.

7.8 **High Pressure Teflon Hose**

- This hose is constructed with a seamless extruded Teflon resin inner tube.
- Hose has one layer of stainless steel wire braid reinforcement in sizes -4 through -10.
- The -12 size has two layers of stainless steel wire braid reinforcement.
- Hose is for use in high pressure, 3,000 p.s.i., hydraulic systems.

7.9 Bend Radii For Conduit and Fluid Lines

Minimum Bend Radii[2] Steel Tubing
Bend Radii Measured to Inside of Bend

Nominal tube OD (in.)	1100-1/2 H, 5052-0 (in.)	Corrosion resistant[3] (in.)	Desirable radius (in.)	Minimum radius[4] (in.)
1/8	3/8	–	–	–
3/16	7/16	21/32	3/4	3/8
1/4	9/16	7/8	1	3/8
5/16	11/16	–	1-1/4	3/8
3/8	15/16	1-5/16	1-1/2	3/8
1/2	1-1/4	1-3/4	2	1/2
5/8	1-1/2	2-3/16	2-1/2	5/8
3/4	1-3/4	2-5/8	3	3/4
7/8	2	–	3-1/2	7/8
1	3	3-1/2	4	1
1-1/8	3-1/2	–	4-1/2	1-1/4
1-1/4	3-3/4	4-3/8	5	1-1/2

NOTES: Increase bend radii when wall thickness is below standard
Equal to 3 1/2 times tube diameter
The minimum radius will be used only when the desirable radius cannot be used.
All dimensions are in inches

7.10 Pressure Drop Data for Smooth Tubing

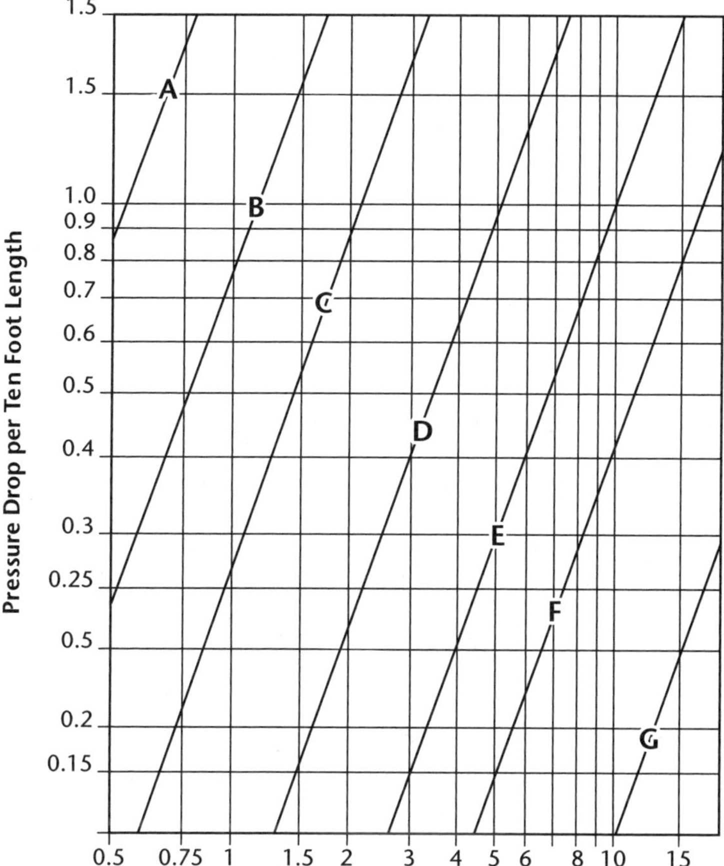

Tubing Size & Wall Thickness

A. $1/4$ x 0.035   E. $5/8$ x 0.042

B. $5/16$ x 0.035   F. $3/4$ x 0.049

C. $3/8$ x 0.035   G. 1 x 0.049

D. $1/2$ x 0.042

7.11 Dimensions for Single Flared Tubing

Tube Size Outside Diameter	Diameter		Radius +0.010
	Aluminum Alloy Tubing	Steel Tubing	
3/16	0.302 (+0.000, -0.010)	0.302 (+0.000, -0.010)	0.032
1/4	0.359 (+0.000, -0.010)	0.359 (+0.000, -0.010)	0.032
5/16	0.421 (+0.000, -0.010)	0.421 (+0.000, -0.010)	0.032
3/8	0.484 (+0.000, -0.010)	0.484 (+0.000, -0.010)	0.046
1/2	0.656 (+0.000, -0.010)	0.656 (+0.000, -0.010)	0.062
5/8	0.781 (+0.000, -0.010)	0.781 (+0.000, -0.010)	0.062
3/4	0.937 (+0.000, -0.010)	0.937 (+0.000, -0.010)	0.078
1	1.187 (+0.000, -0.015)	1.187 (+0.000, -0.015)	0.093
1-1/4	1.500 (+0.000, -0.015)	1.500 (+0.000, -0.015)	0.093
1-1/2	1.721 (+0.000, -0.015)	1.721 (+0.000, -0.015)	0.109
1-3/4	2.106 (+0.000, -0.015)	2.106 (+0.000, -0.015)	0.109
2	2.356 (+0.000, -0.015)	2.356 (+0.000, -0.015)	0.109
2-1/2	2.856 (+0.000, -0.015)	2.856 (+0.000, -0.015)	0.109
3	3.356 (+0.000, -0.015)	3.356 (+0.000, -0.015)	0.109

NOTE: All dimensions are in inches

Maximum Distance Between Supports for Fluid Tubing

Tubing O.D.	Distance between supports	
	Aluminum Alloy	Steel
1/8	9-1/2	11-1/2
3/16	12	14
1/4	13-1/2	16
5/16	15	18
3/8	16-1/2	20
1/2	19	23
5/8	22	25-1/2
3/4	24	27-1/2
1	26-1/2	30-1/2
1-1/4	28-1/2	31-1/2
1-1/2	29-1/2	32-1/2

NOTE: All dimensions are in inches

7.13 **Pressure Drops for Tubing**

Equivalent Straight Tube Line Drops for 90° Elbows

Tubing size		Pressure drop in a 90° elbow in terms of length of straight tube equivalent to a 90° elbow
O.D.	Wall thickness	Feet
1/4	0.035	0.28
3/8	0.035	0.46
1/2	0.042	0.62
5/8	0.042	0.81
3/4	0.049	0.98
1	0.049	1.35

NOTE: All dimensions are in inches

7.14 **Fluid Line Installation Practices**

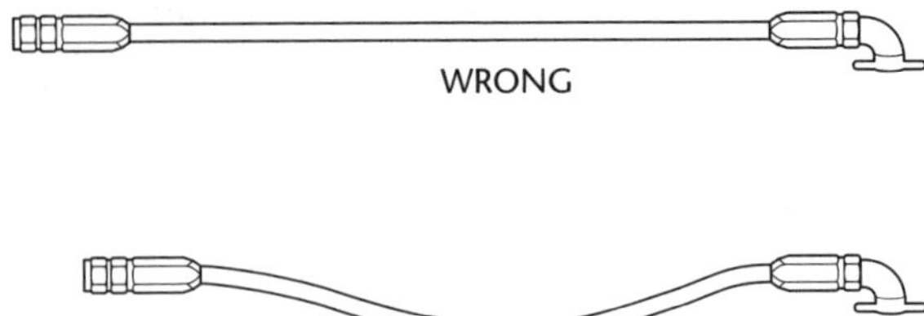

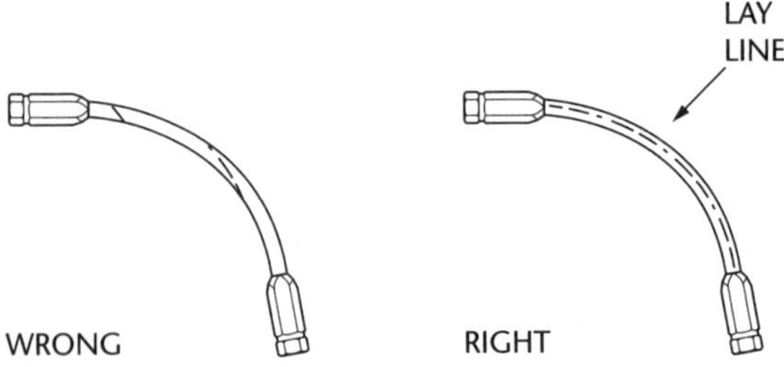

Provide slack in the hose to allow for a 2% to 4% change in length when pressurized.

Observe linear shape. The hose must not be twisted. High pressure applied to a twisted hose may cause hose to fail or loosen.

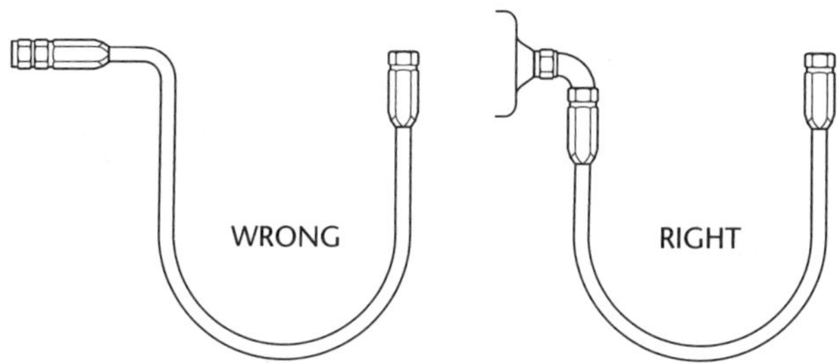

Provide additional bend radius when lines are subject to flexing and remember that the metal and fittings are not flexible. Place support clamps so as not to restrict hose flexing.

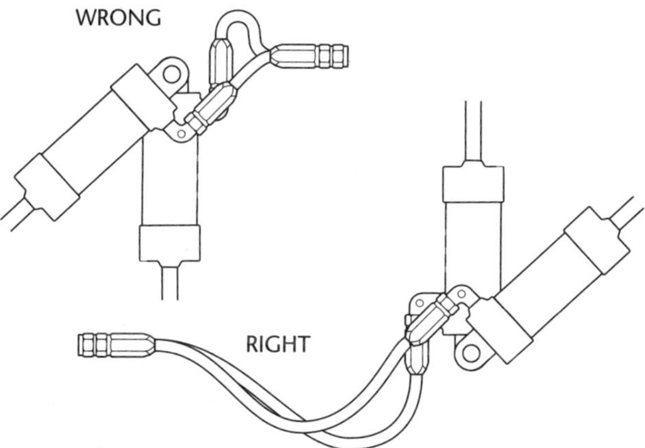

Relieve sharp bends, avoid strain or hose collapse and make cleaner installations by using elbows or other adapter fittings. Provide as large a bend radius as possible. Never use less than the recommended minimum bend radius specified for the hose.

7.14 Fluid Line Installation Practices (cont'd)

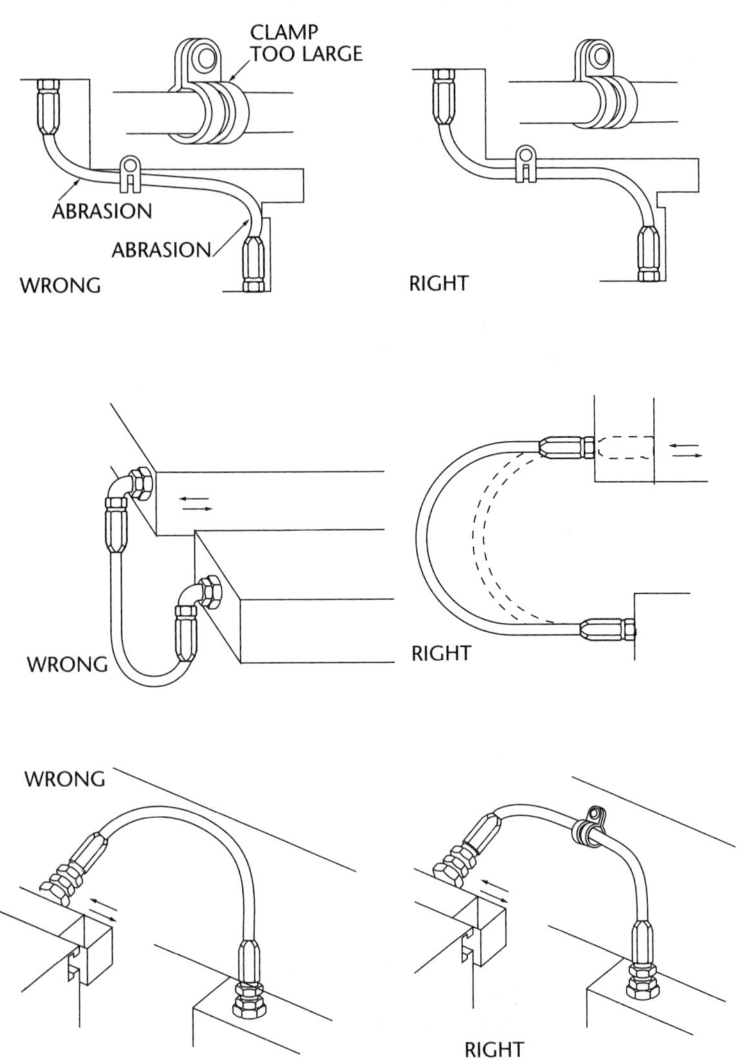

7.14 Fluid Line Installation Practices (cont'd)

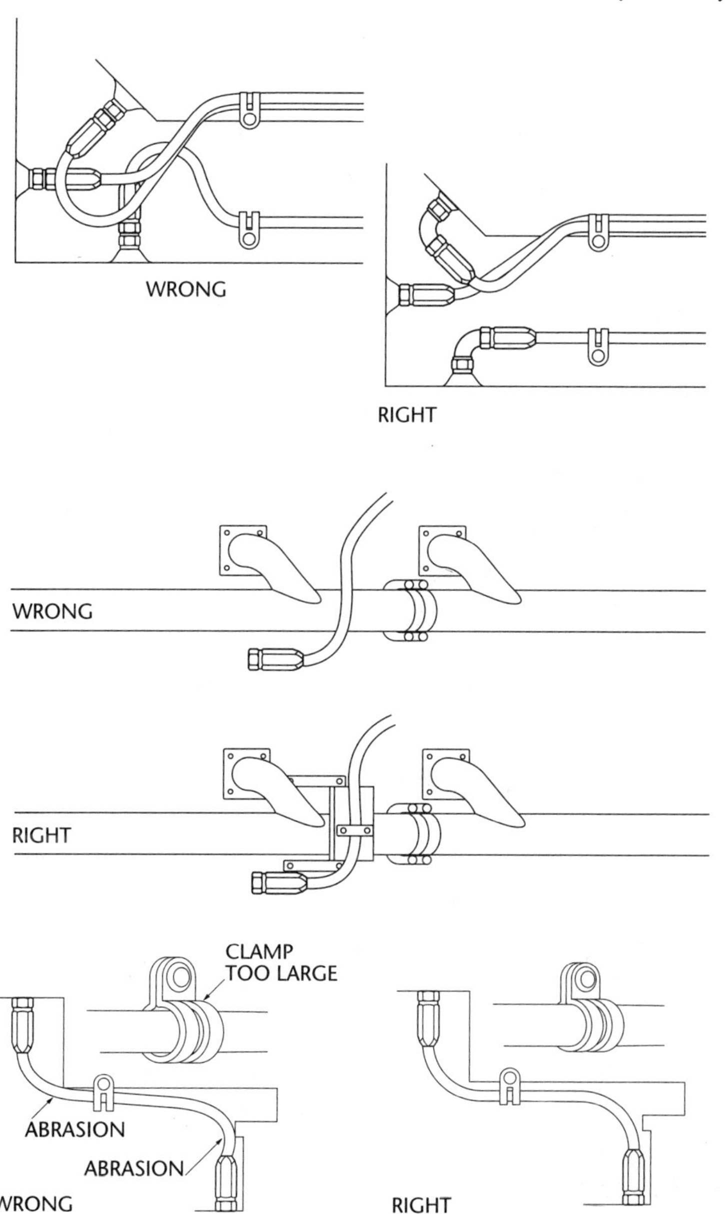

7.15 Recommended Torque Values for Fittings

| Nominal Tube OD (in) | Filling Thread Size | Torque in Inch-Pounds For Gasketed Aluminum or Steel Fittings* | | | | | | For Jamnuts and Fittings Without Gaskets** | | | |
| | | AN924 nut AN815 union | | AN814 plug | | AN6289 nut | | Aluminum | | Steel | |
		Min	Max	Min	Max	Min	Max	Min	Max	Min	Max
1/8	5/16-24	25	35	10	16	25	35	35	50	–	–
3/16	3/8-24	50	75	30	40	50	75	65	80	70	90
1/4	7/16-20	55	80	40	65	75	100	90	105	110	130
5/16	1/2-20	75	100	60	80	90	120	105	125	140	160
3/8	9/16-18	100	150	80	120	150	200	125	145	225	275
1/2	3/4-16	180	230	150	200	200	250	240	280	400	450
5/8	7/8-14	250	350	200	350	275	400	330	370	550	650
3/4	1-1/6-12	420	600	300	500	450	650	540	660	800	960
1	1-5/16-12	600	840	450	600	650	900	840	960	1,000	1,200
1-1/4	1-5/8-12	720	960	600	720	800	1,000	960	1,200	–	–
1-1/2	1-7/8-12	840	1,080	600	800	900	1,100	1,200	1,400	–	–

NOTE: *For use with O rings and aluminum, Teflon, gaskets, or washers
**For combinations of materials (either jamnut, fittings, or boss), use the lowest applicable values shown
All dimensions are in inches

7.16 Recommended Torque Values for Flared and Flex Tubing B Nuts

Flared & Flex Tubing B Nuts

Torque in Inch-Pounds

Nominal Tube O.D.	6061-O & 5052-O Aluminum Alloy Tubing		Flex Hose Assembly and 6061-T6 Aluminum Alloy Tubing		Specification MIL-T-6845 Stainless (CRES.) Steel Tubing	
	Min	Max	Min	Max	Min	Max
1/8	20	25	–	–	35	40
3/16	25	35	30	70	90	140
1/4	40	65	70	120	135	185
5/16	60	80	70	120	180	230
3/8	75	125	130	180	270	345
1/2	150	250	300	400	450	525
5/8	200	350	430	550	650	750
3/4	300	500	650	800	900	1,100
1	500	700	900	1,100	1,200	1,400
1-1/4	600	900	1,200	1,450	1,500	1,800
1-1/2	600	900	1,550	1,850	2,000	2,300
1-3/4	700	1,000	2,000	2,300	2,600	2,900
2	800	1,100	2,500	2,900	3,200	3,600

NOTE: For combinations of tempers for materials, use the applicable values shown for the material of the tubing flare
All dimensions are in inches

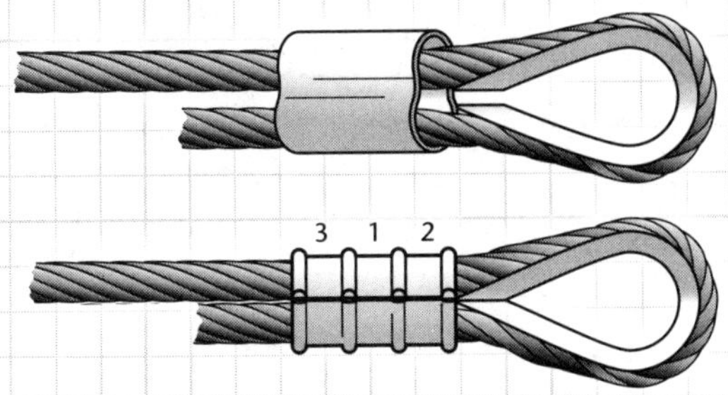

8
Aircraft Cable

8.1 Cable Cross Section

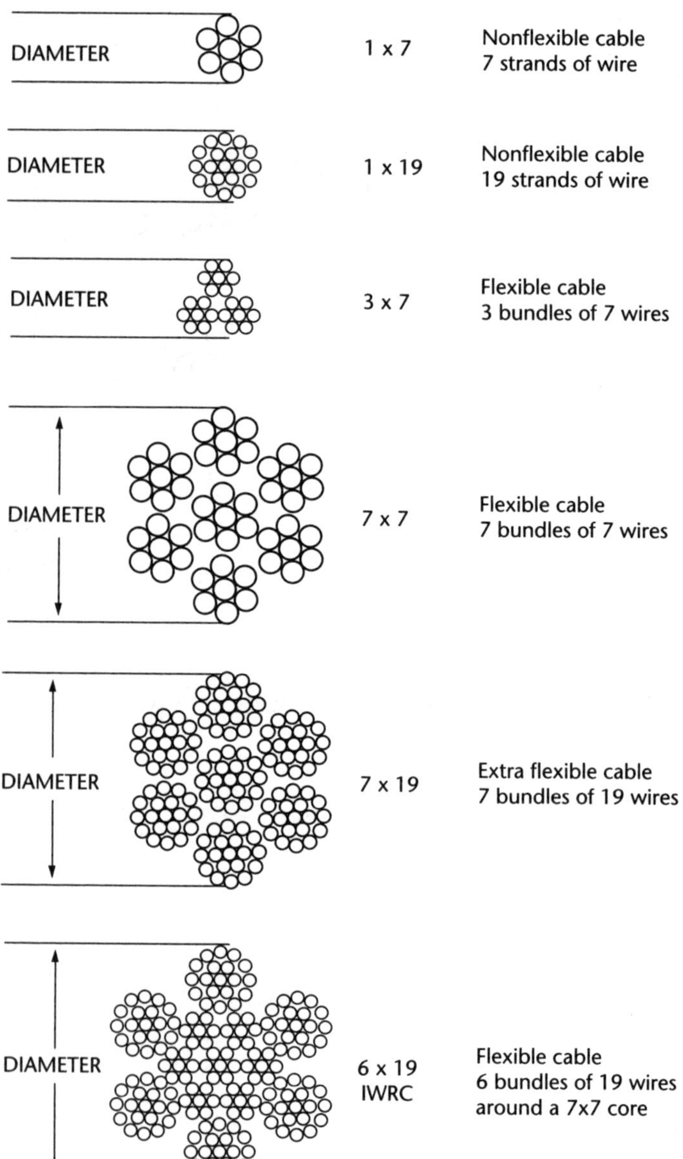

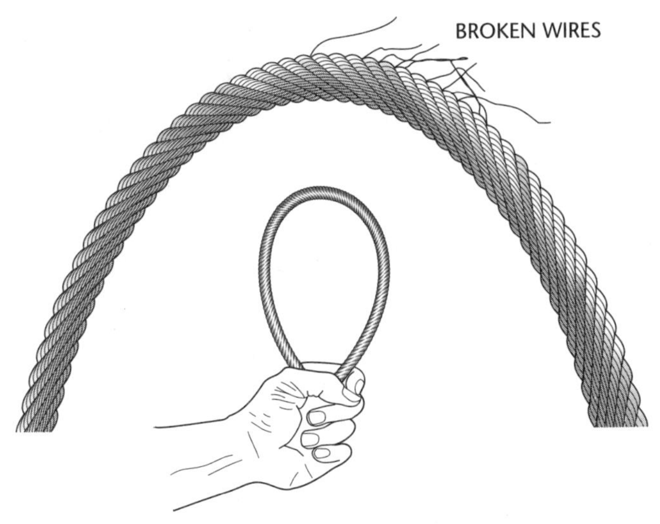

Inspect cable for broken wires when the cable is not installed and therefore not under tension.

8.3 Cable Wear Patterns

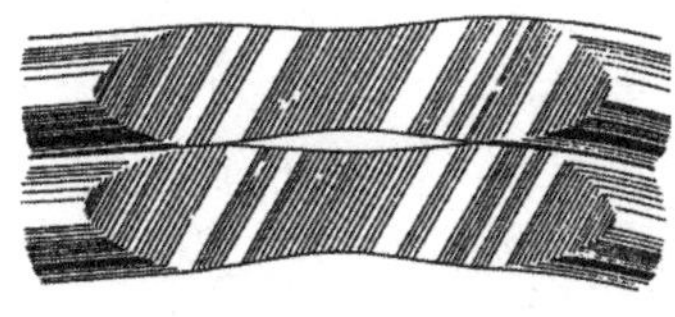

Individual outer wires worn more than 50%.

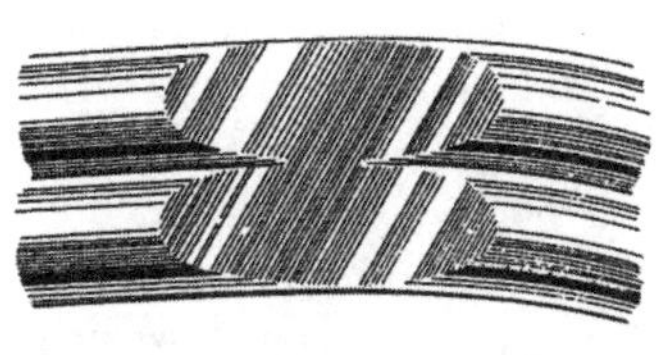

Individual outer wires worn more than 40-50%. (Note blending of worn areas)

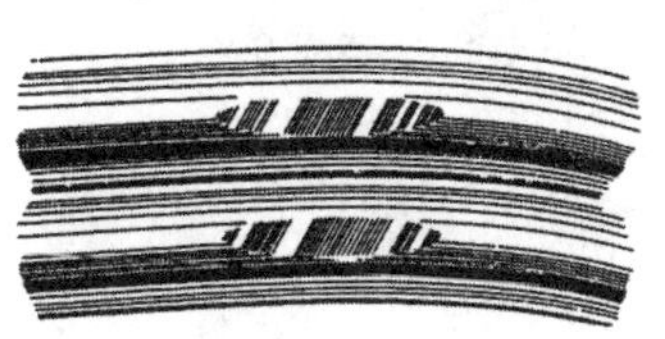

Individual outer wires worn less than 40%. (Worn areas individually distinguishable)

8.4 Flexible Cable Construction and Physical Properties

Nominal Diameter of Wire Rope Cable	Construction	Tolerance On Diameter (Plus Only)	Allowable Increase of Diam. at Cut End	Min. Breaking Strength (lbs)		
				MIL-W83420	MIL-W83420 (CRES.)	MIL-C18375 (CRES.)
Inches		Inches	Inches	lbs	lbs	lbs
1/32	3x7	0.006	0.006	110	110	–
3/64	7x7	0.008	0.008	270	270	–
1/16	7x7	0.010	0.009	480	480	360
1/16	7x19	0.010	0.009	480	480	–
3/32	7x7	0.012	0.010	920	920	700
3/32	7x19	0.012	0.010	1,000	920	–
1/8	7x19	0.014	0.011	2,000	1,760	1,300
5/32	7x19	0.016	0.017	2,800	2,400	2,000
3/16	7x19	0.018	0.019	4,200	3,700	2,900
7/32	7x19	0.018	0.020	5,600	5,000	3,800
1/4	7x19	0.018	0.021	7,000	6,400	4,900
9/32	7x19	0.020	0.023	8,000	7,800	6,100
5/16	7x19	0.022	0.024	9,800	9,000	7,600
11/32	7x19	0.024	0.025	12,500	–	–
3/8	7x19	0.026	0.027	14,400	12,000	11,000
7/16	6x19 IWRC	0.030	0.030	17,600	16,300	14,900
1/2	6x19 IWRC	0.033	0.033	22,800	22,800	19,300
9/16	6x19 IWRC	0.036	0.036	28,500	28,500	24,300
5/8	6x19 IWRC	0.039	0.039	35,000	35,000	30,100
3/4	6x19 IWRC	0.045	0.045	49,600	49,600	42,900
7/8	6x19 IWRC	0.048	0.048	66,500	66,500	58,000
1	6x19 IWRC	0.050	0.050	85,400	85,400	75,200
1-1/8	6x19 IWRC	0.054	0.054	106,400	106,400	–
1-1/4	6x19 IWRC	0.057	0.057	129,400	129,400	–
1-3/8	6x19 IWRC	0.060	0.060	153,600	153,600	–
1-1/2	6x19 IWRC	0.062	0.062	180,500	180,500	–

NOTE: IWRC Independent Wire Rope Center

8.5 Swaged Copper Sleeves

| Cable Size | Copper Oval Sleeve Stock No. | | Manual Tool No. | Sleeve Length Before Compression (in) | Sleeve Length After Compression (in) | # of Presses | Tested Strength (pounds) |
	Plain	Plated					
3/64	18-11-B4	28-11-B4	51-B4-887	3/8	7/16	1	340
1/16	18-1-C	28-1 -C	51-C-887	3/8	7/16	1	550
3/32	18-2-G	28-2-G	51-G-887	7/16	1/2	1	1,180
1/8	18-3-M	28-3-M	51-M-850	9/16	3/4	3	2,300
5/32	18-4-P	28-4-P	51-P-850	5/8	7/8	3	3,050
3/16	18-6-X	28-6-X	51-X-850	1	1-1/4	4	4,350
7/32	18-8-F2	28-8-F2	51-F2-850	7/8	1-1/16	4	5,790
1/4	18-10-F6	28-10-F6	3-F6-950	1-1/8	1-1/2	3	7,180
5/16	18-13-G9	28-13-G9	3-G9-950	1-1/4	1-5/8	3	11,130
No. 635 Hydraulic Tool Dies							
3/8	18-23-H5	28-23-H5	Oval H5	1-1/2	1-7/8	1	16,800
7/16	18-24-J8	28-24-J8	Oval J8	1-3/4	2-1/8	2	19,700
1/2	18-25-K8	28-25-K8	Oval K8	1-7/8	2-1/2	2	25,200
9/16	18-27-M1	28-27-M1	Oval M1	2	2-5/8	3	31,025
5/8	18-28-N5	28-28-N5	Oval N5	2-3/8	3-1/8	3	39,200

8.6 Go No-Go Gauge

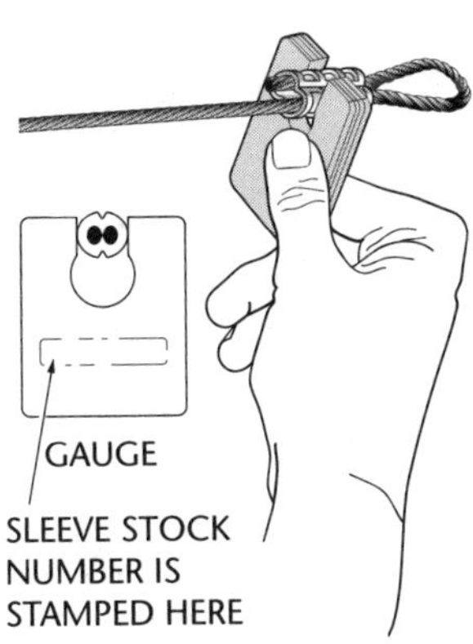

8.7 Copper Sleeve Installation

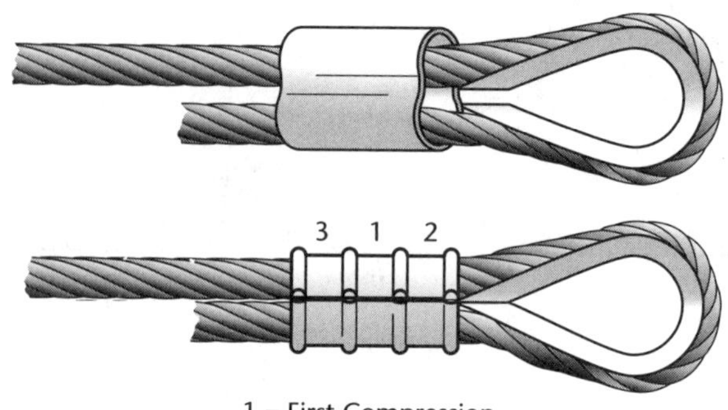

1 = First Compression

2 = Second Compression

3 = Third Compression

8.8 Turnbuckle Safetying Guide

Cable Size	Type of Wrap	Diameter of Safety Wire	Material (Annealed Condition)
1/16	Single	0.040	Copper, brass[1]
3/32	Single	0.040	Copper, brass[1]
1/8	Single	0.040	Stainless steel, Monel and "K" Monel
1/8	Double	0.040	Copper, brass[1]
1/8	Single	0.057 min.	Copper, brass[1]
5/32 and greater	Double	0.040	Stainless steel, Monel or "K" Monel[1]
5/32 and greater	Single	0.057 min.	Stainless steel, Monel or "K" Monel[1]
5/32 and greater	Double	0.051[2]	Copper, brass

NOTE: [1]Galvanized or tinned steel, or soft iron wires are also acceptable
[2]The safety wire holes in 5/32-inch diameter and larger turnbuckle terminals for swaging may be drilled sufficiently to accommodate the double 0.051-inch diameter copper or brass wires when used

8.8 Turnbuckle Safetying Guide (cont'd)

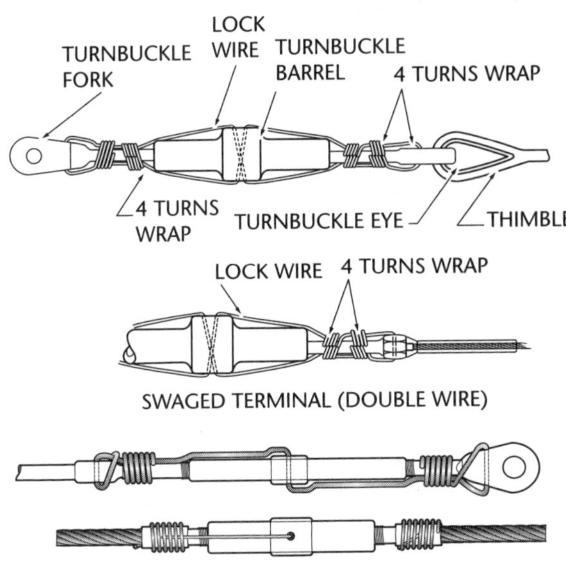

8.9 Locking-clip Application

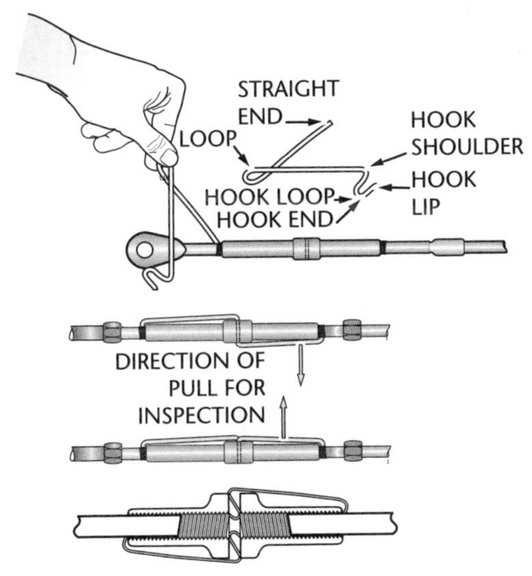

8.9 **Locking-clip Application (cont'd)**

Nominal Cable Diameter	Thread UNF-3	Locking Clip MS21256	Turnbuckle Body MS21251
1/16	#6-40	-1	-2S
3/32	#10-32	-1	-3S
3/32	#10-32	-2	-3L
1/8	1/4-28	-1	-4S
1/8	1/4-28	-2	-4L
5/32	1/4-28	-1	-5S
5/32	1/4-28	-2	-5L
3/16	5/16-24	-1	-6S
3/16	5/16-24	-2	-6L
7/32	3/8-24	-2	-7L
1/4	3/8-24	-2	-8L
9/32	7/16-20	-3	-9L
5/16	1/2-20	-3	-10L

NOTE: All dimensions are in inches

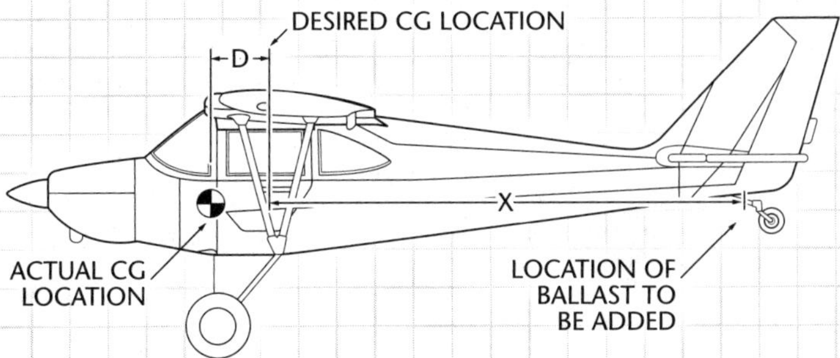

9
Weight and Balance

9.1 **Preparation for Weighing**

The major considerations when preparing an aircraft for weighing are as follows:

- The aircraft should be weighed inside a hangar where wind cannot blow over the surface and cause fluctuating or false scale readings.

- The aircraft should be clean inside and out, with special attention paid to the bilge area to be sure no water or debris is trapped there, and the outside of the aircraft should be as free as possible of all mud and dirt.

Equipment List
All of the required equipment must be properly installed, and there should be no equipment installed that is not included in the equipment list. If such equipment is installed, the weight and balance record must be corrected to indicate it.

Ballast
All required permanent ballast must be properly secured in place and all temporary ballast must be removed.

Draining the Fuel
Drain fuel from the tanks in the manner specified by the aircraft manufacturer. If there are no specific instructions, drain the fuel until the fuel quantity gauges read empty when the aircraft is in level flight attitude. Any fuel remaining in the system is called residual, or unusable fuel and is part of the aircraft empty weight.

If it is not feasible to drain the fuel, the tanks can be topped off to be sure of the quantity they contain and the aircraft weighed with full fuel. After the weighing is complete, the weight of the fuel and its moment are subtracted from those of the aircraft as weighed. To correct the empty weight for the residual fuel, add its weight and moment. The amount of residual fuel and its arm are normally found in NOTE 1 in the section of the TCDS, "Data Pertaining to All Models."

When computing the weight of the fuel, for example a tank full of jet fuel, measure its specific gravity (s.g.) with a hydrometer and multiply it by 8.345 (the nominal weight of 1 gallon of pure water whose s.g. is 1.0). If the ambient temperature is high and the jet fuel in the tank is hot enough for its specific gravity to reach 0.81, rather than its nominal s.g. of 0.82, the fuel will actually weigh 6.76 pounds per gallon rather than its nominal weight of 6.84 pounds per gallon. The standard weight of aviation gasoline (Avgas) is 6 pounds per gallon.

Oil
The empty weight of aircraft certificated under the CAR, Part 3 does not include the engine lubricating oil. The oil must either be drained before the aircraft is weighed, or its weight must be subtracted from the scale readings to determine the empty weight. To weigh an aircraft that does not include the engine lubricating oil as part of the empty weight, place it in level flight attitude, then open the drain valves and allow all of the oil that is able to, to drain out. Any oil remaining is undrainable oil and is part of the empty weight. Aircraft certificated under 14 CFR, Parts 23 and 25 include full oil as part of the empty weight.

If it is impractical to drain the oil, the reservoir can be filled to the specified level and the weight of the oil computed at 7.5 pounds per gallon. Then its weight and moment are subtracted from the weight and moment of the aircraft as weighed. The amount and arm of the undrainable oil are found in NOTE 1 of the TCDS, and this must be added to the empty weight.

Other Fluids

The hydraulic fluid reservoir and all other reservoirs containing fluids required for normal operation of the aircraft should be full. Fluids not considered to he part of the empty weight of the aircraft are potable (drinkable) water, lavatory precharge water, and water for injection into the engines.

Configuration of the Aircraft

Consult the aircraft service manual regarding the position of the landing gear shock struts and the control surfaces for weighing; when weighing a helicopter, the main rotor must be in its correct position.

Jacking the Aircraft

Large aircraft are often weighed by rolling them onto ramps in which load cells are embedded. This eliminates the problems associated with jacking the aircraft off the ground. But most smaller aircraft are actually lifted off the ground onto scales or load cells.

You must exercise special care when raising an aircraft on jacks for weighing. If the aircraft has spring steel landing gear and it is jacked at the wheel, the landing gear will slide inward as the weight is taken off of the tire, and care must be taken to prevent the jack from tipping over.

For some aircraft, stress panels or plates must be installed before they are raised with wing jacks, to distribute the weight over the jack pad. Be sure to follow the recommendations of the aircraft manufacturer in detail anytime an aircraft is jacked. When using two wing jacks, take special care to raise them simultaneously, keeping the aircraft level so it will not slip off the jacks. As the jacks are raised, keep the safety collars screwed down against the jack cylinder to prevent the aircraft from tilting if one of the jacks should lose hydraulic pressure.

Leveling the Aircraft

When an aircraft is weighed, it must be in its level flight attitude so that all of the components will be at their correct distance from the datum.

9.2 **Empty Weight Center of Gravity Formulas**

Nose Wheel Aircraft

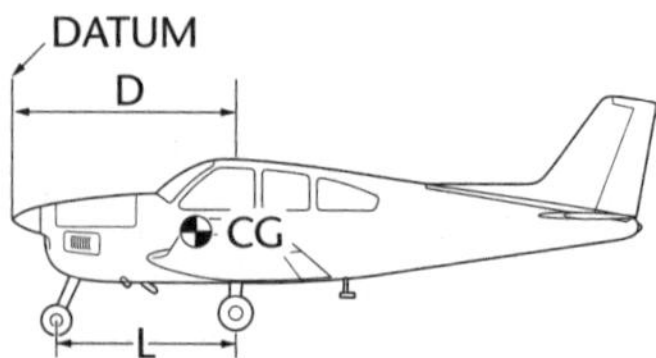

Datum located forward of the main wheels:

$$CG = D - \left[\frac{F \times L}{W}\right]$$

Nose Wheel Aircraft

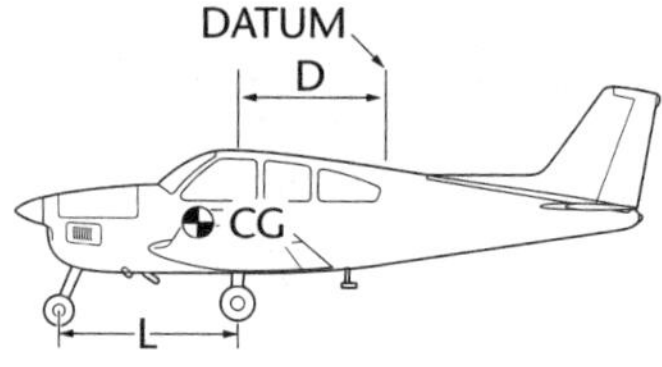

Datum located aft of the main wheels:

$$CG = \left[D + \frac{F \times L}{W}\right]$$

Tail Wheel Aircraft

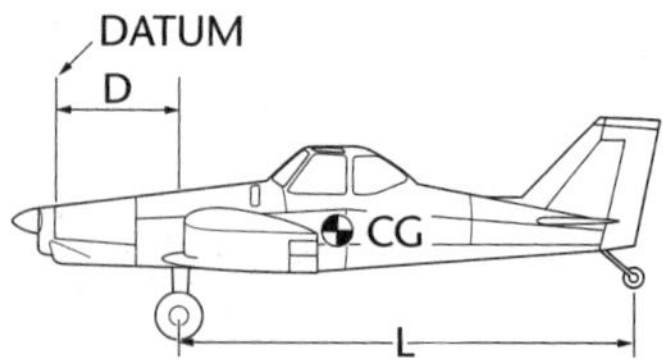

Datum located forward of the main wheels:

$$CG = D + \left[\frac{R \times L}{W}\right]$$

Tail Wheel Aircraft

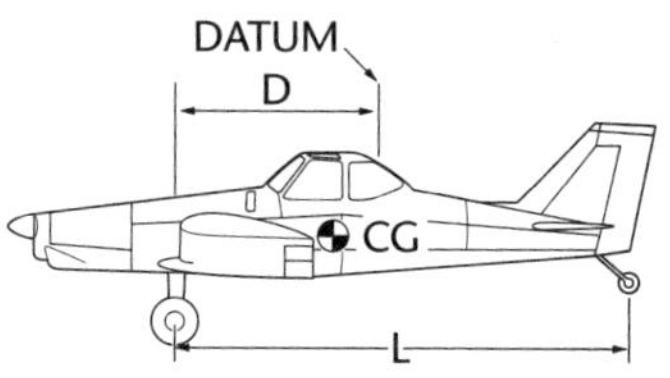

Datum located aft of the main wheels:

$$CG = D + \left[\frac{R \times L}{W}\right]$$

CG = Distance from datum to center of gravity of the aircraft

W = The weight of the aircraft at the time of weighing

D = The horizontal distance measured from the datum to the main wheel weighing point

L = The horizontal distance measured from the main wheel weighing point to the nose or tail weighing point

F = The weight at the nose weighing point

R = The weight at the tail weighing point

9.3 **Permanent Ballast Computation Formula**

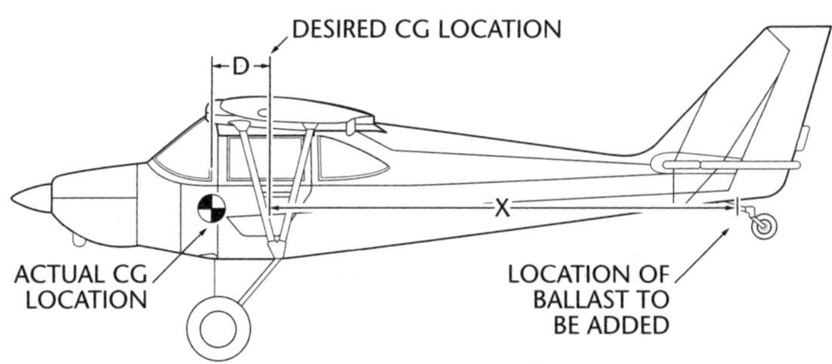

$$B = \frac{D \times W}{X}$$

D = Distance in inches desired to move CG of airplane.

W = Weight of airplane as loaded.

X = Distance in inches from point where ballast is to be installed, to the desired location of the new CG.

B = Weight of ballast required in pounds.

Compute the new CG of the aircraft with ballast installed.

NOTE: If greater accuracy is desired, repeat the entire formula using the NEW aircraft weight and the new CG in the second operation

9.4 **Mean Aerodynamic Chord**

Location with Respect to the Mean Aerodynamic Chord

AMTs are primarily concerned with the location of the CG relative to the datum, an identifiable physical location from which measurements can be made. But because the aerodynamic characteristics of a wing relate to its chord length, pilots and flight engineers are more concerned with the location of the CG relative to the chord; and because the mean, or average, physical chord of a tapered wing is difficult to measure, the mean aerodynamic chord (MAC) is used. The allowable CG range is expressed in percentages of the MAC.

The MAC is the chord of an imaginary airfoil that has all of the aerodynamic characteristics of the actual airfoil. It can also be thought of as the chord drawn through the geographic center of the plan area of the wing.

The relative positions of the CG and the aerodynamic center of lift of the wing have critical effects on the flight characteristics of the aircraft. Conse-

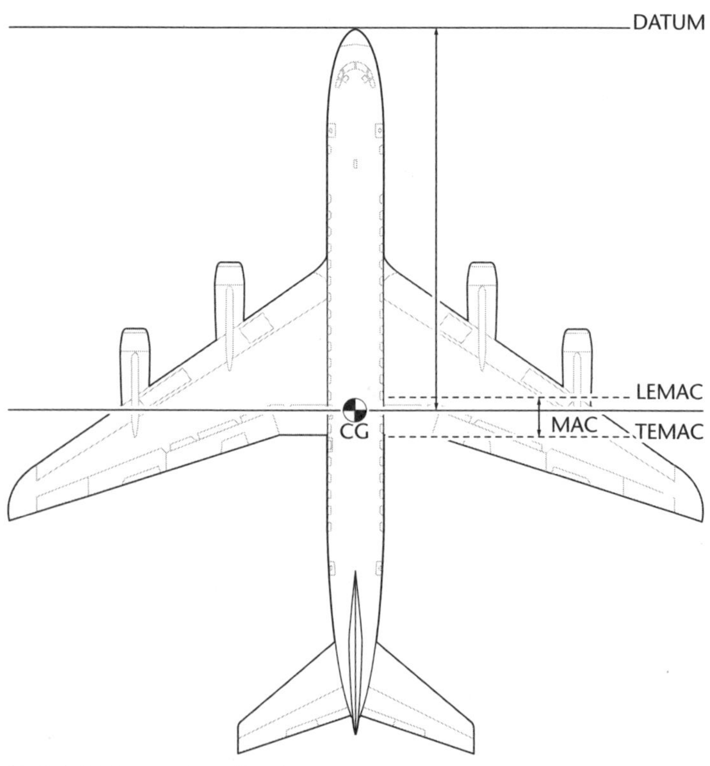

quently, relating the CG location to the chord of the wing is convenient from a design and operations standpoint. Normally, an aircraft will have acceptable flight characteristics if the CG is located somewhere near the 25% average chord point. This means the CG is located one fourth of the total distance back from the leading edge of the wing section. Such a location will place the CG forward of the aerodynamic center for most airfoils. In order to relate the percent MAC to the datum, all weight and balance information includes two items: the length of MAC in inches and the location of the leading edge of MAC (LE-MAC) in inches from the datum.

Refer to the airplane below. The MAC is from stations 1,022 to 1,198 and the CG is located at station 1,070.

MAC = 1,198-1,022 = 176 inches
LEMAC = Station 1,022
CG is 48 inches behind LEMAC
(1,070 - 1,022 = 48 inches)

The location of the CG expressed in percentage of MAC is determined using this formula:

$$CG \text{ in } \% \text{ MAC} = \frac{\text{Dist. aft of LEMAC} \times 100}{\text{MAC}}$$

$$= \frac{48 \times 100}{176}$$

$$= 27.3$$

The CG of the airplane is located at 27.3% MAC.

It is sometimes necessary to determine the location of the CG in inches from the datum when its location in % MAC is known.

The CG of the airplane is located at 27.3% MAC
MAC = 1,198 - 1,022 = 176 inches
LEMAC = station 1022

Determine the location of the CG in inches from the datum by using this formula:

$$CG \text{ ins. fr. datum} = \frac{\text{LEMAC} + \text{MAC} \times CG \% \text{ MAC}}{\text{MAC}}$$

$$= \frac{1,022 + 176 \times 27.3}{100}$$

$$= 1,070$$

The CG of this airplane is located at station 1,070 which is 1,070 inches aft of the datum.

It is important for longitudinal stability that the CG be located ahead of the center of lift of a wing. Since the center of lift is expressed as a percentage of the MAC, the location of the CG is expressed in the same terms.

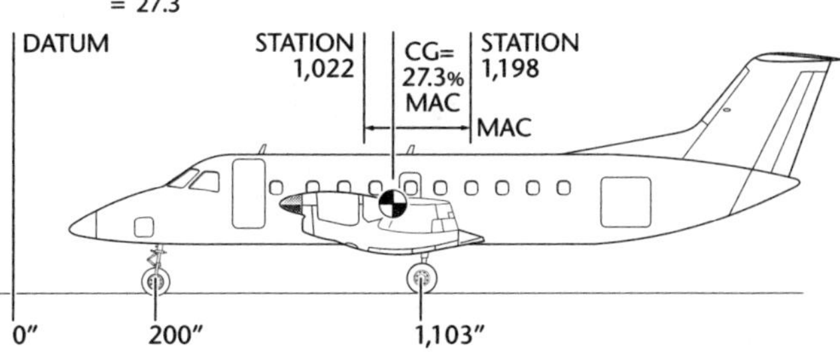

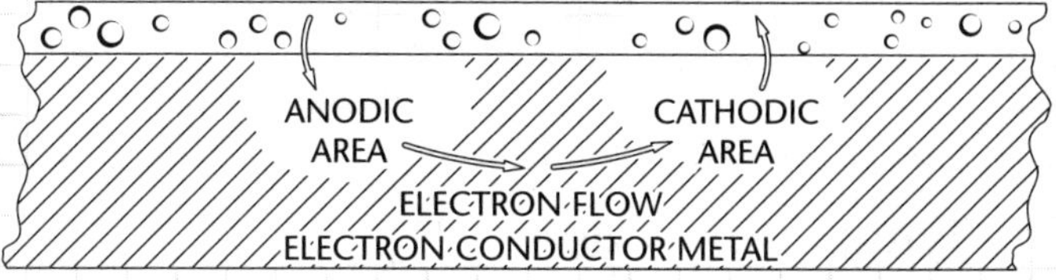

10

Corrosion Control

10.1 Conditions Contributing to Corrosion

Four conditions must exist before electrochemical corrosion can occur:
• A metal that is anodic and subject to corrosion
• A dissimilar conductive material that has fewer tendencies to corrode (cathode).
• Presence of a continuous, conductive path (electrolyte)
• Electrical contact between the anode and the cathode

Elimination of any one of the above will stop electrochemical corrosion

10.2 Types of Corrosion

General Surface Corrosion
General surface corrosion results from a direct chemical attack on a metal surface, and involves only the metal surface. If usually occurs over a wide area and is more or less equal in distribution. A general dulling of the surface is the first sign of this form of corrosion. Allowed to continue the surface becomes rough and possibly frosted in appearance.

Pitting Corrosion
Pitting corrosion is one of the most destructive and intense forms of corrosion. It can occur in any metal but is most common on metals that form protective oxide films, such as aluminum and magnesium. It is first noticeable as white or gray powdery deposits, on the surface. When the deposits are cleaned away, tiny holes or pits can be seen in the surface. These may penetrate deeply into structural members and cause damage completely out of proportion to their appearance.

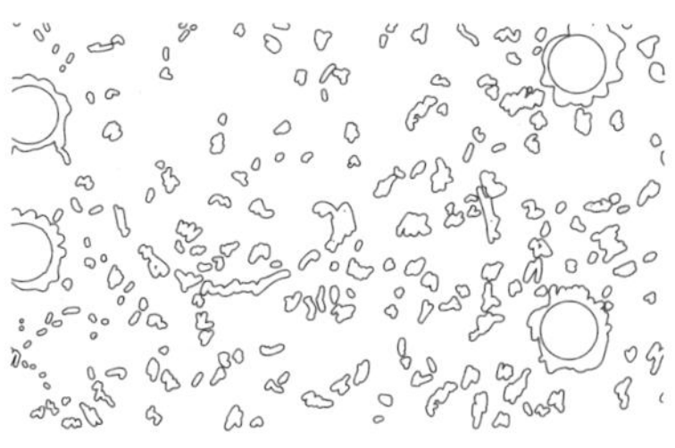

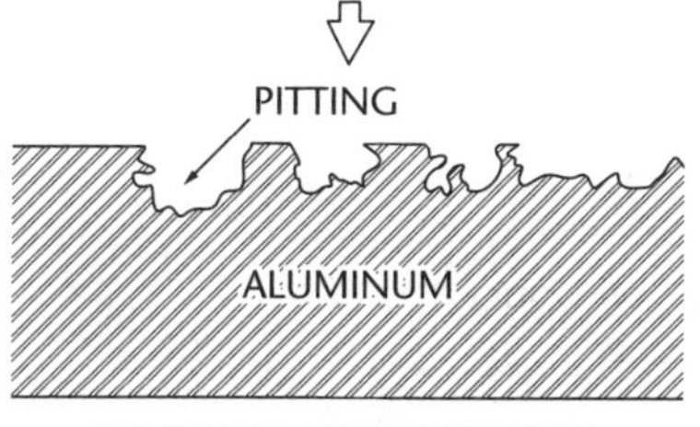

Pitting Corrosion

Concentration Cell Corrosion

This is corrosion in a metal-to-metal joint, at the end of a joint, or of a spot on the metal surface covered by a foreign material. Metal ion concentration cell and oxygen concentration cell are the two general types of concentration cell corrosion.

Metal ion concentration: A high concentration of metal ions will normally exist under faying surfaces. When a solution of water and metallic ions is in contact with the metal, a low concentration of metallic ions will exist near the crevice created by the faying surface. An electrical potential will exist between the low concentration point (anode) and the high (cathode) point. The anodic side will corrode while the cathode will not.

Oxygen cell concentration: Moisture in contact with the surface will normally contain dissolved oxygen. An oxygen cell will develop at any point where the oxygen in the air does not diffuse into the moisture. This creates a difference in oxygen concentration between two points. Corrosion occurs in the area of low concentration, which is anodic.

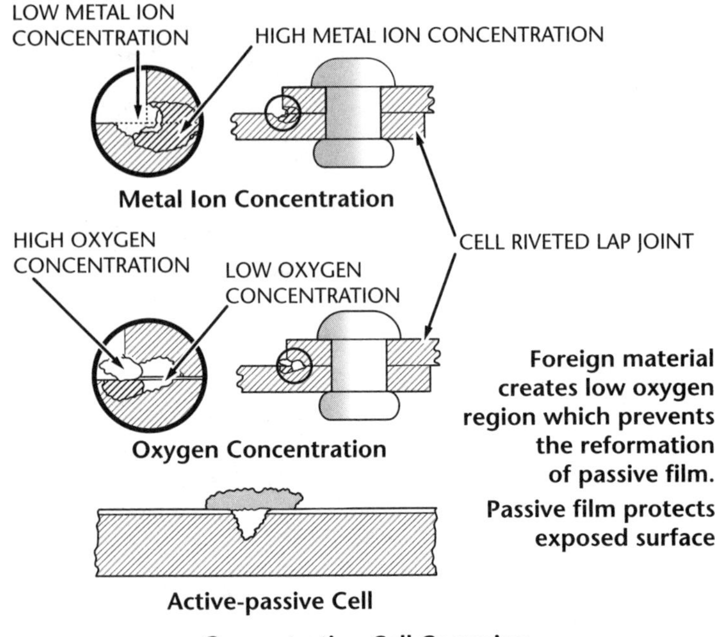

Active-Passive Cells

Metals that depend on a tightly adhering passive film, usually an oxide, for corrosion protection are prone to rapid corrosive attacks by active-passive cells. The corrosion action usually starts as an oxygen concentration cell. Once the passive film is broken, the active metal beneath is exposed to corrosive attack.

Filiform Corrosion

Filiform corrosion is a special form of oxygen concentration cell, which occurs on metal surfaces having an organic coating system. Filiform occurs when the relative humidity of the air is between 78 and 90 percent and the surface is slightly acidic. It is recognized by its characteristic worm-like trace of corrosion products beneath the paint film. This corrosion usually attacks steel and aluminum surfaces. On steel, the traces never cross but will on aluminum, which causes the damage to be deeper and more severe. If not removed and the surface treated it can lead to intergranular corrosion.

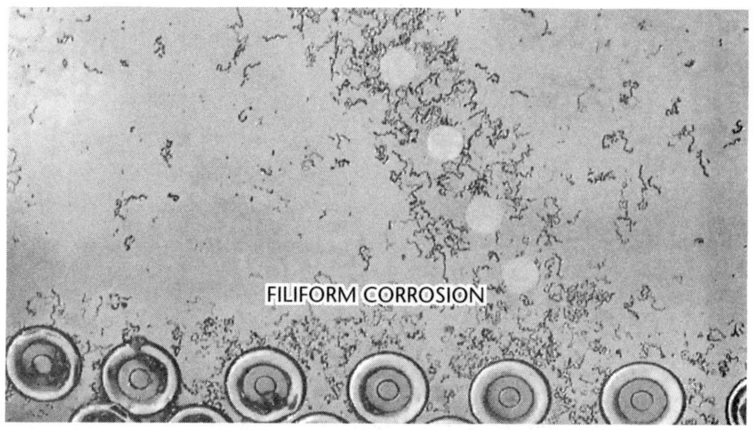

Intergranular Corrosion

A magnified cross section of any commercial alloy shows the granular structure of the metal. Each of the grains has a clearly defined boundary, which chemically differs from the metal within the grain. The grain boundary and the grain center can react with each other as anode and cathode when in contact with an electrolyte. Intergranular corrosion is an attack on the grain boundaries of a metal.

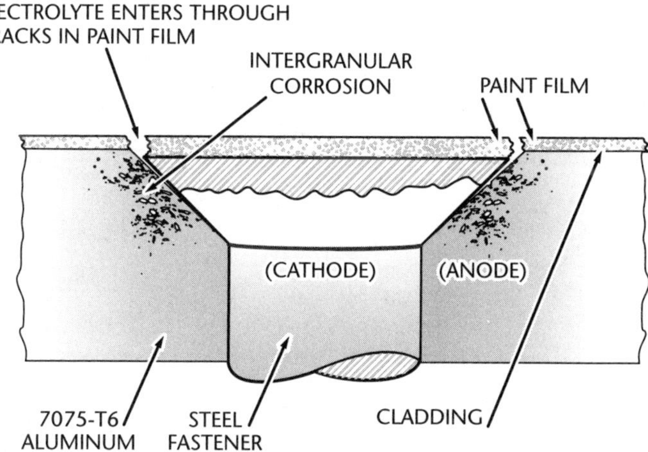

Intergranular Corrosion

Exfoliation Corrosion

Exfoliation is an advanced form of intergranular corrosion. It is visible by lifting up of the surface grains of a metal by the force of expanding corrosion products occurring at the grain boundaries just below the surface. It is most often seen on extruded sections that have been heat treated for strength.

Galvanic Corrosion

Galvanic corrosion occurs when two dissimilar metals make contact in the presence of an electrolyte. It is recognizable by the presence of a build-up of corrosion at the joint between the metals.

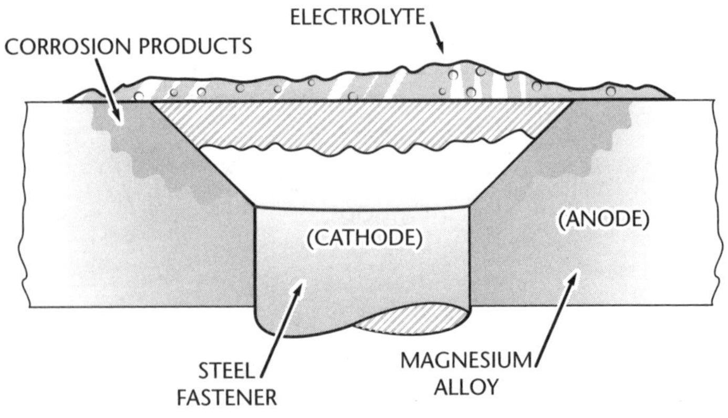

Galvanic Corrosion

Stress Corrosion Cracking

This form of corrosion involves a constant or cyclic stress, acting in conjunction with a damaging chemical environment. Internal or external loads may cause the stress.

Cold working or uneven cooling from elevated temperatures during manufacturing will create internal loads.

External loads can be introduced into the structure by riveting, welding, bolting, clamping etc. Internal stresses are created if a fastener is over torqued.

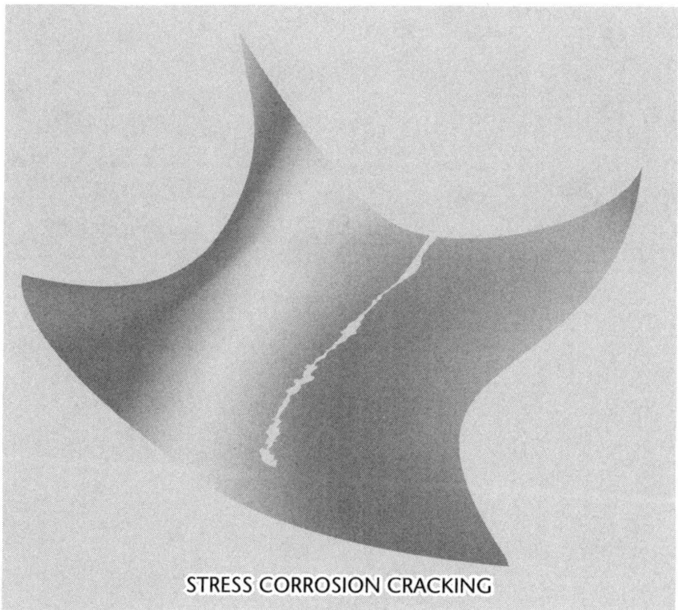

Fatigue Corrosion

Cyclic stress and a corrosive environment contribute to fatigue corrosion. Metals can withstand cyclic stress for an infinite number of cycles as long as the stress is below the endurance limit for the metal. When a part or structure undergoing cyclic stress is exposed to a corrosive environment, the stress level for failure may be reduced many times.

Fretting Corrosion

Fretting corrosion occurs at the interface of two highly loaded surfaces that are not supposed to move against each other. Vibration may cause the surfaces to rub together resulting in abrasive wear known as fretting. With continued rubbing, metal particles sheared from the surface of the metal combine with oxygen to form metal oxides. As these oxides accumulate, they cause damage by abrasive action and increased local stress.

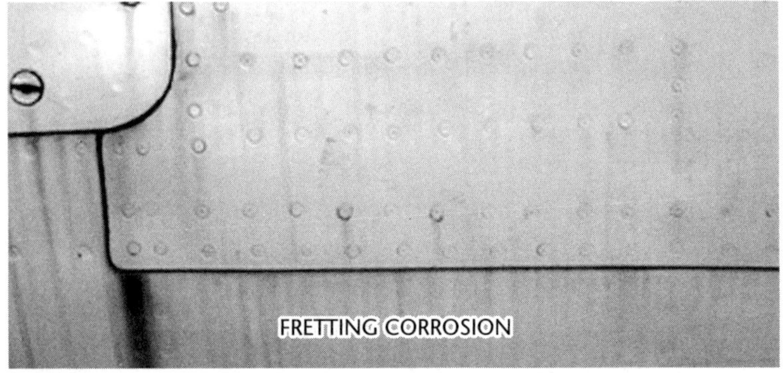

10.3 Corrosion Identification

Alloy	Type of Attack to Which Alloy is Susceptible	Appearance of Corrosion Product
Magnesium	Highly susceptible to pitting	White, powdery, snowlike mounds and white spots on surface
Low Alloy Steel (4000-8000 series)	Surface oxidation and pitting, surface, and intergranular	Reddish-brown oxide (rust)
Aluminum	Surface pitting, intergranular, exfoliation stress corrosion and fatigue cracking, and fretting	White to gray powder
Titanium	Highly corrosion resistant; extended or repeated contact with chlorinated solvents may result in degradation of the metal's structural properties at high temperature	No visible corrosion products at low temperature. Colored surface oxides develop above 700°F (370°C)
Cadmium	Uniform surface corrosion; used as sacrificial plating to protect steel	From white powdery deposit to brown or black mottling of the surface
Stainless Steels (300-400 series)	Crevice corrosion; some pitting in marine environments; corrosion cracking; intergranular corrosion (300 series); surface corrosion (400 series)	Rough surface; sometimes a uniform red, brown, stain
Nickel base (Inconel, Monel)	Generally has good corrosion resistant qualities; susceptible to pitting in sea water	Green powdery deposit
Copper base Brass, Bronze	Surface and intergranular corrosion	Blue or blue-green powdery deposit
Chromium (Plate)	Pitting (promotes rusting of steel where pits occur in plating)	No visible corrosion products; blistering of plating due to rusting and lifting
Silver	Will tarnish in the presence of sulfur	Brown to black film
Gold	Highly corrosion resistant	Deposits cause darkening of reflective surfaces
Tin	Subject to whisker growth	Whiskerlike deposit

10.4 Abrasives for Corrosion Removal

Metals or Materials to be Processed	Operation	Restrictions	Abrasive Paper or Cloth — Aluminum Oxide	Abrasive Paper or Cloth — Silicon Carbide	Abrasive Paper or Cloth — Garnet	Abrasive Fabric or Pad	Aluminum	Stainless Steel	Pumice 350 Mesh or Finer	Abrasive Wheel
Ferrous Alloys	Corrosion Removal or Fairing	—	150 Grit or Finer	—	—	Fine to Ultra Fine	X	X	X	X
Ferrous Alloys	Finishing	—	400	—	—	—	X	X	X	—
Aluminum Alloys Except Clad Aluminum	Corrosion Removal or Fairing	Do Not Use Silicon Carbide Abrasive	150 Grit or Finer	—	7/0 Grit or Finer	Very Fine and Ultra Fine	X	—	X	X
Aluminum Alloys Except Clad Aluminum	Finishing	Do Not Use Silicon Carbide Abrasive	400	—	—	—	X	—	X	—
Clad Aluminum	Corrosion Removal or Fairing	Sanding Limited to the Removal of Minor Scratches	240 Grit or Finer	—	7/0 Grit or Finer	Very Fine and Ultra Fine	X	—	X	X
Clad Aluminum	Finishing	Sanding Limited to the Removal of Minor Scratches	400	—	—	—	X	—	X	—
Magnesium Alloys	Corrosion Removal or Fairing	—	240 Grit or Finer	—	—	Very Fine and Ultra Fine	X	—	X	X
Magnesium Alloys	Finishing	—	400	—	—	—	X	—	X	—
Titanium	Cleaning and Finishing	—	150 Grit or Finer	180 Grit or Finer	—	—	X	X	X	X

10.5 Grouping of Metals and Alloys

Group I	Group II	Group III	Group IV
Magnesium & Magnesium Alloys	Aluminum, Aluminum Alloys, Zinc, Cadmium & Cadmium-Titanium Plate	Iron, Steels (Except Stainless Steels), Lead, Tin & their Alloys	Copper, Brass, Bronze, Copper-Berylium, Copper-Nickel Chromium, Nickel, Nickel Base Alloys, Cobalt Base Alloys, Carbon Graphite, Stainless Steels, Titanium & Titanium Alloys

NOTE: Metals listed in the same group are considered similar to one another
Metals listed in different groups are considered dissimilar to one another

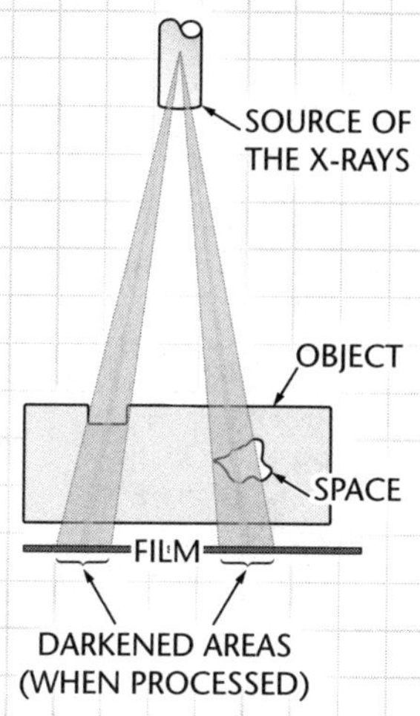

11

Non-destructive Testing of Materials

11.1 **NDT Methods**

Certification can be obtained in a number of NDT methods, which are listed below:

- AE Acoustic Emission Testing
- ET Electromagnetic Testing
- LT Leak Testing
- PT Liquid Penetrant Testing
- MT Magnetic Particle Testing
- NRT Neutron Radiographic Testing
- RT Radiographic Testing
- TIR Thermal/Infrared Testing
- UT Ultrasonic Testing
- VA Vibration Analysis Testing
- VT Visual Testing

AE
Acoustic emission is the technical term for the noise emitted by materials and structures when subjected to stress. Types of stresses can be mechanical, thermal or chemical. The emission is caused by the rapid release of energy within a material due to events such as crack initiation and growth, crack opening and closure, dislocation movement, and phase transformation in monolithic materials and fiber breakage and fiber-matrix debonding in composites. The sensor is a transducer that converts the mechanical sound wave into an electrical signal.

ET
Eddy current, penetrating radar and other electromagnetic techniques are used to detect or measure flaws, bond or weld integrity, thickness, and electrical conductivity. Eddy current is the most widely applied electromagnetic NDT technique. The eddy current method is also useful in sorting alloys and verifying heat treatment. Eddy current testing uses an electromagnet to induce an eddy current in a conductive sample. The response of the material to the induced current is sensed. Since the probe does not have to contact the work surface, eddy current testing is useful on rough surfaces or surfaces with wet films or coatings.

LT
Leak testing is the branch of nondestructive testing that is concerned with the escape of liquids, vacuum or gases from sealed components or systems. Leaks are thought of as specialized flaws. Leaks can result from poor seals and connections, as well as from inadequate welds.

A leak is a hole or porosity in an enclosure capable of passing a fluid from the higher-pressure side to the lower pressure side.

PT
Liquid penetration inspection is used to reveal surface breaking flaws by bleed-out of a colored or fluorescent dye from the flaw. Test objects are coated with visible or fluorescent dye solution. Excess dye is then removed from the surface, and a developer is applied. The developer acts as blotter, drawing trapped penetrant out of imperfections open to the surface.

MT
Magnetic particle inspection (MPI) is used for the detection of surface and near-surface flaws in ferromagnetic materials. A magnetic field is applied to the specimen, either locally or overall, using a permanent magnet, electromagnet, flexible cables or hand-held probes. If the material is sound, most of the magnetic flux is concentrated below the material's surface. If a flaw is present, the flux is distorted locally and 'leaks' from the surface of

the specimen in the region of the flaw. Fine magnetic particles, applied to the surface of the specimen, are attracted to the area of flux leakage, creating a visible indication of the flaw.

In some cases, the particles are coated with a fluorescent material enabling them to be viewed under a UV lamp in darkened conditions.

NRT

Neutron Radiography is an imaging technique which provides images similar to X-ray radiography. The difference between neutron and X-ray interaction mechanisms produce significantly different and often complementary information.

RT

This technique involves the use of penetrating gamma or X-radiation to examine parts and products for imperfections. An X-ray machine or radioactive isotope is used as a source of radiation. Radiation is directed through a part and onto film or other media. The resulting shadowgraph shows the internal soundness of the part. Possible imperfections are indicated as density changes in the film.

TIR

Thermal, or infrared energy, is light that is not visible because its wavelength is too long to be detected by the human eye; it's the part of the electromagnetic spectrum that we perceive as heat.

Thermography is the use of an infrared imaging and measurement camera to "see" and "measure " thermal energy emitted from an object. Infrared thermography cameras produce images of invisible infrared or "heat" radiation and provide precise non-contact temperature measurement capabilities.

UT

Ultrasonic inspection is a nondestructive method in which beams of high-frequency sound waves are introduced into materials for the detection of subsurface flaws in the material. The sound waves travel through the material with some attendant loss of energy (attenuation) and are reflected at interfaces (cracks or flaws). The reflected beam is displayed and then analyzed to define the presence and location of flaws or discontinuities.

VA

Vibration is essentially the heartbeat of all mechanical equipment. Capturing this vibration in a number of different forms allows analysts to diagnose equipment ailments, such as worn bearings or imbalance, by measuring the amplitude and frequency of the vibration. Mechanical vibration records provide valuable detail on the health of rotating equipment.

VT

Visual inspection is one NDT method used extensively to evaluate the condition or the quality of a weld or component. It is easily carried out, inexpensive and usually doesn't require special equipment. It requires good vision, good lighting and the knowledge of what to look for. Visual inspection can be enhanced by various methods ranging from low power magnifying glasses to boroscopes.

11.1 NDT Methods (cont'd)

NDT Certification Levels

NDT personnel are generally certified to several different levels of competence within each of the NDT methods they are working. The levels are Level I Limited, Level I , Level II, and Level III.

Level 1

Level I technicians are only qualified to perform specific calibrations and tests, and acceptance or rejection determinations allow little or no deviation from the procedure. Level I technicians are under close supervision and direction of a higher level tester. The level I position is not the trainee level, but the first level a trainee reaches upon demonstrating ability in specific tests. Level I Limited personnel are restricted even more in what they can do. They are usually trained to a specific procedure and can perform only certain types of inspections on a certain set of components.

Level II

Level II technicians are able to set up and calibrate equipment, conduct the inspection according to procedures, interpret, evaluate and document results in all the testing method(s) utilized by the certificate holder. The technician can provide on the job training for Level I and Level I Limited and act as a supervisor. The technician can also organize and document the results of the inspection. They must be familiar with all applicable codes, standards, and other documents that control the NDT method being utilized.

Level III

Level III technicians are capable of establishing techniques and procedures; interpreting codes, standards, and specifications; and designating the particular nondestructive testing methods, techniques, and procedures to be used. They must also have knowledge of materials, fabrication, and product technology. Level III technicians are responsible for training and examining Level I and Level II's. Usually Level III technicians are in administration, supervision, or management positions, or are owners of a testing laboratory. Some Level III technicians also become consultants.

11.2 Certification Requirements

Certification Requirements

There are a number of organizations that have produced documents that recommended or specify the minimum qualifications for certification. The following is a partial list of documents pertaining to the certification of NDT personnel in the US.

- SNT-TC-1A, The American Society for Nondestructive Testing, Recommended Practice, Personnel Qualification and Certification in Nondestructive Testing.
- ATA-105 Aviation Transport Association, Guidelines for Training and Qualifying Personnel in Nondestructive Testing Methods.
- AIA-NAS-410, Aerospace Industries Association, National Aerospace Standard, NAS Certification and Qualification of Nondestructive Test Personnel.
- ISO 9712, International Organization

for Standards, Nondestructive testing Qualification and certification of personnel.

The education and work experience requirements for the various specification are common or similar. Typical requirements are summarized in the table on page 11.6 for qualification levels I and II. Please consult the certification documents to assure that information is correct for your situation.

NDT training can be obtained at colleges, vocational-technical schools, the Armed Forces, commercial training companies and through individual company training departments. To be considered for certification as a Level III an individual must:

- Have graduated from a university or college with a degree in engineering or science, and have at least one year of experience comparable to that of a Level II in the applicable NDT method(s).
- Have completed with passing grades at least two years of engineering or science study at a university, college or technical school and have two years of experience comparable to that of a Level II in the applicable NDT method(s).
- Have four years of experience comparable to that of a Level II in the applicable NDT method(s).

11.3 Certification Standards

Certification Examinations

Once the education, training and work experience requirements have been met and documented, a certification examination must be taken. The examination process actually includes several exams.

- For certification to Levels I and II a general, a specific, and a practical, exam must be completed with a passing grade of 70 percent for each exam and a composite grade of 80 percent (determined by averaging the results of the three exams).
- The Level III exam process includes completion of a basic, a method, and a specific examination with a passing grade of 70 percent for each exam and a composite grade of 80 percent.
- Level I and II exams must be administered by an NDT Level III and this is often done within a particular company. Level I, II and II exams can also be taken through a central agency such as the American Society of Nondestructive Testing (ASNT).
- Central certifications provides technicians with documentation of qualification that is recognized nationally.

Visual

It is important that NDT personnel have good near visual acuity and color vision. Therefore, an eye test must be taken to insure that natural or corrected near distance acuity is acceptable. Depending on which specification the company uses for certification, an individual must be able to read a Jaeger Number 1 (or equivalent) type and size letter at no less than 12 inches (for one eye). Determining contrast of color or shades of gray is also generally required.

11.4 NDT Training Hours

Examination Method	Level	For Those with High School Diploma or Equivalent	For Those with at Least 2 Years of Engineering or Science Study at a College or Technical School	Minimum Hours of Work Experience in a Method	Permitted Time Frame to Obtain Required Work Experience in a Method (Months)
Acoustic Emission (AE)	I	40	32	210	1.5-9
	II	40	40	630	4.5-27
Electromagnetic (ET)	I	40	24	400	1.5-9
	II	40	40	1,200	4.5-27
Liquid Penetrant (PT)	I	16	4	130	0.5-3
	II	16	4	270	1-6
Magnetic Particle (MT)	I	16	8	130	0.5-3
	II	16	4	400	1.5-9
Neutron Radiography (NRT)	I	28	20	420	3-18
	II	40	40	1,680	12-72
Radiography (RT)	I	40	30	400	1.5-9
	II	40	35	1,200	4.5-27
Thermal/Infrared (TIR)	I	32	30	210	1.5-9
	II	34	32	1,260	9-27
Ultrasonics (UT)	I	40	30	400	1.5-9
	II	40	40	1,200	4.5-27
Vibration Analysis (VA)	I	24	24	420	2-18
	II	72	48	1,680	12-72
Visual (VT)	I	8	4	70	0.5-3
	II	16	8	140	1-6

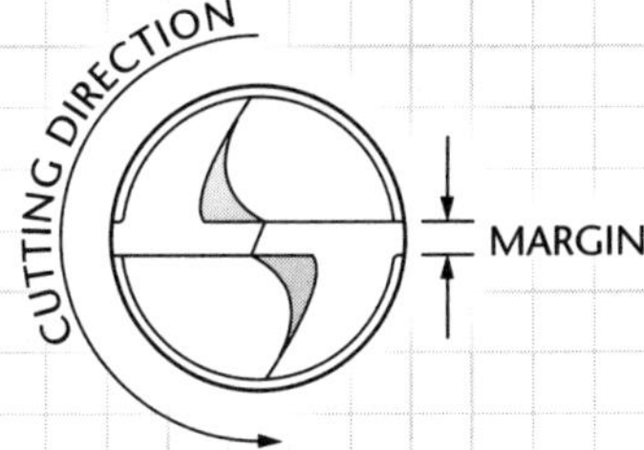

12
Tools

Lubricants for Cutting Tools

Material	Turning	Chucking	Drilling Milling	Reaming	Tapping
Tool Steel	Dry or Oil	Oil or Water	Oil	Lard Oil	Oil
Soft Steel	Dry or Water	Water	Oil or Water	Lard Oil	Oil
Wrought Iron	Dry or Water	Water	Oil or Water	Lard Oil	Oil
Cast Iron	Dry	Dry	Dry	Dry	Oil
Brass	Dry	Dry	Dry	Dry	Oil
Copper	Dry	Oil	Oil	Oil	Oil
Babbitt	Dry	Dry	Dry	Dry	Oil
Glass	–	–	Turpentine or Kerosene		–

NOTE: When two lubricants are mentioned, the first is preferable

12.2 Drill Feeds and Cutting Speeds

The following information is a good general guide. Specific jobs may have to be modified because of varying conditions on the job, such as coolant, equipment, and job requirements.

Drill feeds are governed by the size of the drill and also the material to be drilled; a feed of:

- 0.001" to 0.002" per revolution for drills smaller than 1/8"
- 0.002" to 0.004" for drills 1/8" to 1/4"
- 0.004" to 0.007" for drills 1/4 to ½"
- 0.007" to 0.015" for drills 1/2 to 1"
- 0.015" to 0.025" for drills larger than 1" is recommended. The lower feeds should be used when drilling relatively hard materials such as alloy steels and the higher feeds should be used when drilling relatively soft materials such as aluminum and brass.

These feeds are based an the peripheral speed of a drill. Recommended approximate peripheral speeds for carbon steel twist drills are as follows:

- 30 feet per minute for machinery steel
- 35 feet per minute for cast iron
- 60 feet per minute for brass

Recommended approximate peripheral speeds for high speed steel drills are:

- 80 feet per minute for machinery steel
- 100 feet per minute for cast iron
- 50 feet per minute for alloy steel
- 200 feet per minute for brass

Drill Diam.	Feet Per Minute										
	30	40	50	60	70	80	90	100	150	200	250
	Revolutions Per Minute										
1/16	1,833	2,445	3,056	3,667	4,278	4,889	5,500	6,112	9,167	12,223	15,279
1/8	917	1,222	1,528	1,833	2,139	2,445	2,750	3,056	4,584	6,112	7,639
3/16	611	815	1,019	1,222	1,426	1,630	1,833	2,037	3,056	4,074	5,093
1/4	458	611	764	917	1,070	1,222	1,375	1,528	2,292	3,056	3,820
5/16	367	489	611	733	856	978	1,100	1,222	1,833	2,445	3,056
3/8	306	407	509	611	713	815	917	1,019	1,528	2,037	2,546
7/16	262	349	437	524	611	698	786	873	1,310	1,746	2,183
1/2	229	306	382	458	535	611	688	764	1,146	1,528	1,910
5/8	183	244	306	367	428	489	550	611	917	1,222	1,528
3/4	153	204	255	306	357	407	458	509	764	1,019	1,273
7/8	131	175	218	262	306	349	393	473	655	873	1,091
1	115	153	191	229	267	306	344	382	573	764	955
1-1/8	102	136	170	204	238	272	306	340	509	679	849
1-1/4	92	122	153	183	214	244	275	306	458	611	764
1-3/8	83	111	139	167	194	222	250	278	417	556	694
1-1/2	76	102	127	153	178	204	229	255	382	509	637
1-5/8	71	94	118	141	165	188	212	235	353	470	588
1-3/4	66	87	109	131	153	175	196	218	327	437	546

NOTE: All dimensions are in inches

Tap Drill Sizes

National Fine Thread Series Medium Fit, Class 3 (NF)

Size & Threads	Body Diameter	Body Drill	Preferred Hole Dia.	Tap Drill
0-80	0.060	52	0.0472	3/64
1-72	0.073	47	0.0591	53
2-64	0.086	42	0.7000	50
3-56	0.099	37	0.0810	46
4-48	0.112	31	0.0911	42
5-44	0.125	29	0.1024	38
6-40	0.138	27	0.1130	33
8-36	0.164	18	0.1360	29
10-32	0.190	10	0.1590	21
12-28	0.216	2	0.1800	15
1/4-28	0.250	F	0.2130	3
5/16-24	0.3125	5/16	0.2703	I
3/8-24	0.375	3/8	0.3320	Q
7/16-20	0.4375	7/16	0.3860	W
1/2-20	0.500	1/2	0.4490	7/16
9/16-18	0.5625	9/16	0.5060	1/2
5/8-18	0.625	5/8	0.5680	9/16
3/4-16	0.750	3/4	0.6688	11/16
7/8-14	0.875	7/8	0.7822	51/64
1-14	1.000	1	0.9072	59/64

NOTE: All dimensions are in inches

12.4 Coarse Thread Tap Drills

Tap Drill Sizes

National Coarse Thread Series Medium Fit, Class 3 (NC)

Size & Threads	Body Diameter	Body Drill	Preferred Hole Dia.	Tap Drill
1-64	0.073	47	0.0575	53
2-56	0.086	42	0.0682	51
3-48	0.099	37	0.078	5/64
4-40	0.122	31	0.0866	44
5-40	0.125	29	0.0995	39
6-32	0.138	27	0.1063	36
8-32	0.164	18	0.1324	29
10-24	0.190	10	0.1476	26
12-24	0.216	2	0.1732	17
1/4-20	0.250	1/4	0.1990	8
5/16-18	0.3125	5/16	0.2559	F
3/8-16	0.375	3/8	0.3110	5/16
7/16-14	0.4375	7/16	0.3642	U
1/2-13	0.500	1/2	0.4219	27/64
9/16-12	0.5625	9/16	0.4776	31/64
5/8-11	0.625	5/8	0.5315	17/32
3/4-10	0.750	3/4	0.6480	41/64
7/8-9	0.875	7/8	0.7307	49/64
1-8	1.000	1	0.8376	7/8

NOTE: All dimensions are in inches

TAPER TAP

PLUG TAP

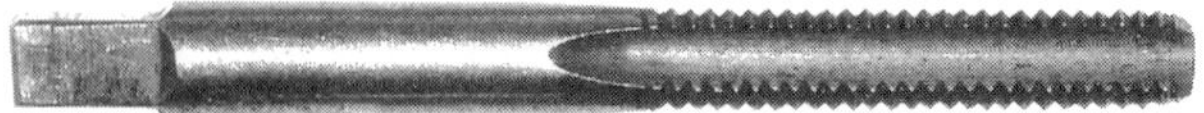

BOTTOMING TAP

American Standard Pipe Thread and Tap Drill Sizes

Pipe Size Inches	Threads per Inch	Root Diameter Small End of Pipe and Gauge	Tap Drill	
			Taper NPT	Straight NPS
1/8	27	0.3339	Q	11/32
1/4	18	0.4329	7/16	7/16
3/8	18	0.5676	9/16	37/64
1/2	14	0.7013	45/64	23/32
3/4	14	0.9105	29/32	59/64
1	11-1/2	1.1441	1-9/64	1-5/32
1-1/4	11-1/2	1.4876	1-31/64	1-1/2
1-1/2	11-1/2	1.7265	1-47/64	1-3/4
2	11-1/2	2.1995	2-13/64	2-7/32

NOTE: All dimensions are in inches

12.6 Tap Drill Sizes for Fractional Size Threads

Approximately 65% Depth Thread
American National Thread Form

Tap Size	Threads per Inch	Diam. Hole	Drill	Tap Size	Threads per Inch	Diam. Hole	Drill
1/16	72	0.049	3/64	1/2	20	0.451	29/64
1/16	64	0.047	3/64	1/2	13	0.425	27/64
1/16	60	0.046	56	1/2	12	0.419	27/64
5/64	72	0.065	52	9/16	27	0.526	17/32
5/64	64	0.063	1/16	9/16	18	0.508	33/64
5/64	60	0.062	1/16	9/16	12	0.481	31/64
5/64	56	0.061	53	5/8	27	0.589	19/32
3/32	60	0.077	5/64	5/8	18	0.571	37/64
3/32	56	0.076	48	5/8	12	0.544	35/64
3/32	50	0.074	49	5/8	11	0.536	17/32
3/32	48	0.073	49	11/16	16	0.627	5/8
7/64	56	0.092	42	11/16	11	0.599	19/32
7/64	50	0.090	43	3/4	27	0.714	23/32
7/64	48	0.089	43	3/4	16	0.689	11/16
1/8	48	0.105	36	3/4	12	0.669	13/64
1/8	40	0.101	38	3/4	10	0.653	21/32
1/8	36	0.098	40	13/16	12	0.731	47/64
1/8	32	0.095	3/32	13/16	10	0.715	23/32
9/64	40	0.116	32	7/8	27	0.839	27/32
9/64	36	0.114	33	7/8	18	0.821	53/64
9/64	32	0.110	35	7/8	14	0.805	13/16
5/32	40	0.132	30	7/8	12	0.794	51/64
5/32	36	0.129	30	7/8	9	0.767	49/64
5/32	32	0.126	1/8	15/16	12	0.856	55/64
11/64	36	0.145	27	15/16	9	0.829	53/64
11/64	32	0.141	9/64	1	27	0.964	31/32
3/16	36	0.161	20	1	14	0.930	15/16
3/16	32	0.157	22	1	12	0.919	59/64
3/16	30	0.155	23	1	8	0.878	7/8
3/16	24	0.147	26	1-1/16	8	0.941	15/16
13/64	32	0.173	17	1-1/8	12	1.044	1-3/64
13/64	30	0.171	11/64	1-1/8	7	0.986	63/64

12.6 Tap Drill Sizes for Fractional Size Threads (cont'd)

Approximately 65% Depth Thread
American National Thread Form

Tap Size	Threads per Inch	Diam. Hole	Drill	Tap Size	Threads per Inch	Diam. Hole	Drill
13/64	24	0.163	20	1-3/16	7	1.048	1-3/64
7/32	32	0.188	12	1-1/4	12	1.169	1-11/64
7/32	28	0.184	13	1-1/4	7	1.111	1-7/64
7/32	24	0.178	16	1-5/16	7	1.173	1-11/64
15/64	32	0.204	6	1-3/8	12	1.294	1-19/64
15/64	28	0.200	8	1-3/8	6	1.213	1-7/32
15/64	24	0.194	10	1-1/2	12	1.419	1-27/64
1/4	32	0.220	7/32	1-1/2	6	1.338	1-11/32
1/4	28	0.215	3	1-5/8	5-1/2	1.448	1-29/64
1/4	27	0.214	3	1-3/4	5	1.555	1-9/16
1/4	24	0.209	4	1-7/8	5	1.680	1-11/16
1/4	20	0.201	7	2	4-1/2	1.783	1-25/32
5/16	32	0.282	9/32	2-1/8	4-1/2	1.909	1-29/32
5/16	27	0.276	J	2-1/4	4-1/2	2.034	2-1/32
5/16	24	0.272	I	2-3/8	4	2.131	2-1/8
5/16	20	0.264	17/64	2-1/2	4	2.256	2-1/4
5/16	18	0.258	F	2-5/8	4	2.381	2-3/8
5/16	27	0.339	R	2-3/4	4	2.506	2-1/2
3/8	24	0.334	Q	2-7/8	3-1/2	2.597	2-19/32
3/8	20	0.326	21/64	3	3-1/2	2.722	2-23/32
3/8	16	0.314	5/16	3-1/8	3-1/2	2.847	2-27/32
7/16	27	0.401	Y	3-1/4	3-1/2	2.972	2-31/32
7/16	24	0.397	X	3-3/8	3-1/4	3.075	3-3/16
7/16	20	0.389	25/64	3-1/2	3-1/4	3.200	3-3/16
7/16	14	0.368	U	3-5/8	3-1/4	3.325	3-5/16
1/2	27	0.464	15/32	3-3/4	3	3.425	3-7/16
1/2	24	0.460	29/64	4	3	3.675	3-11/16

NOTE: All dimensions are in inches

12.7 Types of Drill Motors

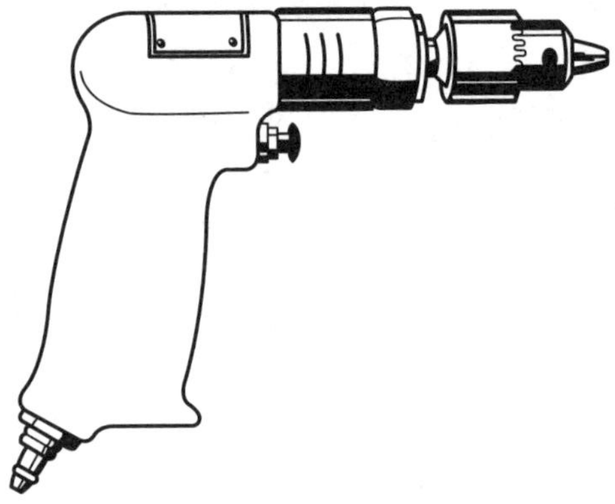

TYPICAL PNEUMATIC DRILL MOTOR

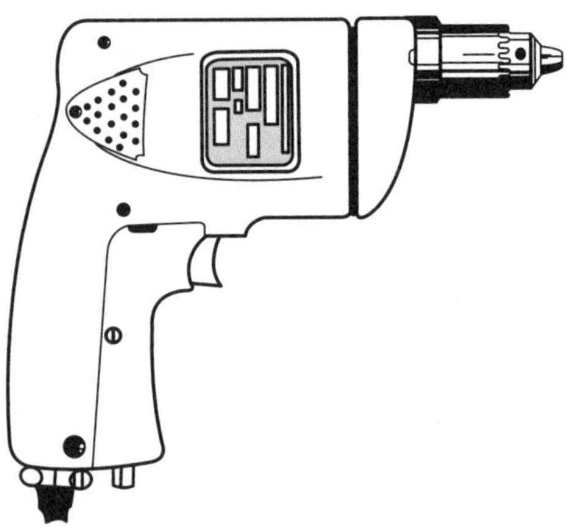

TYPICAL ELECTRIC DRILL MOTOR

12.8 **Chucking the Drill**

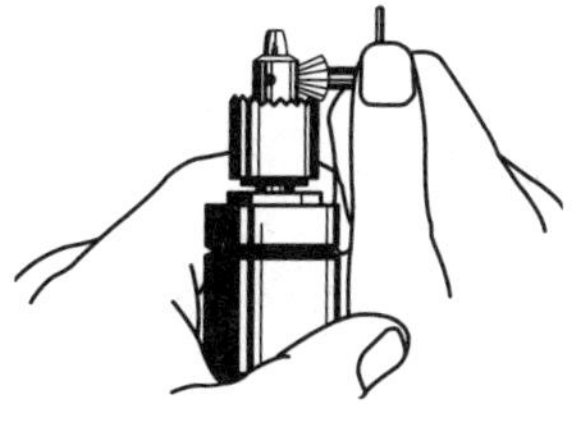

1. Use a chuck key to open the jaws just far enough to admit the shank of the drill. Be sure drill shank and chuck jaws are clean.

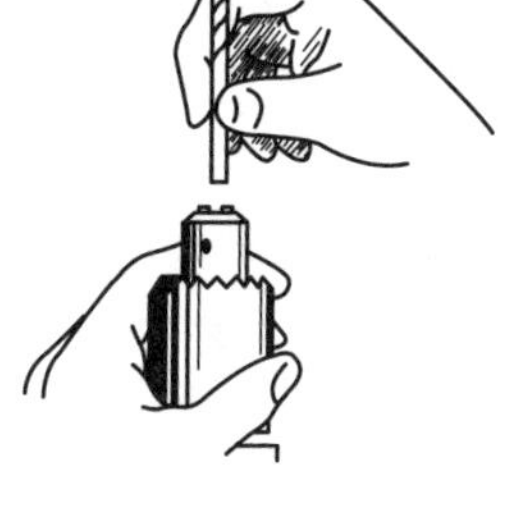

2. Insert drill shank into chuck. CAUTION: Do not allow the flutes to enter chuck.

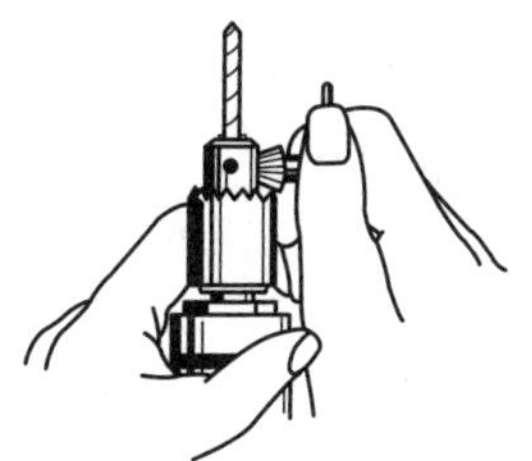

3. Tighten the chuck firmly with the chuck key, inserting the key in all three key holes. This prevents unequal clamping on the drill.

12.9 **Safety Precautions**

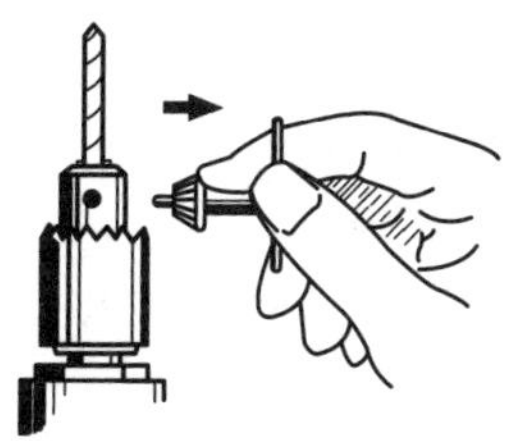

1. Remove the key before starting the drill motor.

2. Serious injury may result if this is not done.

3. The trigger of the motor must be OFF before connecting to power.

12.10 **Drilling a Hole**

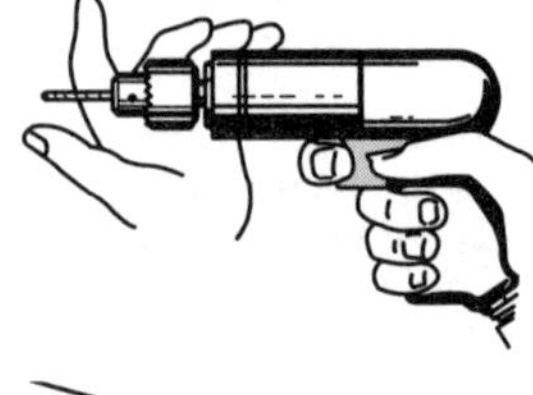

1. Hold the drill firmly.

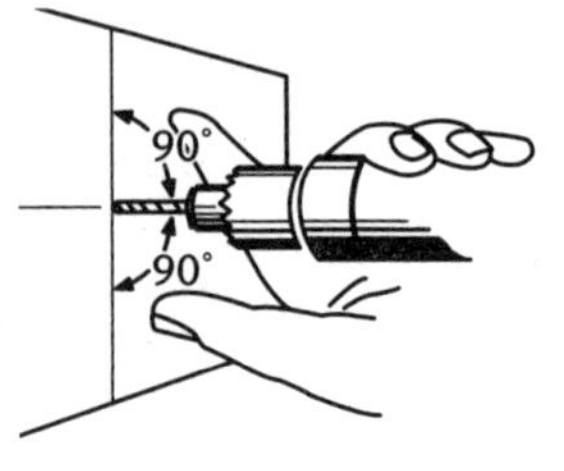

2. Put drill point on the spot to be drilled. Hold drill at a 90° angle to the material's surface. Start motor by squeezing trigger. Support drill motor to prevent chuck from touching aircraft part.

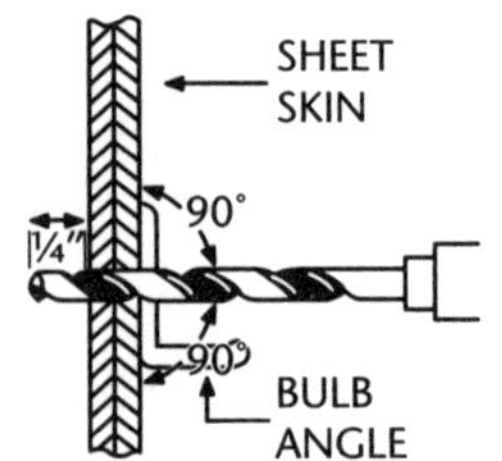

3. Push drill with sufficient pressure to drill hole. Drill through material no more than 1/4 inch. Keep motor running while withdrawing drill from hole. Be sure drill is held at an angle 90° to the drilled surface.

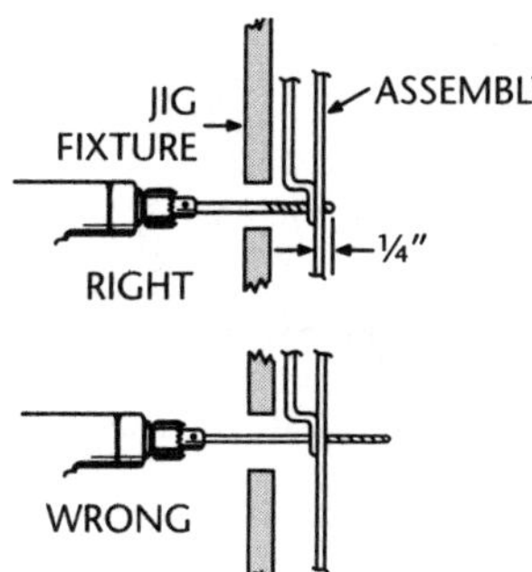

1. Select a drill of the correct length
   and size. It should be no longer than
   necessary to clear the obstruction and
   go through the material 1/4 inch.

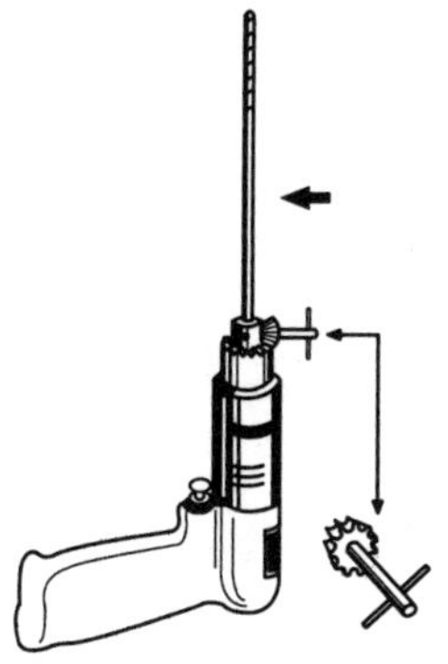

2. Disconnect the power.
   Place the drill in the chuck as usual.
   Remove the chuck key.

12.12 **Safety Precautions**

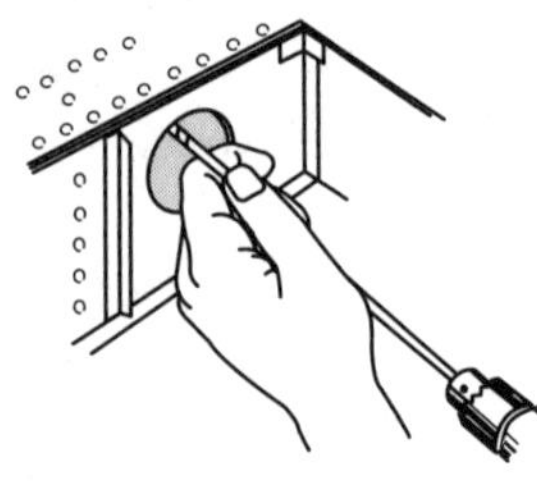

1. Before starting the motor, hold the extension near the flute end with one hand.

   Don't touch the flutes and don't forget to wear safety glasses or face shield.

2. If the end of the drill is not supported, it may whip around and cut your face or injure another worker. USE CAUTION.

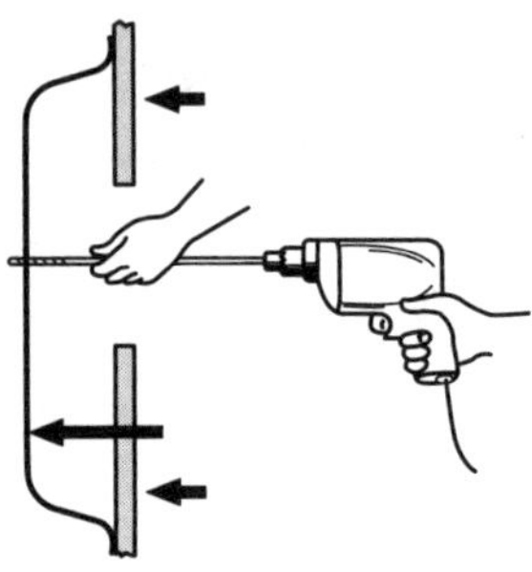

3. Drill through the part. Do not let go of the drill shank. Keep the motor running as the drill is removed.

   Support the extension drill until the motor stops.

Angle Drills

90° ANGLE

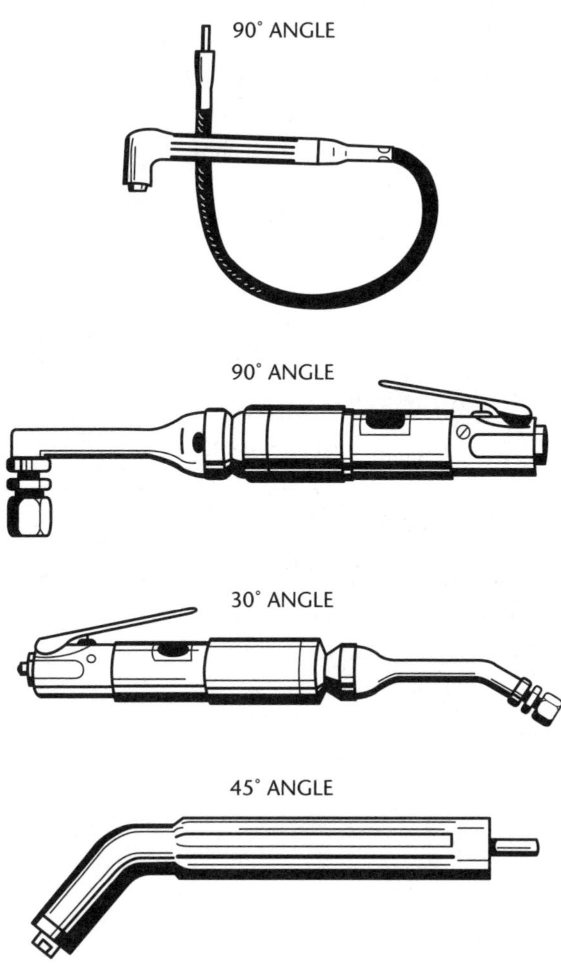

NOTE: Avoid accidents. Hold angle drilling accessory firmly; do not let it spin.

Close Ream - Hand Feed

Nominal Hole Size (inches)	Required Hole Size (inches)	Reamer Diameter (inches)	Depth of Cut	Speed (r.p.m.)	Pilot Clearance
5/32	0.1635 to 0.1645	0.1632 + 0.0003 +0.0001	1/64	1,000	0.001 - 0.003
3/16	0.1895 to 0.1905	0.1892 + 0.0003 +0.0001	1/64	1,000	0.001 - 0.003
1/4	0.2495 to 0.2505	0.2492 + 0.0003 + 0.0001	1/32	1,000	0.001 - 0.003
5/16	0.3120 to 0.3130	0.3117 + 0.0003 + 0.0001	1/32	500	0.001 - 0.003
3/8	0.3745 to 0.3755	0.3742 + 0.0003 + 0.0001	1/32	500	0.001 - 0.003
7/16	0.4370 to 0.4380	0.4367 + 0.0003 + 0.0001	1/32	500	0.001 - 0.003
1/2	0.4995 to 0.5005	0.4992 + 0.0003 +0.0001	1/32	500	0.001 - 0.003
9/16	0.5620 to 0.5630	0.5617 + 0.0003 + 0.0001	1/32	500	0.001 - 0.003

NOTES: Hole tolerance: Close ream, 0.001 to 0.003 inch
Cutting agent Boelube, Freon TB1 or cetyl alcohol paste
Reamer material: high-speed steel (M-2, M-7, M-10)
All dimensions are in inches

12.15 RPM - Reaming Aluminum Alloys - Transition Fit

Transition Fit - Hand Feed

Nominal Hole Size	Required Hole Size	Reamer Diameter	Depth of Cut	Speed (r.p.m.)	Pilot Clearance
5/32	0.1610 to 0.1640	0.1610 + 0.0004 +0.0001	1/64	1,000	0.001 - 0.004
3/16	0.1870 to 0.1900	0.1870 + 0.0004 +0.0001	1/64	1,000	0.001 - 0.004
1/4	0.2470 to 0.2500	0.2470 + 0.0004 + 0.0001	1/32	1,000	0.001 - 0.004
5/16	0.3090 to 0.3130	0.3090 + 0.0005 + 0.0001	1/32	1,000	0.001 - 0.004
3/8	0.3710 to 0.3750	0.3710 + 0.0005 + 0.0001	1/32	1,000	0.001 - 0.004
7/16	0.4340 to 0.4380	0.4340 + 0.0005 + 0.0001	1/32	500	0.001 - 0.004
1/2	0.4960 to 0.5000	0.4960 + 0.0005 +0.0001	1/32	500	0.001 - 0.004
9/16	0.5590 to 0.5630	0.5590 + 0.0005 + 0.0001	1/32	500	0.001 - 0.004

12.16 RPM - Reaming Aluminum Alloys - Class One Fit

NOTES: Hole tolerance: Transition fit, 0.001 to 0.004 inch
Cutting agent: Boelube, Freon T-B1 or cetyl alcohol paste
Reamer material: high-speed steel (M-2, M-7, M-10)
All dimensions are in inches

Class One Fit Hand Feed

Nominal Hole Size	Required Hole Size	Reamer Diameter	Depth of Cut	Speed (r.p.m.)	Pilot Clearance
5/32	0.164 to 0.168	0.1640 + 0.0004 +0.0001	1/64	1,000	0.001 - 0.004
3/16	0.190 to 0.194	0.1900 + 0.0004 +0.0001	1/64	1,000	0.001 - 0.004
1/4	0.250 to 0.254	0.2500 + 0.0004 + 0.0001	1/32	1,000	0.001 - 0.004
5/16	0.312 to 0.316	0.3125 + 0.0005 + 0.0001	1/32	1,000	0.001 - 0.004
3/8	0.375 to 0.379	0.3750 + 0.0005 + 0.0001	1/32	1,000	0.001 - 0.004
7/16	0.437 to 0.442	0.4375 + 0.0005 + 0.0001	1/32	500	0.001 - 0.004
1/2	0.500 to 0.505	0.5000 + 0.0005 +0.0001	1/32	500	0.001 - 0.004
9/16	0.562 to 0.567	0.5625 + 0.0005 + 0.0001	1/32	500	0.001 - 0.004

NOTES: For reamer geometry, refer to NAS 097
Hole tolerance: Class 1 fit, 0.001 to 0.004 inch
Cutting agent: Boelube, Freon T-B1 or cetyl alcohol paste
Reamer material: high-speed steel (U-2, 61-7, M-10)
All dimensions are in inches

12.17 Piloted Chucking Reamer

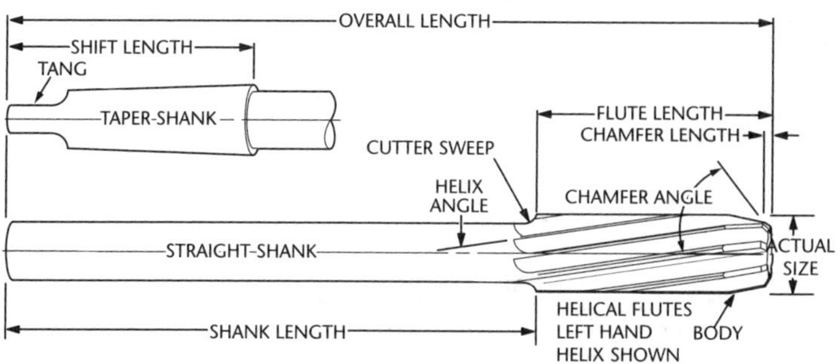

CHUCKING REAMER, STRAIGHT AND TAPER SHANK

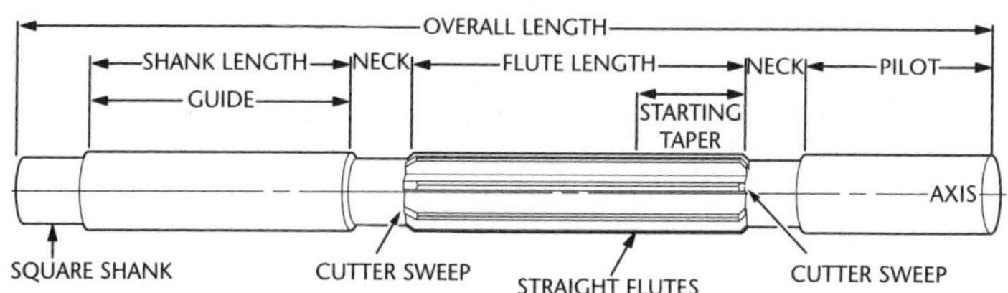

HAND REAMER, PILOT AND GUIDE

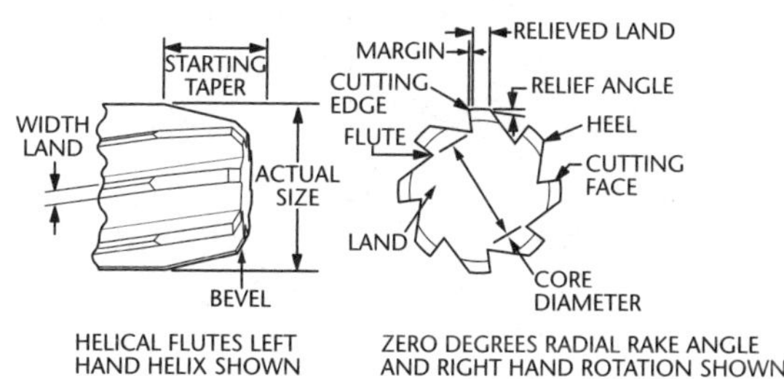

HAND REAMER

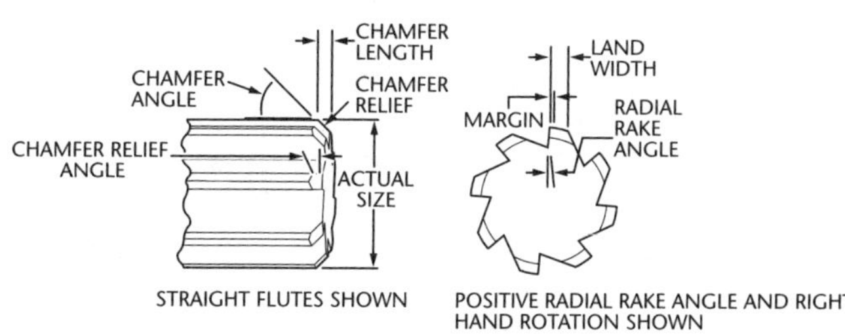

MACHINE REAMER

12.18 **Clecos**

A cleco is a spring loaded clamp used to hold parts together.

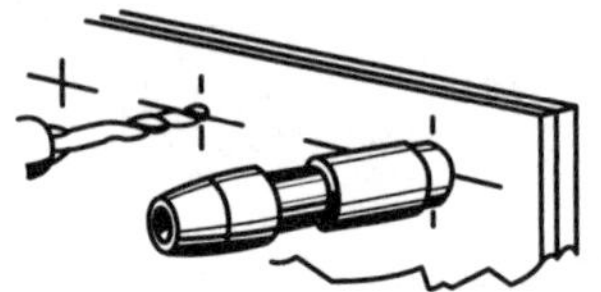

While drilling, parts must be held firmly together.

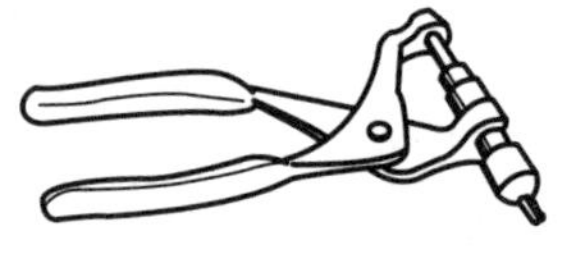

Use special pliers to insert clecos into holes.

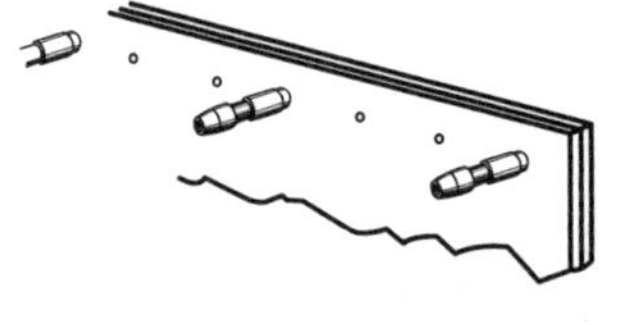

Space clecos as needed.

Wear saftey glasses when using clecos.

Cleco size	Color
3/32	Silver
1/8	Copper
5/32	Black
3/16	Brass

CAUTION: Keep clecos off the floor

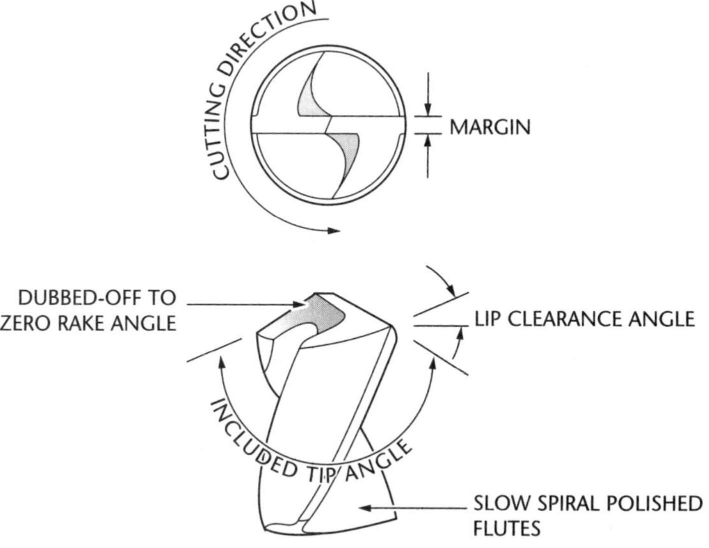

12.20 **Types of Drills**

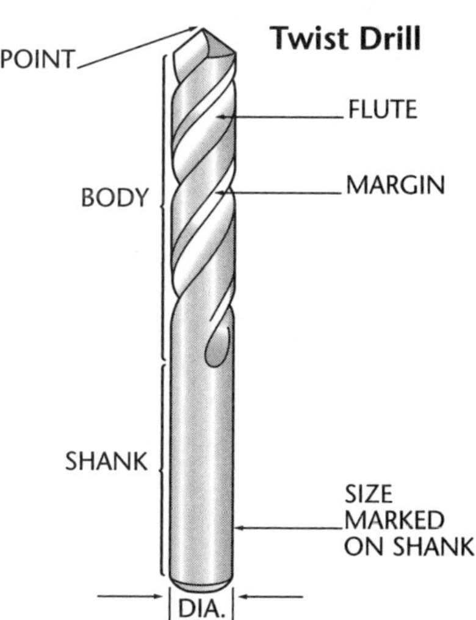

Single Margin   Double Margin

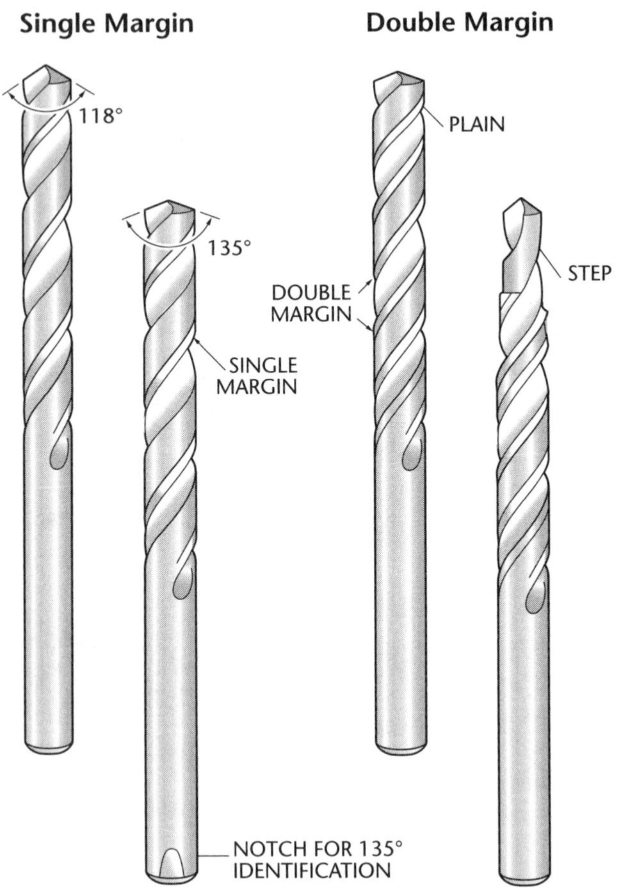

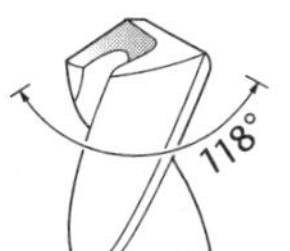

General Purpose:
Aluminum,
Magnesium,
Mild Steel

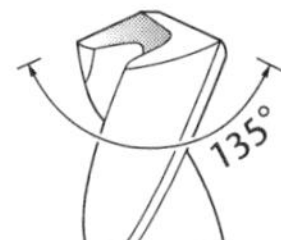

Hard & Tough Materials:
Stainless Steel,
Hard Steel,
Titanium

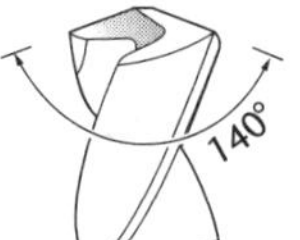

Cobalt Drills:
High Heat
Treat Steels

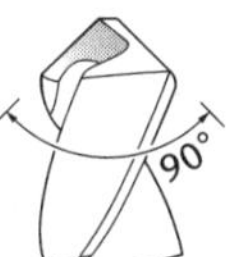

Plexiglas & Kirksite
Also used for
enlarging holes
in thin skin

Drill Points

The proper point angle depends upon the material being drilled. In general, the harder the material the greater the point angle should be. The greater the point angle, the greater the required feeding pressure.

Factors Over Which the Operator has Control:

- Use of a sharp drill
- Method of locating and supporting the drill at the start and through the drilling of the hole
- Use of proper drill (point angle, web thickness, helix) for material being drilled
- Use shortest drill possible
- Select proper speed of drill motor. In general, by increasing speed a larger hole can be expected

Factors Over which the Operator has No Control:

- Method of sharpening
- Amount of back taper
- Nature and structure of material being drilled

Tolerance of Drilled Holes (Close Tolerance Drills)

Close tolerance double margin drills have been designed to create holes that have a closer tolerance than required for common fasteners, such as rivets, screws, etc. A 0.003 hole tolerance can be maintained by use of these tools, however, the hole finish is not comparable to that obtained by reaming. It is possible to obtain closer hole tolerance by using the "step type" close tolerance drill in a class A drill bushings having a minimum overall length of three drill diameters. For reasons of economy, single margin (regular) drills should be used for drilled hole tolerances required for ordinary application.

Drilling Sheet Metal

Special problems are encountered in drilling sheet metal and other thin sections. The main difficulty is the breakage of drills, particularly on the smaller diameter holes. This is due to several factors:

- Hand supported power tools are not held rigidly enough in line of feed,

and feeding pressure is not constant
- There is no rigid support when the drill breaks through, so that a distinct shock is produced at this time.
- The metal will deform because of feeding pressure before the drill actually begins to cut. When the drill begins to cut the entire torque load is thrown on the drill at once.

The deformation may cause the metal to work harden before the cutting begins. For best results use:
- Shortest drill possible and shortest flute length
- Proper point angle
- Heaviest web thickness

For enlarging holes in thin sheet metal use:
- Plastic type drills
- Hole saws for holes over 3/8" diameter

- DO NOT USE counterbores or spotfacers

Drilling Stainless Steel

Stainless steel is more difficult to drill than aluminum alloys and straight carbon steel because of the work hardening properties. Because of work hardening it is most important to keep the cutting tools cutting continuously with a uniform speed and feed. If the tool is permitted to rub or idle on the work, the surface will become work hardened to a point where it is difficult to restart the cut. For best results in cutting stainless steel, following should be adhered to:
- Use sharp drills, point angle 135°
- Use moderate speeds
- Use adequate and uniform feeds
- Use an adequate amount of sulphurized mineral oil or soluble oil as a coolant if possible

RIVET SIZE:			USE THIS SIZE DRILL:
-2 or 1/16"			#51 (0.0670)
-3 or 3/32"			#41 (0.096)
-4 or 1/8"			#30 (0.1285)
-5 or 5/32"			#21 (0.159)
-6 or 3/16"			#11 (0.191)
-8 or 1/4"			F (0.257)

Stainless Steel

Drilling stainless steel requires special techniques because of its work hardening properties. If the drill is allowed to spin on material without cutting, the stainless steel surface will become hard, making it very difficult to drill.

For best results in drilling stainless:
- Use a sharp drill with a 135° point angle
- Use a slow speed drill motor
- Apply sufficient pressure for positive feed of drill
- Support back of material being drilled

When drilling through dissimilar materials, drill through the harder material first to prevent making an egg-shaped hole in the softer material.

Drills Break:
- When side pressure is applied
- When dropped with drill motor
- When dull and forced to cut

Titanium and Titanium Alloys

Titanium and its alloys have low-volume specific heat and low thermal conductivity, causing them to heat readily at the point of putting, and making them difficult to cool.

Thermal problems can best be overcome by reducing either the speed or the feed. Fortunately, titanium alloys do not work harden appreciably, thus lighter feed pressures can be used.

When using super-high-speed drills having high carbon, vanadium, and cobalt to resist abrasion and high drilling heats, the following drilling speeds (RPM) are suggested:

Drill Dia.[1]	Max. Drill Speed (r.p.m.)
1/2	225
3/8	300
5/16	360
1/4	450
7/32	520
3/16	600
5/32	710
1/8	900
#40	1,050

NOTES:[1]Hand-feed drilling. Larger diameters should have positive-feed equipment which should be used if feasible
All dimensions are in inches

Aluminum and Aluminum Alloys

The drilling of these materials has become quite commonplace, however, some newer aluminum alloys of high silicon content and some cast alloys still present a few problems.

In drilling aluminum, high rates of penetration can be used; hence disposal of chips or cuttings is very important. To permit these high penetration rates and still dispose of the chips, drills must be free cutting to reduce the heat generated and have large flute areas for passage of chips.

12.23 Proper Torque for Threaded Fasteners

- To obtain the maximum strength from a joint using threaded fasteners, the load applied to the fastener must be greater than the maximum load that will be applied to the joint.

- If a threaded fastener does not fail when it is being properly torqued, it will not fail in service. When the fastener is being torqued, it is subjected to both torsional and tensile stresses. After installation is complete, the fastener is subjected only to the tensile stress. Unless otherwise stated, torque values specified are normally for clean, dry threads. When lubricated threads are called for, the type of lubricant will be specified.

- When torquing a self locking nut on a bolt, first determine the amount of torque needed to run the nut down on the bolt before it contacts the surface (this is called prevailing torque). The final torque on the nut must be the prevailing torque plus the desired torque.

- When using a click type torque wrench, stop the pull as soon as the wrench snaps. The snapping action is an indicator of the desired torque. It does not limit further torque.

- Torque applied to a threaded fastener by measuring the amount the nut is turned after it reaches its bearing surface is not affected by prevailing torque of the nut, or by lubrication or lack of lubrication of the threads.

- When using an adapter on a torque wrench, the arm of the adapter must be considered when determining the torque applied to the fastener.

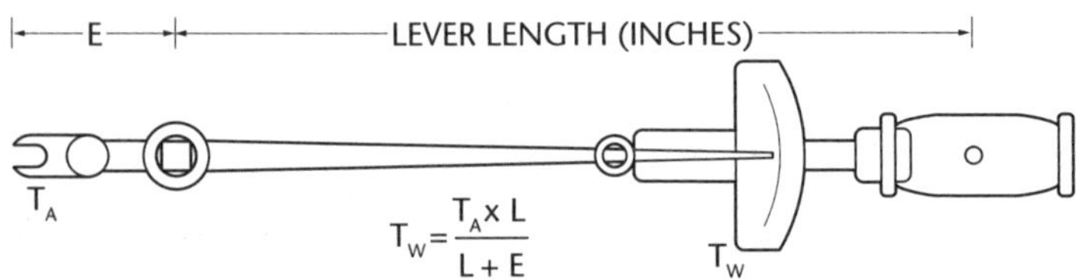

T_W = Torque indicated on the wrench

T_A = Torque applied at the adapter

L = Lever length of torque wrench

E = Arm of the adapter

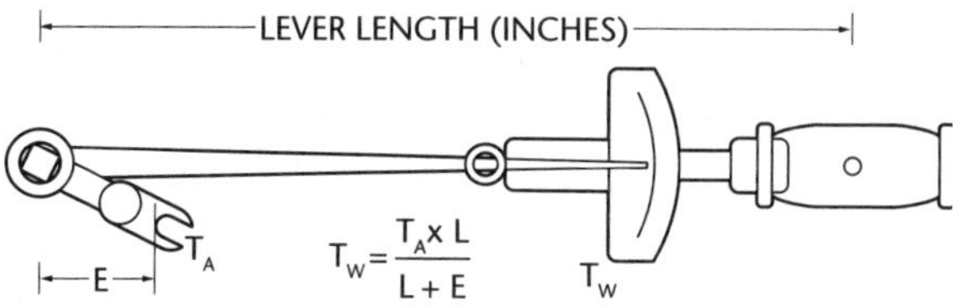

T_W = Torque indicated on the wrench

T_A = Torque applied at the adapter

L = Lever length of torque wrench

E = Arm of the adapter

Inch Grams	Inch Ounces	Inch Pounds	Foot Pounds	Centimeter Kilograms	Meter Kilograms
7.09	0.25	–	–	–	–
14.17	0.50	–	–	–	–
21.26	0.75	–	–	–	–
28.35	1.00	–	–	–	–
113.40	4.00	0.25	–	–	–
226.80	8.00	0.50	–	–	–
453.59	16.00	1.00	0.08	1.11	–
–	96.00	6.00	0.50	6.92	–
–	192.00	12.00	1.00	13.83	0.138
–	384.00	24.00	2.00	27.66	0.277
–	576.00	36.00	3.00	41.49	0.415
–	768.00	48.00	4.00	55.32	0.553
–	960.00	60.00	5.00	69.15	0.692
–	–	72.00	6.00	82.98	0.830
–	–	84.00	7.00	96.81	0.968
–	–	96.00	8.00	110.64	1.106
–	–	108.00	9.00	124.47	1.245
–	–	120.00	10.00	138.31	1.383

NOTE: All dimensions are in inches

12.25 **Micrometers**

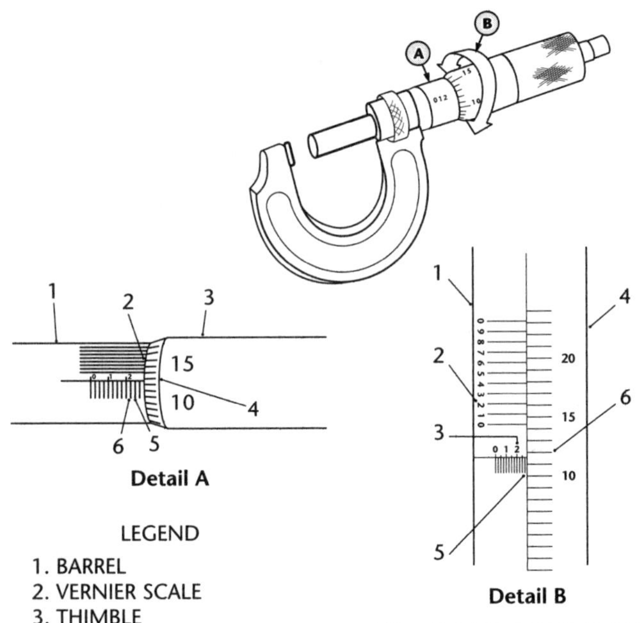

Detail A

LEGEND

1. BARREL
2. VERNIER SCALE
3. THIMBLE
4. 0.001 INCH DIVISIONS
5. 0.0025 INCH DIVISIONS
6. 0.1 INCH DIVISIONS

Detail B

VIEW SHOWS SCALES FLATTENED
FOR CLARITY

12.26 **Bevel Protractor**

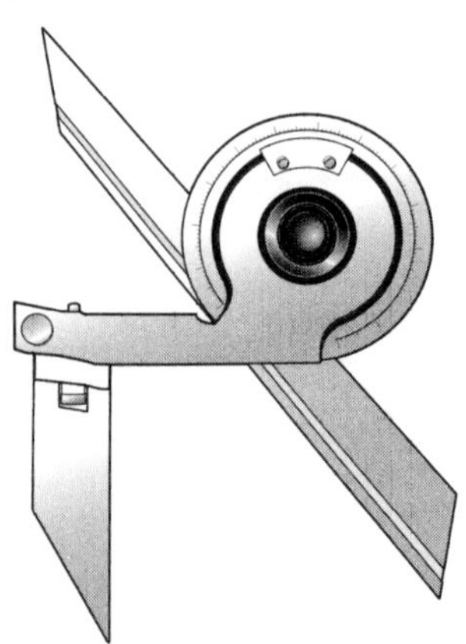

12.27 **Combination Square**

12.28 **Carpenter's Square**

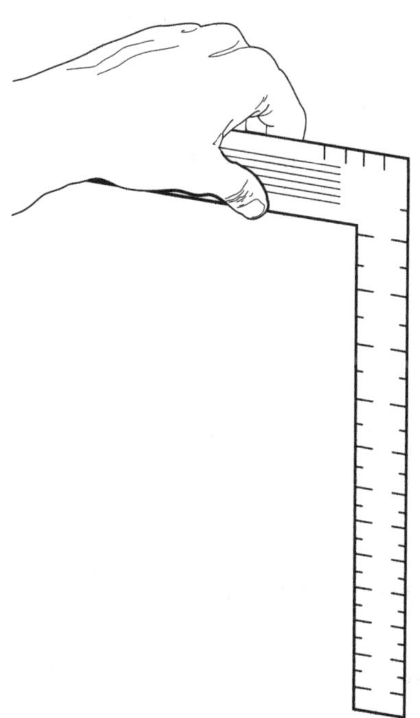

12.29 Steel Rulers

12.30 Tape Measures

12.31 Machinist's Scribe

12.32 Plumb Bobs

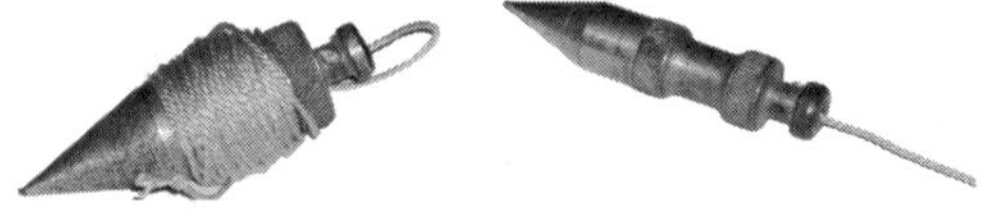

12.33 Bubble Level

C
D
E/2 RADIUS
B DIA
PART NO.
HERE
(LOCATION
OPTIONAL)
E
R
S
H
B
F
THREAD T
COUNTERSINK
OPPOSITE END
ONLY 110° TO
O.D. OF THREAD

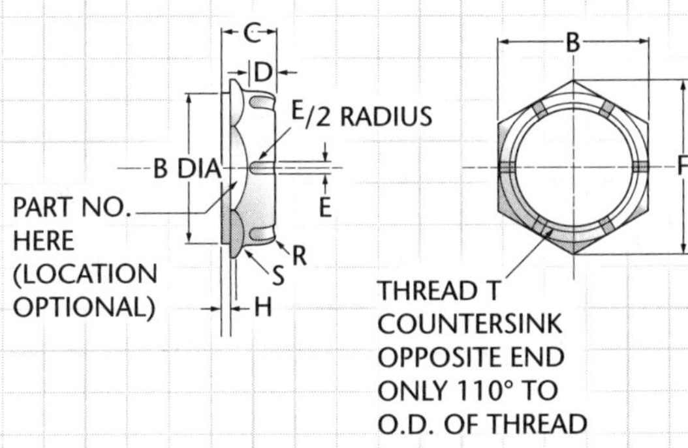

13

Hardware

13.1 AN3 - AN20 Bolts

AN # Basic	Thread Dia./ pitch	Dia. Max	Dia. Min	Wrench Size	Hole, Shank +0.010, -0.000	Hole, Head +0.010, -0.000	Commnoly Used Steel Cotter Pin	Commonly Used Stainless Cotter Pin
AN3	10-32	0.189	0.186	$3/8$	0.070	0.046	MS24665-132	MS24665-151
AN4	$1/4$-28	0.249	0.246	$7/16$	0.076	0.046	MS24665-132	MS24665-151
AN5	$5/16$-24	0.312	0.309	$1/2$	0.076	0.070	MS24665-210	MS24665-229
AN6	$3/8$-24	0.374	0.371	$9/16$	0.106	0.070	MS24665-283	MS24665-300
AN7	$7/16$-20	0.437	0.433	$5/8$	0.106	0.070	MS24665-283	MS24665-300
AN8	$1/2$-20	0.499	0.495	$3/4$	0.106	0.070	MS24665-285	MS24665-302
AN9	$9/16$-18	0.562	0.558	$7/8$	0.141	0.070	MS24665-353	MS24665-370
AN10	$5/8$-18	0.624	0.620	$15/16$	0.141	0.070	MS24665-355	MS24665-372
AN12	$3/4$-16	0.749	0.744	1-$1/16$	0.141	0.070	MS24665-355	MS24665-372
AN14	$7/8$-14	0.874	0.869	1-$1/4$	0.141	0.070	MS24665-357	MS24665-374
AN16	1-14	0.999	0.993	1-$1/2$	0.141	0.070	MS24665-359	MS24665-376
AN17	1-12	0.999	0.993	1-$1/2$	0.141	0.070	MS24665-359	MS24665-376
AN18	1-$1/8$-12	1.124	1.118	1-$5/8$	0.141	0.070	MS24665-359	MS24665-376
AN20	1-$1/4$-12	1.249	1.243	1-$7/8$	0.141	0.070	MS24665-360	MS24665-377

NOTE: All dimensions are in inches

AN # Basic	Thread DIA/ Pitch	Dia. +0.000 -0.002	Hole Shank +0.010 -0.000	Head Dia.	Nylon Locknut	Castle Nut	Commonly Used Steel Cotter Pin	Commonly Used Stainless Cotter Pin
AN23	10-32	0.186	0.070	3/8	MS21083N3	AN320-3	MS24665-132	MS24665-151
AN24	1/4-28	0.248	0.076	1/2	MS21083N4	AN320-4	MS24665-132	MS24665-151
AN25	5/16-24	0.311	0.076	5/8	MS21083N5	AN320-5	MS24665-210	MS24665-229
AN26	3/8-24	0.373	0.106	11/16	MS21083N6	AN320-6	MS24665-283	MS24665-300

NOTE: All dimensions are in inches

Dash # / Grip Length / Overall Length

-#	AN23-GRIP + or -1/64	AN23-OAL + or -1/64	AN24-GRIP + or -1/64	AN24-OAL + or -1/64	AN25-GRIP + or -1/64	AN25-OAL + or -1/64	AN26-GRIP + or -1/64	AN26-OAL + or -1/64
8	0.188	0.531	0.188	0.531				
9	0.250	0.594	0.250	0.594	0.250	0.609	0.250	0.609
10	0.313	0.656	0.313	0.656	0.313	0.672	0.313	0.672
11	0.375	0.719	0.375	0.719	0.375	0.734	0.375	0.734
12	0.438	0.781	0.438	0.781	0.438	0.797	0.438	0.797
13	0.500	0.844	0.500	0.844	0.500	0.859	0.500	0.859
14	0.563	0.906	0.563	0.906	0.563	0.922	0.563	0.922
15	0.625	0.969	0.625	0.969	0.625	0.984	0.625	0.984
16	0.688	1.031	0.688	1.031	0.688	1.047	0.688	1.047
17	0.750	1.094	0.500	1.094	0.750	1.109	0.750	1.109
18	0.813	1.156	0.813	1.156	0.813	1.172	0.813	1.172

13.2 AN23 - AN26 Clevis Bolts (cont'd)

Dash # / Grip Length / Overall Length

-#	AN23-GRIP + or -1/64	AN23-OAL + or -1/64	AN24-GRIP + or -1/64	AN24-OAL + or -1/64	AN25-GRIP + or -1/64	AN25-OAL + or -1/64	AN26-GRIP + or -1/64	AN26-OAL + or -1/64
19	0.875	1.219	0.875	1.219	0.875	1.234	0.875	1.234
20	0.938	1.281	0.938	1.281	0.938	1.29	0.938	1.297
21	1.000	1.344	1.000	1.344	1.000	1.359	1.000	1.359
22	1.063	1.406	1.063	1.406	1.063	1.422	1.063	1.422
23	1.125	1.469	1.125	1.469	1.125	1.484	1.125	1.484
24	1.188	1.531	1.188	1.531	1.188	1.547	1.188	1.547
25	1.250	1.594	1.250	1.594	1.250	1.609	1.250	1.609
26	1.313	1.656	1.313	1.656	1.313	1.672	1.313	1.672
27	1.375	1.719	1.375	1.719	1.375	1.734	1.375	1.734
28	1.438	1.781	1.438	1.781	1.438	1.797	1.438	1.797
29	1.500	1.844	1.500	1.844	1.500	1.859	1.500	1.859
30	1.563	1.906	1.563	1.906	1.563	1.922	1.563	1.922
31	1.625	1.969	1.625	1.969	1.625	1.984	1.625	1.984
32	1.688	2.031	1.688	2.031	1.688	2.047	1.688	2.047
33	1.750	2.094	1.750	2.094	1.750	2.109	1.750	2.109
34	1.813	2.156	1.813	2.156	1.813	2.172	1.813	2.172
35	1.875	2.219	1.875	2.219	1.875	2.234	1.875	2.234
36	1.938	2.281	1.938	2.281	1.938	2.297	1.938	2.297
37	2.000	2.344	2.000	2.344	2.000	2.359	2.000	2.359
38	2.063	2.406	2.063	2.406	2.063	2.422	2.063	2.422
39	2.125	2.469	2.125	2.469	2.125	2.484	2.125	2.484
40	2.188	2.531	2.188	2.531	2.188	2.547	2.188	2.547

NOTE: All dimensions are in inches

Standard Head
Bolt

Drilled Hex
Head Bolt

Countersunk Head
Bolt

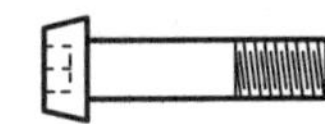

Internal Hex
Head Bolt

Eyebolt

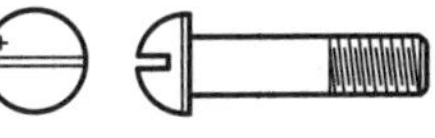

Clevis Bolt

AN Standard
Steel Bolt
(Corrosion
Resistant)

AN Standard
Steel Bolt

Special Bolt

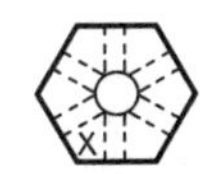

Drilled Head
Bolt

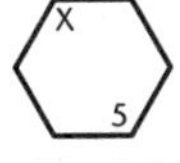

Special
Bolt

NAS Close
Tolerance Bolt

Aluminum Alloy
(2024) Bolt

Magnetically
Inspected

Orange Dyed
Magnetic Ins.

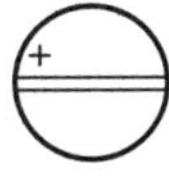

Clevis Bolt

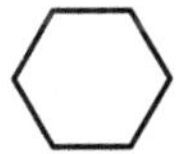

Low Strength
Material Bolt

13.4 MS2003 - MS20036, 1200°F Bolts

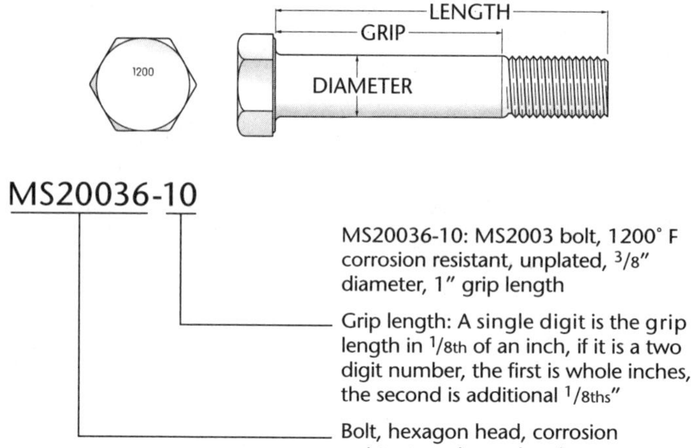

MS20036-10

MS20036-10: MS2003 bolt, 1200° F corrosion resistant, unplated, 3/8" diameter, 1" grip length

Grip length: A single digit is the grip length in 1/8th of an inch, if it is a two digit number, the first is whole inches, the second is additional 1/8ths"

Bolt, hexagon head, corrosion resistant steel, un-plated

13.5 MS20004 - MS20024 Bolts

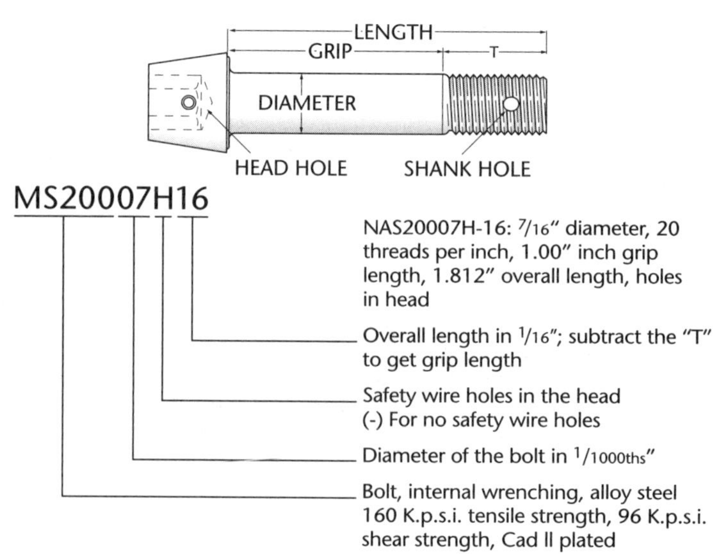

MS20007H16

NAS20007H-16: 7/16" diameter, 20 threads per inch, 1.00" inch grip length, 1.812" overall length, holes in head

Overall length in 1/16"; subtract the "T" to get grip length

Safety wire holes in the head (-) For no safety wire holes

Diameter of the bolt in 1/1000ths"

Bolt, internal wrenching, alloy steel 160 K.p.s.i. tensile strength, 96 K.p.s.i. shear strength, Cad II plated

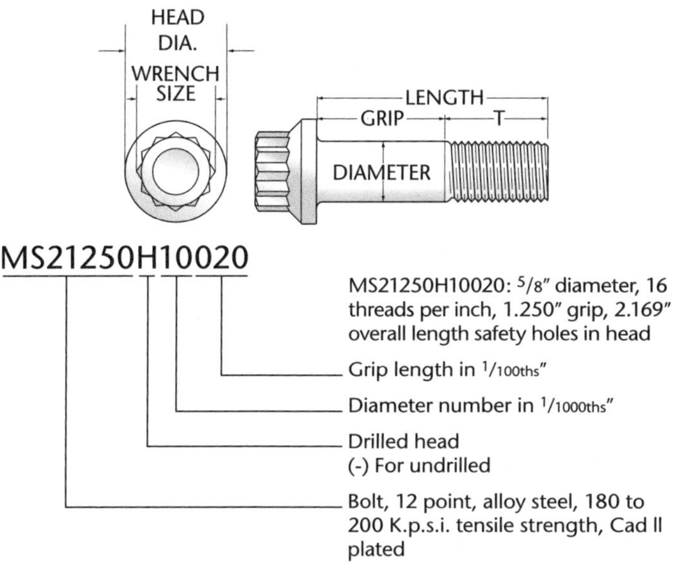

MS21250H10020

MS21250H10020: $^5/_8$" diameter, 16 threads per inch, 1.250" grip, 2.169" overall length safety holes in head

Grip length in $^1/_{100ths}$"

Diameter number in $^1/_{1000ths}$"

Drilled head
(-) For undrilled

Bolt, 12 point, alloy steel, 180 to 200 K.p.s.i. tensile strength, Cad ll plated

13.7 NAS144 - NAS158 Bolts

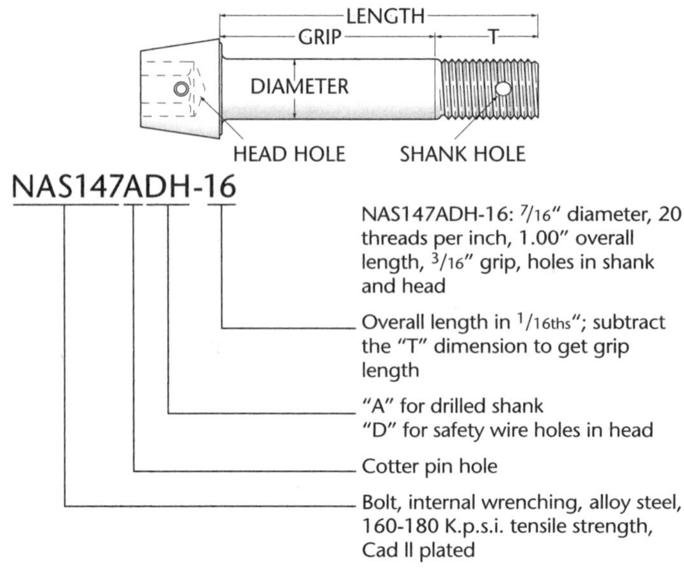

NAS147ADH-16: $^7/16$" diameter, 20 threads per inch, 1.00" overall length, $^3/16$" grip, holes in shank and head

Overall length in $^1/16$ths"; subtract the "T" dimension to get grip length

"A" for drilled shank
"D" for safety wire holes in head

Cotter pin hole

Bolt, internal wrenching, alloy steel, 160-180 K.p.s.i. tensile strength, Cad II plated

13.8 NAS464 Series Bolts

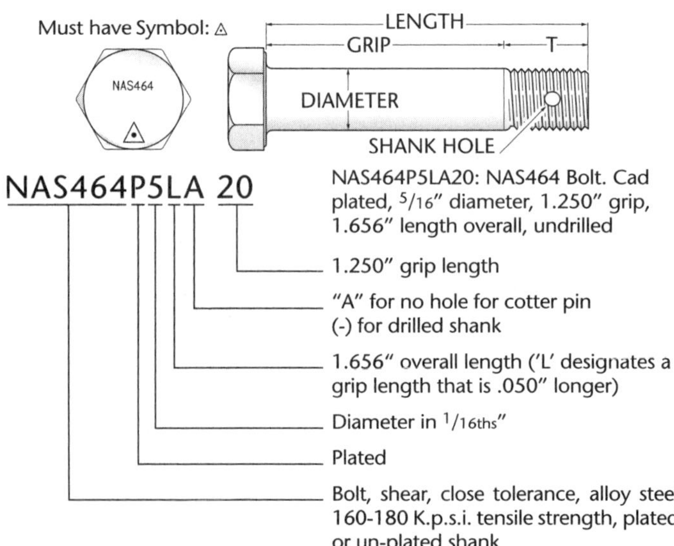

NAS464P5LA20: NAS464 Bolt. Cad plated, $^5/16$" diameter, 1.250" grip, 1.656" length overall, undrilled

1.250" grip length

"A" for no hole for cotter pin
(-) for drilled shank

1.656" overall length ('L' designates a grip length that is .050" longer)

Diameter in $^1/16$ths"

Plated

Bolt, shear, close tolerance, alloy steel 160-180 K.p.s.i. tensile strength, plated or un-plated shank

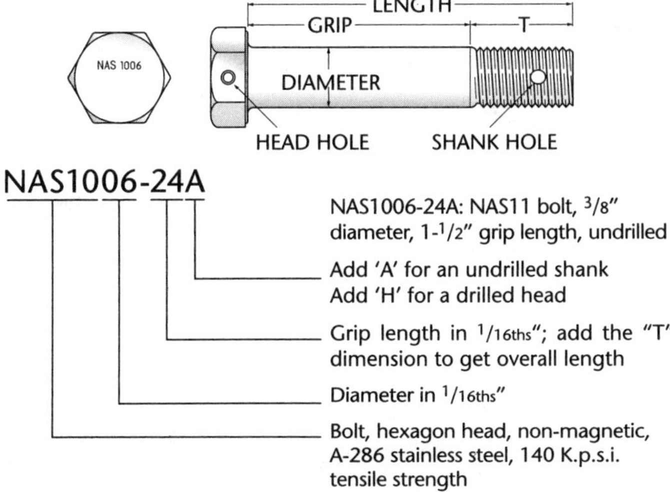

NAS1006-24A

NAS1006-24A: NAS11 bolt, 3/8" diameter, 1-1/2" grip length, undrilled

Add 'A' for an undrilled shank
Add 'H' for a drilled head

Grip length in 1/16ths"; add the "T" dimension to get overall length

Diameter in 1/16ths"

Bolt, hexagon head, non-magnetic, A-286 stainless steel, 140 K.p.s.i. tensile strength

NAS Basic Part #	Thread Diam./Pitch	Diameter (max.)	Diameter (min.)	Wrench Size	Hole, Shank +.010, -.000	Hole, head +.010, -.000	NAS10 Length	Commonly Used Stainless Cotter
1003	10-32	0.1895	0.1870	3/8	0.070	0.046	0.481	MS24665-151
1004	1/4-28	0.2495	0.2470	7/16	0.076	0.046	0.544	MS24665-151
1005	5/16-24	0.3120	0.3095	1/2	0.076	0.070	0.632	MS24665-229
1006	3/8-24	0.3745	0.3720	9/16	0.106	0.070	0.663	MS24665-300
1007	7/16-20	0.4370	0.4345	5/8	0.106	0.070	0.745	MS24665-300
1008	1/2-20	0.4995	0.4970	3/4	0.106	0.070	0.842	M524665-302
1009	9/16-18	0.5615	0.5585	7/8	0.141	0.070	0.947	MS24665-370
1010	5/8-18	0.6240	0.6210	15/16	0.141	0.070	1.042	MS24665-372
1012	3/4-16	0.7490	0.7460	1-1/16	0.141	0.070	1.189	MS24665-372
1014	7/8-14	0.8740	0.8710	1-1/4	0.141	0.070	1.356	MS24665-374
1016	1-12	0.9990	0.9960	1-1/2	0.141	0.070	1.481	MS24665-376
1018	1-1/8-12	1.1240	1.1200	1-5/8	0.141	0.070	1.658	MS24665-376

NOTE: All dimensions are in inches

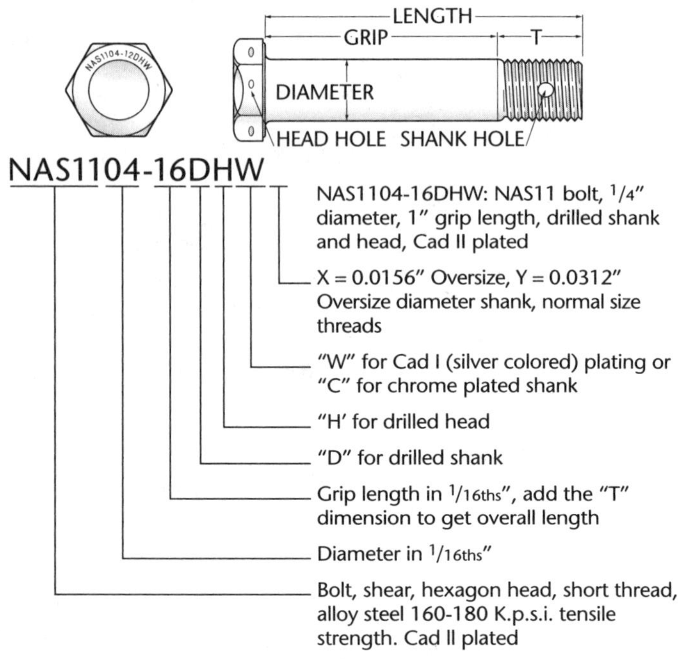

NAS1104-16DHW: NAS11 bolt, $^1/4$" diameter, 1" grip length, drilled shank and head, Cad II plated

X = 0.0156" Oversize, Y = 0.0312" Oversize diameter shank, normal size threads

"W" for Cad I (silver colored) plating or "C" for chrome plated shank

"H' for drilled head

"D" for drilled shank

Grip length in $^1/16$ths", add the "T" dimension to get overall length

Diameter in $^1/16$ths"

Bolt, shear, hexagon head, short thread, alloy steel 160-180 K.p.s.i. tensile strength. Cad II plated

13.11 990FR12-(XX) 1200°F Hi-Beam Locknut

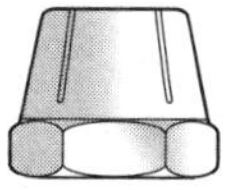

Part Number	Thread Size	Wrench Size	Height (+0.005/ -0.010)
990FR12-832	8-32	11/32	0.297
990FR12-1032	10-32	3/8	0.350
990FR12-428	1/4-28	7/16	0.406
990FR12-524	5/16-24	1/2	0.469
990FR12-624	3/8-24	9/16	0.500

NOTE: All dimensions are in inches

13.12 Tinnerman Clip-on Sheet Metal Nuts

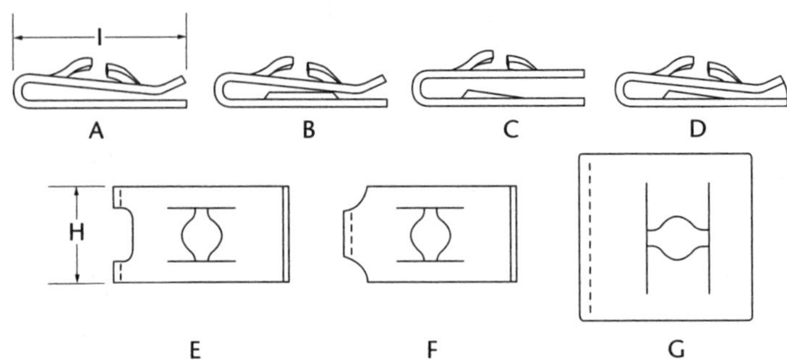

Tinnerman "U" Type Clip-on Sheet Metal Nuts

Screw Size	Panel Thickness	Design Variation	Tinnerman Part #	"I" Length	"H" Width	Max. Panel Edge Distance	Panel Hole Diameter
6	0.025-0.051	E	A1784-6Z1D	0.61	0.44	0.281	0.250
6	0.025-0.032	D, E, G	D1274-8-1	0.50	0.50	0.250	0.281
6	0.025-0.051	E	A1789-8Z1D	0.61	0.50	0.281	0.250
8	0.025-0.064	A,E	A1348-8Z1D	0.73	0.50	0.343	0.170
8	0.032-0.051	B, E	A1932-8Z1D	0.58	0.50	0.265	0.343
8	0.040-0.051	C, E, G	A1786-8Z1D	0.53	0.50	0.218	0.250
10	0.025-0.064	A, E	A1350-10Z1D	0.73	0.50	0.343	0.218
10	0.025-0.064	E	A1787-10Z1D	0.84	0.44	0.500	0.281
10	0.081-0.094	E	A1758-10Z1D	0.62	0.44	0.281	0.281

NOTE: All dimensions are in inches

Tinnerman 2 Lug Nutplate Sheet Metal Nuts

13.13 Tinnerman Flat Sheet Metal Nuts

 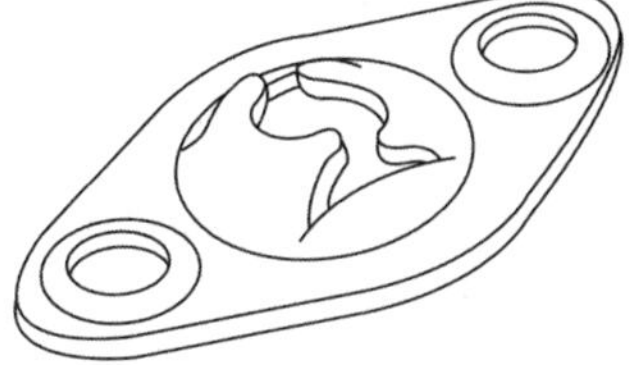

Screw Size	Fits Type of Sheet Metal Screws	Part #	Rivet Hole Diam./ Design
6	#6 Protruding	A6195-6Z1	0.105, Plain
8	#8 Protruding	A6195-68Z1	0.105, Dimpled
8	#8 Protruding	A6191-8Z1	0.105, Plain
8	#8 100 deg, C/S	A8577-8Z1	0.105, Dimpled
8	#8 100 deg, C/S	A6162-8Z1	0.135, Dimpled

NOTE: All dimensions are in inches

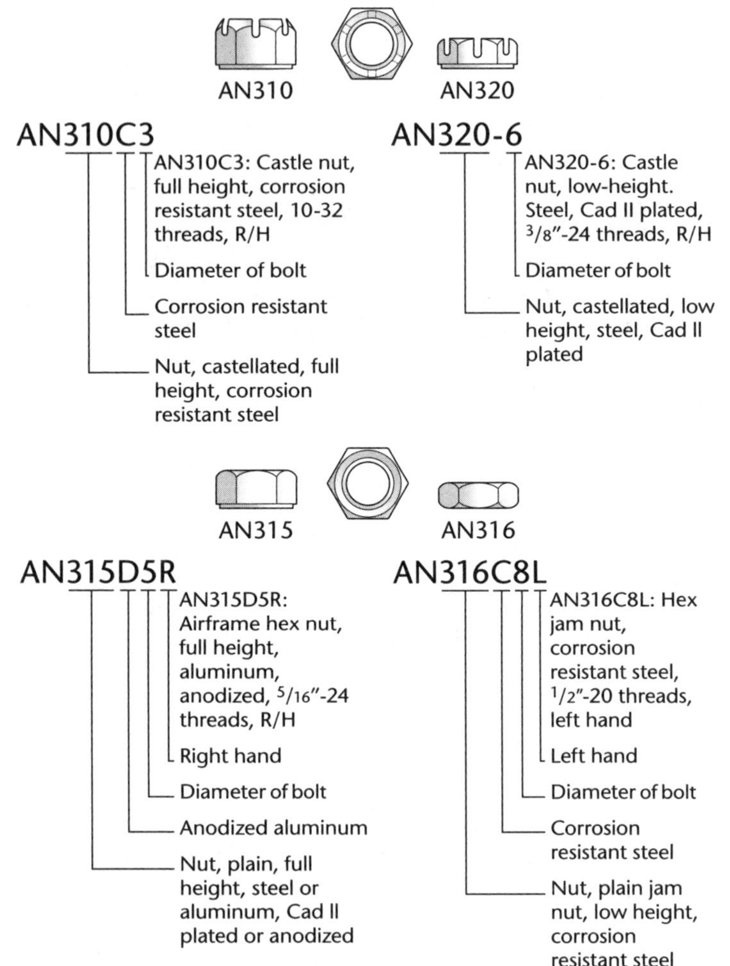

AN310
AN320
AN315
AN316

AN310C3
AN310C3: Castle nut, full height, corrosion resistant steel, 10-32 threads, R/H
Diameter of bolt
Corrosion resistant steel
Nut, castellated, full height, corrosion resistant steel

AN320-6
AN320-6: Castle nut, low-height. Steel, Cad II plated, 3/8"-24 threads, R/H
Diameter of bolt
Nut, castellated, low height, steel, Cad II plated

AN315D5R
AN315D5R: Airframe hex nut, full height, aluminum, anodized, 5/16"-24 threads, R/H
Right hand
Diameter of bolt
Anodized aluminum
Nut, plain, full height, steel or aluminum, Cad II plated or anodized

AN316C8L
AN316C8L: Hex jam nut, corrosion resistant steel, 1/2"-20 threads, left hand
Left hand
Diameter of bolt
Corrosion resistant steel
Nut, plain jam nut, low height, corrosion resistant steel

Type of Nut and Basic Part Number				Threads / Wrench		Approx. Heights			
Castellated Nut Full Height	Castellated Nut Low Height	Airframe Hex Nut Full Height	Hexagon Jam Nut Low Height	Thread Size per MIL-S-7742	Wrench Size, All	AN310	AN320	AN315	AN316
N/A	AN320-1	AN315-640	N/A	#6-40 UNF-3B	5/16	N/A	–	0.109	N/A
N/A	AN320-2	N/A	N/A	#8-36 UNF-3B	11/32	N/A	0.156	N/A	N/A
AN310-3	AN-320-3	AN315-3	N/A	#10-32 UNF-3B	3/8	0.250	–	0.141	N/A
AN310-4	AN320-4	AN315-4	AN316-4	1/4-28 UNF-3B	7/16	0.281	0.188	0.188	0.125
AN310-5	AN320-5	AN315-5	AN316-5	5/16-24 UNF-3B	1/2	0.328	–	0.234	0.156
AN310-6	AN320-6	AN315-6	AN316-6	3/8-24 UNF-3B	9/16	0.406	–	0.281	0.188
AN310-7	AN320-7	AN315-7	AN316-7	7/16-20 UNF-3B	5/8	0.453	0.219	0.328	0.219
AN310-8	AN320-8	AN315-8	AN316-8	1/2-20 UNF-3B	3/4	0.563	0.250	0.375	0.250
AN310-9	AN320-9	AN315-9	AN316-9	9/16-18 UNF-3B	7/8	0.609	–	0.422	0.281
AN310-10	AN320-10	AN315-10	AN316-10	5/8-18 UNF-3B	1	0.719	0.313	0.469	0.313

NOTE: All dimensions are in inches

13.15 Locknut Styles and Sizes

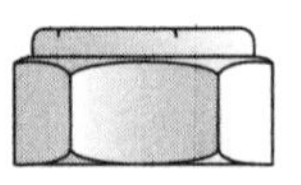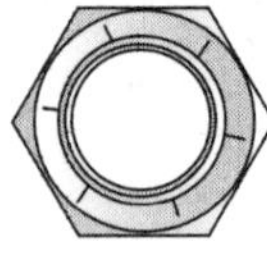

MS21044(C) or (N) (XX)

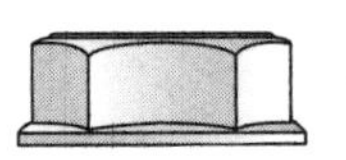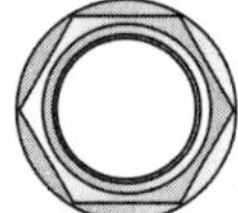

MS21042 (XX)

Old Style (XXX):		New Style (XX):
		MS14144-(XX)
		MS14145-(XX)
		MS17825-(XX)
		MS17826-(XX)
		NAS1804-(XX)
		NAS1805-(XX)
	NAS679(A)(XX)	MS21040-(XX)
	NAS1291-(XX)	MS21042L(XX)
	NAS1291C(XX)	MS21043-(XX)
AN365-(XXX)A MS20365-(XXX)A	NAS1021N(XX)	MS21044N(XX)
AN365-(XXX)C MS20365-(XXX)C AN363-(XXX)	NAS1021AX(XX)	MS21045-(XX)
AN363C(XXX)	MS21021C(XX)	MS21046C(XX)
AN364-(XXX)A MS20364-(XXX)A	NAS1022N(XX)	MS21083N(XX)
AN364-(XXX)C MS20364-(XXX)C	M521022AX(XX)	MS21245-(XX)
MS20500-(XXX)		

Old Style (XXX) Number	New Style (XX) Number	Thread Diameter/Pitch
256	02	2-56
440	04	4-40
632	06	6-32
832	08	8-32
1024	N/A	10-24
1032	3	10-32
420	N/A	1/4-20
428	4	1/4-28
518	N/A	5/16-18
524	5	5/16-24

NOTE: All dimensions are in inches

 # Nuts: Non Locking: Machine Nuts, Finished Hex Nuts

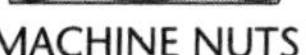

MACHINE NUTS

FINISHED HEX NUTS

Thread Size	AN340 Use MS35649 Steel Grade A Cad I 90 K.p.s.i.	AN345 Use MS35650 Steel Grade A Cad I 90 K.p.s.i.	MS35649 Coarse, Machine Steel Grade A Cad II 90 K.p.s.i.	MS35650 Fine, Machine Steel Grade A Cad II 80 K.p.s.i.	MS51967 Coarse Fin. Hex Steel Grade B Cad II 120 K.p.s.i.	MS51967 Coarse, Fin. Hex Steel Grade C Cad II 144 K.p.s.i.	MS9356 Fine Fin. Hex A286 Stainless 145 K.p.s.i.	MS9357 Fine Fin. Hex A286 Stainless 145 K.p.s.i.
				Dash Numbers				
4-40	-4	–	-242	–	–	–	–	–
4-48	–	-4	–	-342	–	–	-04	-04
6-32	-6	–	-262	–	–	–	–	–
6-40	–	-6	–	-362	–	–	-06	-06
8-32	-8	–	-282	–	–	–	–	–
8-36	–	-8	–	-382	–	–	-08	-08
10-24	-10	–	-202	–	–	–	–	–
10-32	–	-10	–	-302	–	–	-09	-09
1/4-20	-416	–	-2252	–	-2	-3	–	–

NOTE: All dimensions are in inches

 # NAS509, NAS1423 Corner Drilled Jam Nuts

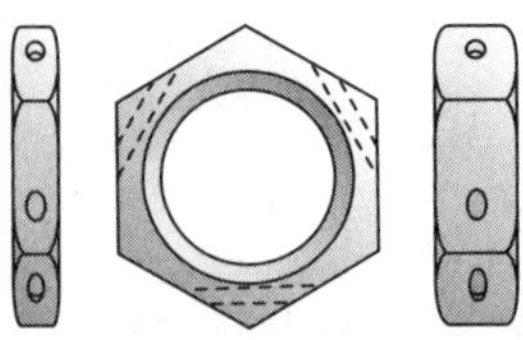

NAS509-L-4-C

— Material C for A286 staples (-) for 4130 steel

— Size and threads

— L for L/H, blank for R/H

— Nut, drilled jam nut, low height, 150 K.p.s.i., 4130 steel or A286 stainless steel

NAS1423-6-L

— NAS1423-6L Corner drilled jam nut, 4130 steel $3/8''$ - 24, left hand thread.

— Thread direction - L for L/H, blank for R/H

— Size and threads

— Material (-) for 4130 steel C for A286 stainless

— Nut, drilled jam nut, full height, 150 K.p.s.i., 4130 steel or A286 stainless steel

Dash #	Thread Size	Wrench Size	Height NAS509	Height NAS1423
06	6-32	5/16	0.125	0.100
08	8-32	1-1/32	0.125	0.112
3	10-32	3/8	0.156	0.125
4	1/4-28	7/16	0.188	0.125
5	5/16-24	1/2	0.219	0.125
6	3/8-24	9/16	0.250	0.125
7	7/16-20	5/8	0.281	0.156
8	1/2-20	3/4	0.313	0.156
9	9/16-18	7/8	0.375	0.203
10	5/8-18	1-5/16	0.406	0.203
12	3/4-16	1-1/16	0.469	0.250
14	7/8-14	1-1/4	0.500	0.250
17	1-12	1-1/2	0.500	0.250
18	1-1/8-12	1-5/8	0.531	0.265

NOTE: All dimensions are in inches

 # MS21047, MS21048, MS21049, MS21050, MS21059, MS21060, NAS1473 Nutplates

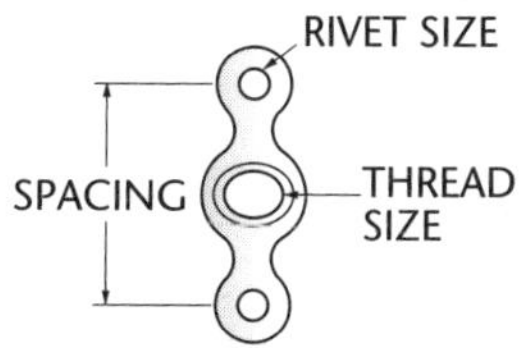

MS21047: Steel, fixed
MS21048: CRES, fixed

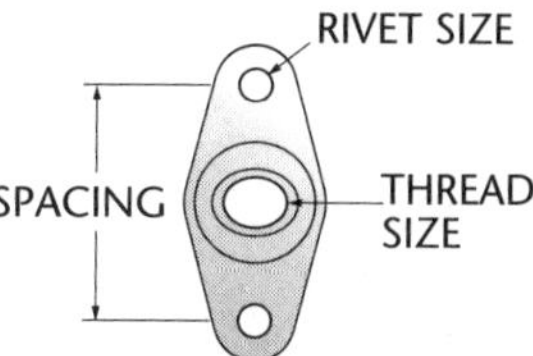

MS21049: Steel, fixed, countersunk
MS21050: CRES, fixed, countersunk

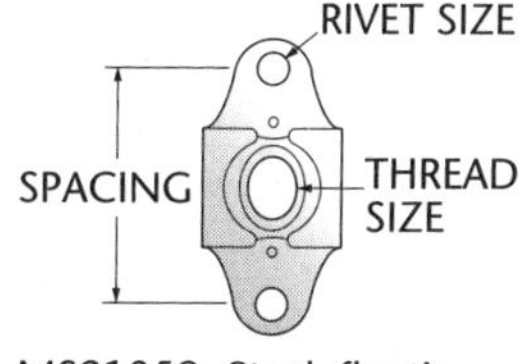

MS21059: Steel, floating
MS21060: CRES, floating

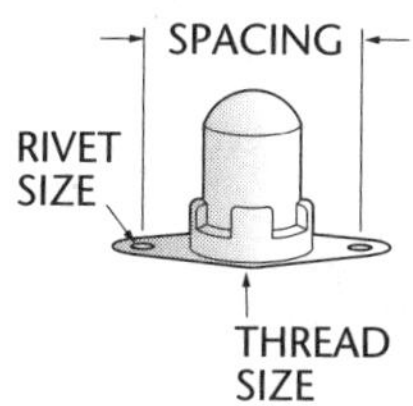

NAS1473: Self-sealing, standard spacing

MS21047L08K

MS21047L08K: Fixed nutplate, steel, black moly lubricant, 8-32 threads, dimpled $3/32''$ rivet holes

(K) for dimpled rivet hole

Thread size

(L) Lubricant black moly
(-) for silver none

Nutplate, riveted, fixed or floating, double leg, corrosion resistant steel or alloy steel

Nut Threads Dia. -Pitch	Rivet Spacing
4-40 through 10-32	0.688
$1/4$-28 through $3/8$-24	1.000

NOTE: All dimensions are in inches

13.19 MS21051, MS21052, MS21053, MS21054, MS21061, MS21062 Nutplates

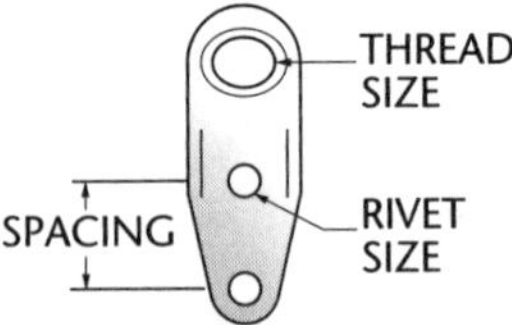

MS21051: Steel, fixed, std spacing, one leg
MS21052: CRES, fixed, std spacing, one leg

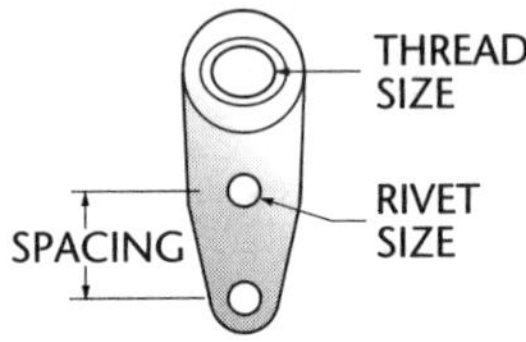

MS21053: Steel, fixed, countersunk, one leg
MS21054: CRES, fixed, countersunk, one leg

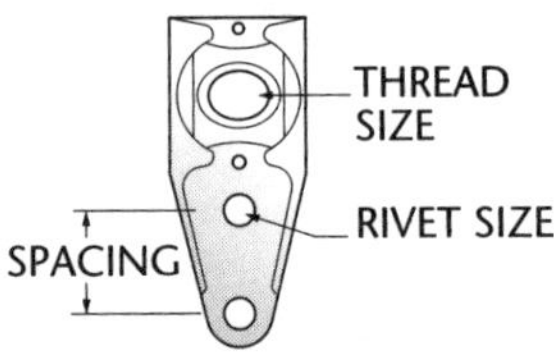

MS21061: Steel, floating, one leg
MS21062: CRES, floating, one leg

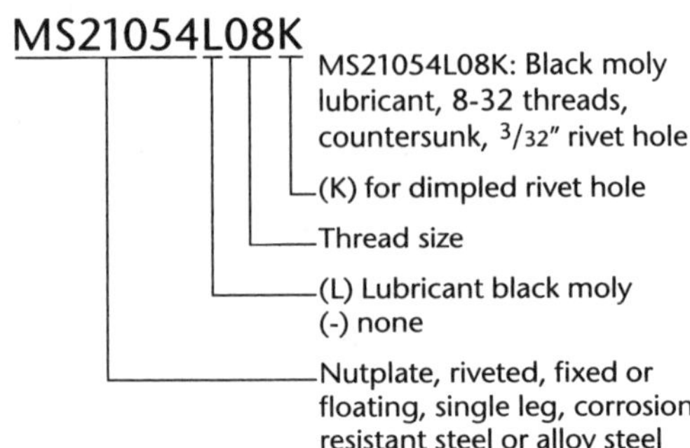

Nut Threads Dia. -Pitch	Rivet Spacing
4-40 through $3/8$-24	0.312

NOTE: All dimensions are in inches

13.20 MS21055, MS21056, MS21057, MS21058 Nutplates

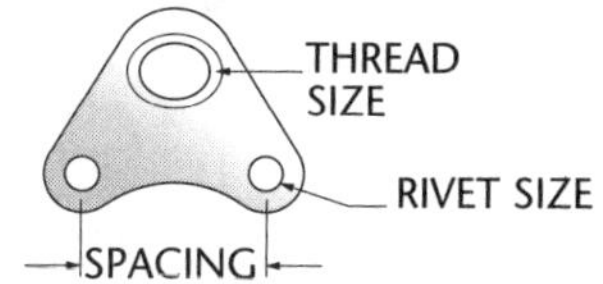

MS21055: Steel, fixed, std spacing, corner
MS21056: CRES, fixed, std spacing, corner
MS21057: Steel, fixed, countersunk, corner
MS21058: CRE., fixed, countersunk, corner

MS21057L08K

MS21057L08K: Fixed nutplate, steel, dimpled rivet holes, 8-32 threads. $3/32''$ rivets

(K) for dimpled rivet hole

Thread size

(L) Lubricant black moly
(-) none

Nutplate, corner, riveted, fixed, single leg, corrosion resistant steel or alloy steel

Nut Threads Dia. -Pitch	Rivet Spacing
4-40 Through 10-32	0.485
$1/4$-28 Through $3/8$-24	0.101

NOTE: All dimensions are in inches

13.21 MS21071, MS21072 Nutplates

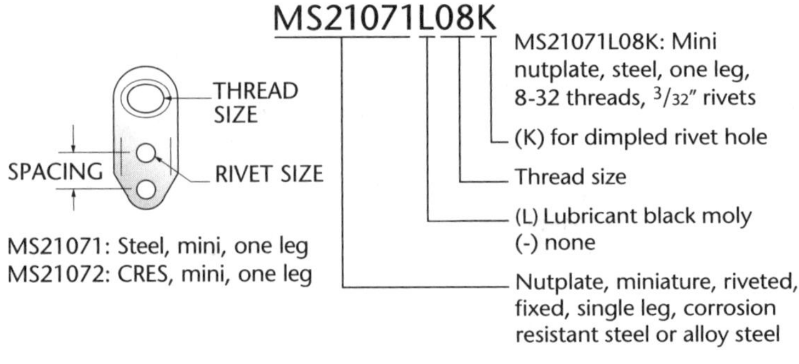

Nut Threads Dia. -Pitch	Rivet Spacing
4-40 Through 10-32	0.485
1/4-28 Through 3/8-24	0.101

NOTE: All dimensions are in inches

13.22 NAS1474 Nutplates

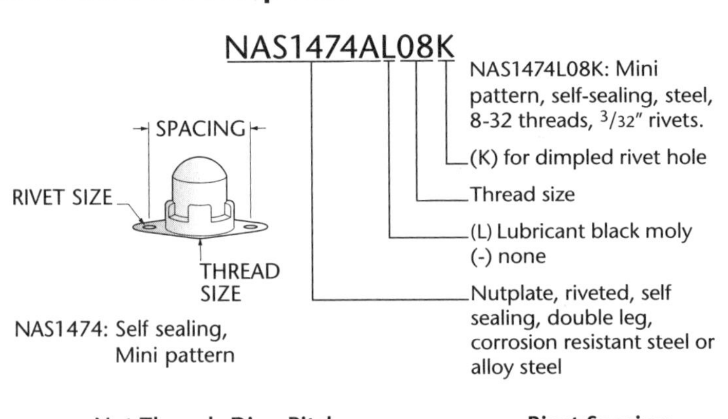

Nut Threads Dia. -Pitch	Rivet Spacing
4-40 through 10-32	0.590
1/4-28	0.752

NOTE: All dimensions are in inches

13.23 **Nutplate Thread Sizes**

Dash #	Dia. - Pitch
04	4-40
06	6-32
08	8-32
3	10-32
4	1/4-28
5	5/16-24
6	3/6-24

NOTE: All dimensions are in inches

13.24 **MS33737 Nut Sheet Spring Instrument Mounting**

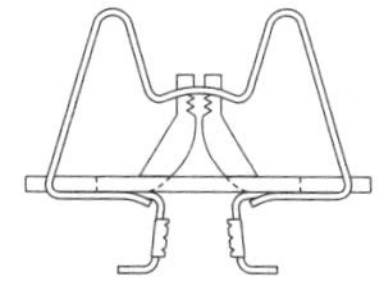
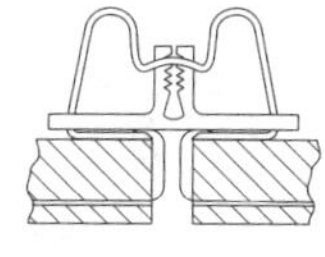

MS33737-(XX)	Tinnerman #	Old NAS #
MS33737- 9C	A8938-632-493	NAS487-13
MS33737-10C	A8939-632-493	NAS487-14
MS33737-11C	A6939-632-493	NAS487-15
MS33737-12C	A8940-632-493	NAS487-16
MS33737-13C	A8941-632-493	NAS487-17
MS33737-14C	A8942-632-493	NAS487-18
MS33737-15C	A8943-632-493	NAS487-20
MS33737-16C	A8944-632-493	NAS487-21

13.25 AN502 and 503 Series: Structural Screws

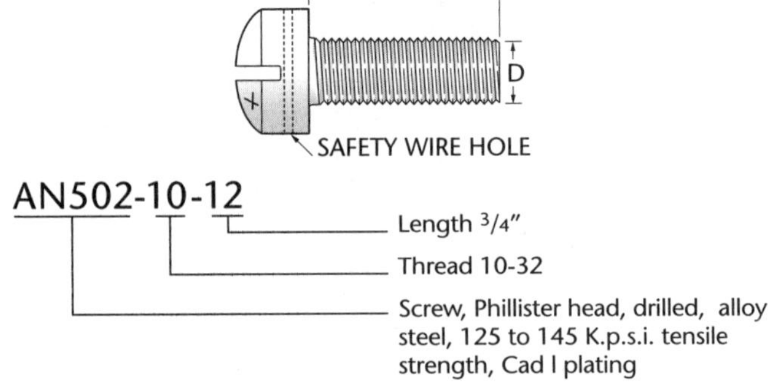

Diameter	6-32 Coarse	8-32 Coarse	10-24 Coarse	10-32 Fine	1/4-20 Coarse	1/4-28 Fine
	AN503	AN503	AN503	AN502	AN503	AN502
1/4	-6-4	-8-4	–	-10-4	–	–
3/8	-6-6	-8-6	-10-6	-10-6	-416-6	–
1/2	-6-8	-8-8	-10-8	-10-8	-416-8	-416-8
5/8	–	-8-10	-10-10	-10-10	-416-10	-416-10
3/4	–	-8-12	-10-12	-10-12	-416-12	-416-12
7/8	–	-8-14	-10-14	-10-14	-416-14	-416-14

NOTE: All dimensions are in inches

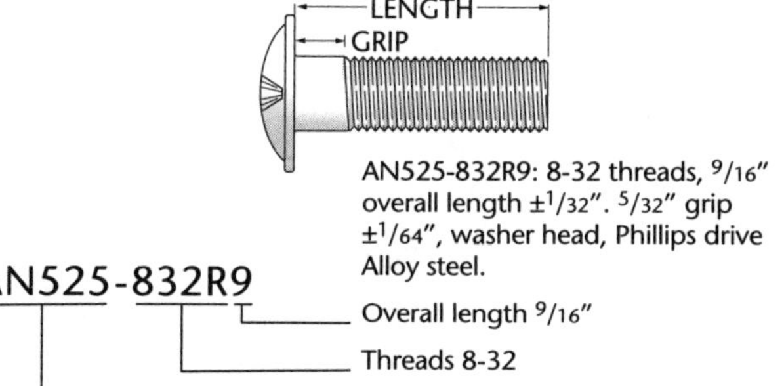

AN525-832R9: 8-32 threads, $9/16$" overall length $\pm 1/32$". $5/32$" grip $\pm 1/64$", washer head, Phillips drive Alloy steel.

AN525-832R9

Overall length $9/16$"

Threads 8-32

Washer head, Phillips drive, alloy steel, 125 K.p.s.i. tensile strength, Cad II plated

D= Threads Dia - Pitch (Length)	AN525-(Diam./Threads) R (Length)					
	8-32 Grip Length	8-32 Size #	10-32 Grip Length	10-32 Size #	1/4-28 Grip Length	1/4-28 Size #
3/8	1/32	832R6	1/32	10R6	1/32	416R6
7/16	1/16	832R7	1/16	10R7	1/16	416R7
1/2	1/8	832R8	1/8	10R8	1/8	416R8
9/16	5/32	832R9	5/32	10R9	5/32	416R9
5/8	7/32	832R10	7/32	10R10	7/32	416R10
11/16	9/32	832R11	9/32	10R11	9/32	416R11

NOTE: All dimensions are in inches

13.27 Commercial Stainless Screws

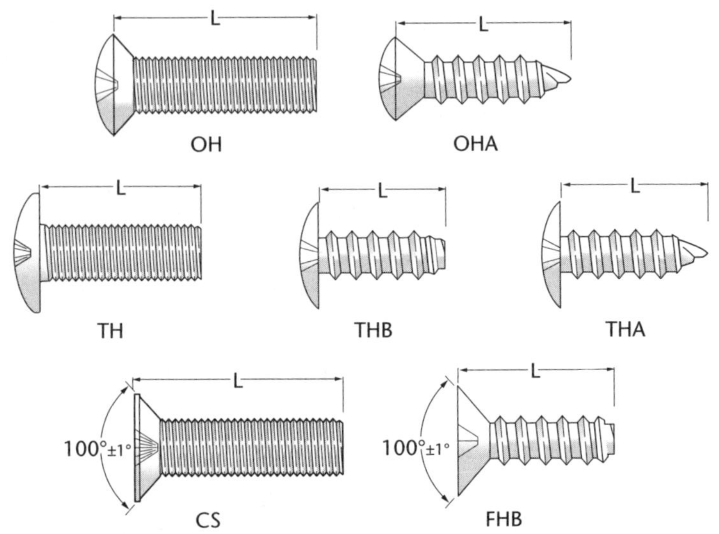

- Commonly used for interiors and non structural fastening
- Phillips drive only

Available Lengths		Available Threads Sheet Metal	Available Threads Machine Screws
1/4	3/4	4R	4-40
3/8	1	6R	6-32
1/2	1-1/4	8R	8-32
5/8	1-1/2	10R	10-32

Threads	X	Length	Style of Screw	Material	Part Number
8-32	X	1"	TH	SS	8-32X1/2THSS
8-32	X	1/2	OH	SS	8-32X1/2OHSS
8-32	X	1/2	CS	SS	8-32X1/2CSSS
8R	X	5/8	OHA	SS	8RX5/8OHASS
8R	X	1/2	THA	SS	8RX1/2THASS
8R	X	1/2	FHB	SS	8RX1/2FHBSS
8R	X	1/2	THB	SS	8RX1/2THBSS

NOTE: All dimensions are in inches

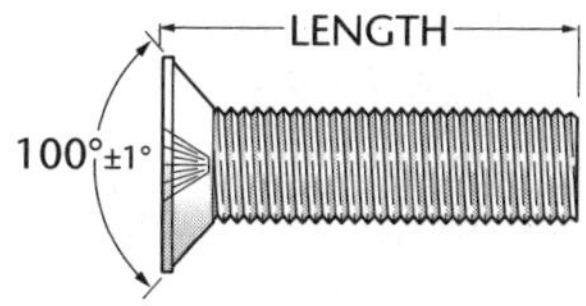

MS24693C272

MS24693C272: 10-32 threads, $^1/_2$" overall length, unplated, 300 series, stainless

Threads and length overall

Use (C) for 300 series stainless steel, unplated
Use (S) for low carbon steel Cad II plated
Use (BB) for brass with black chemical finish

Screw, non structural, 100° countersunk, Phillips drive, low carbon steel, Cad II plating or unplated

D=threads, Diam.-Pitch (Length)	Coarse Threads					Fine Threads	
	4-40 Size #	6-32 Size #	8-32 Size #	10-24 Size #	1/4-20 Size #	10-32 Size #	1/4-28 Size #
1/4	-2	-24	-46	–	-268	–	–
5/16	-3	-25	-47	-69	-91	-269	–
3/8	-4	-26	-48	-70	-92	-270	-292
7/16	-5	-27	-49	-71	-93	-271	-293
1/2	-6	-28	-50	-72	-94	-272	-294
5/8	-7	-29	-51	-73	-95	-273	-295

NOTE: All dimensions are in inches

13.29 MS24694 Series: Structural Screws

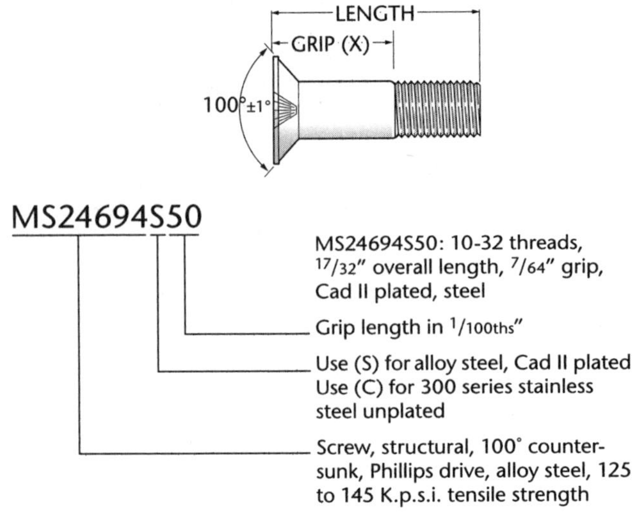

MS24694S50

MS24694S50: 10-32 threads, $^{17}/_{32}$" overall length, $^{7}/_{64}$" grip, Cad II plated, steel

Grip length in $^{1}/_{100}$ths"

Use (S) for alloy steel, Cad II plated
Use (C) for 300 series stainless steel unplated

Screw, structural, 100° countersunk, Phillips drive, alloy steel, 125 to 145 K.p.s.i. tensile strength

13.30 MS27039 Series: Structural Screws

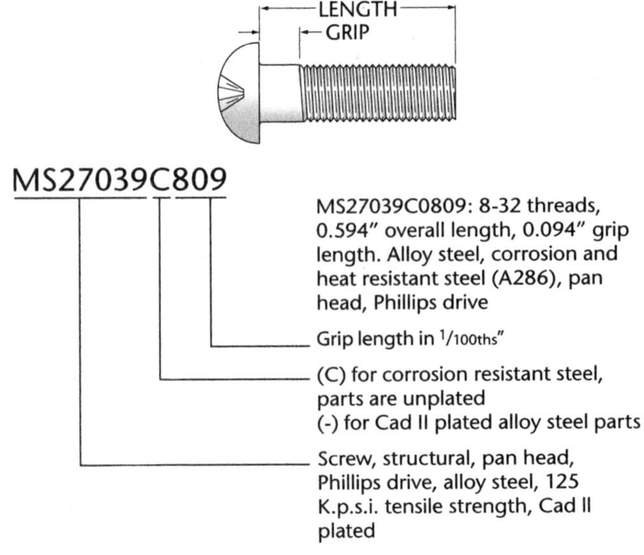

MS27039C809

MS27039C0809: 8-32 threads, 0.594" overall length, 0.094" grip length. Alloy steel, corrosion and heat resistant steel (A286), pan head, Phillips drive

Grip length in $^{1}/_{100}$ths"

(C) for corrosion resistant steel, parts are unplated
(-) for Cad II plated alloy steel parts

Screw, structural, pan head, Phillips drive, alloy steel, 125 K.p.s.i. tensile strength, Cad II plated

 # MS35206 and MS35207 Non-structural Screws

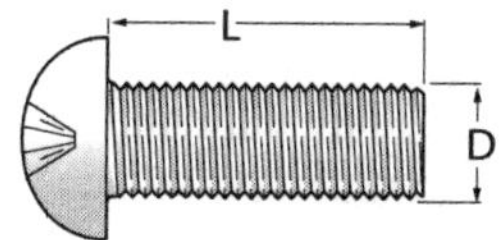

MS35206-261

MS35206-261: Nonstructural pan head, coarse thread 10-24, $^3/_8''$ length overall

Thread and length

Screw, non structural, pan head, Phillips drive, low carbon steel, 125 K.p.s.i. tensile strength, Cad II plated

Overall Length	MS35206 Coarse Threads				MS35207 Fine Threads		
	4-40 Dash#	6-32 Dash#	8-32 Dash#	10-24 Dash#	1/4-20 Dash#	10-32 Dash#	1/4-28 Dash#
1/4	-213	-226	-241	-259	–	-259	–
5/16	-214	-227	-242	-260	-276	-260	-276
3/8	-215	-228	-243	-261	-277	-261	-277
7/16	-216	-229	-244	-262	-278	-262	-278
1/2	-217	-230	-245	-263	-279	-263	-279
9/16	-323	-327	-331	-337	-343	–	–

NOTE: All dimensions are in inches

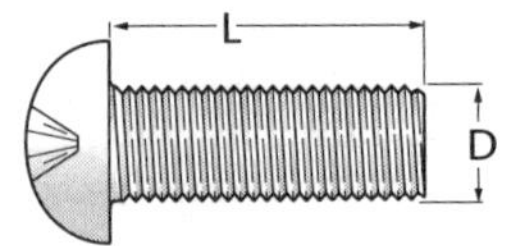

MS35214-120

MS35214-120: Nonstructural pan head brass black oxide Phillips head screw, 10-24 coarse threads, 9/16″ length overall

Thread and length

Screw, non structural, pan head, Phillips drive, brass, black oxide finish

Overall Length	MS35214 Coarse Threads					MS35215 Fine Threads	
	4-40 Dash#	6-32 Dash#	8-32 Dash#	10-24 Dash#	1/4-20 Dash#	10-32 Dash#	1/4-28 Dash#
1/4	-12	-23	-38	-51	–	-51	–
5/16	-13	-24	-39	-52	-66	-52	-66
3/8	-14	-25	-40	-53	-67	-53	-67
7/16	-15	-26	-41	-54	-68	-54	-68
1/2	-16	-27	-42	-55	-69	-55	-69
9/16	-106	-108	-114	-120	-124	–	–

NOTE: All dimensions are in inches

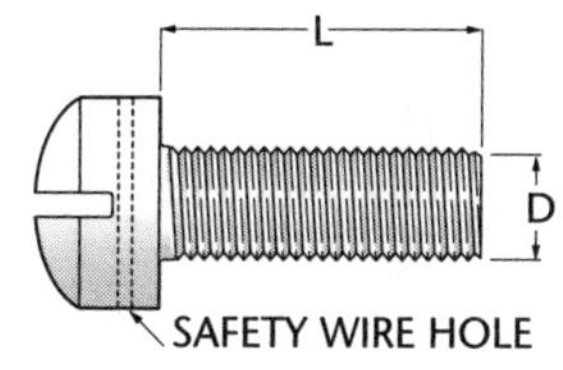

MS35265-63

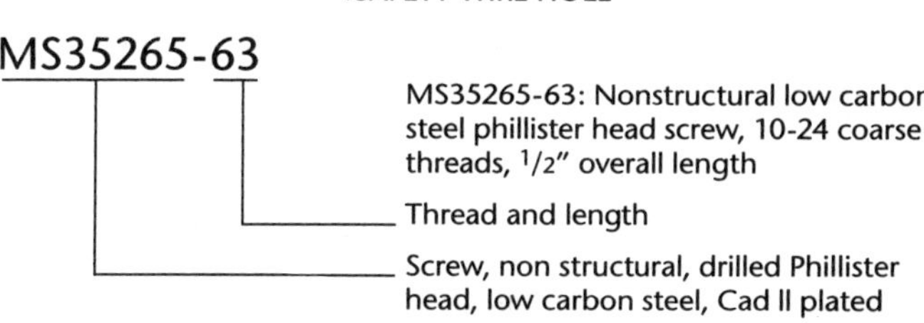

MS35265-63: Nonstructural low carbon steel phillister head screw, 10-24 coarse threads, 1/2" overall length

Thread and length

Screw, non structural, drilled Phillister head, low carbon steel, Cad II plated

Overall Length	MS35265 Coarse Threads					MS35266 Fine Threads	
	4-40 Dash#	6-32 Dash#	8-32 Dash#	10-24 Dash#	1/4-20 Dash#	10-32 Dash#	1/4-28 Dash#
1/4	-13	-26	-41	-59	–	-59	–
5/16	-14	-27	-42	-60	-76	-60	-76
3/8	-15	-28	-43	-61	-77	-61	-77
7/16	-16	-29	-44	-62	-78	-62	-78
1/2	-17	-30	-45	-63	-79	-63	-79

NOTE: All dimensions are in inches

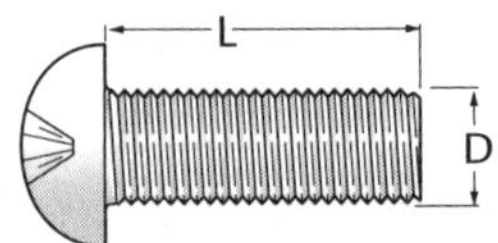

MS51957-126

MS51957-126: Nonstructural stainless steel Phillips head fully threaded screw, 8-32 coarse thread, $^9/_{16}$" length overall

Threads and length

Screw, non structural, pan head, Phillips drive, stainless steel, unplated

Overall Length	MS51957 Coarse Threads					MS51958 Fine Threads	
	4-40 Dash#	6-32 Dash#	8-32 Dash#	10-24 Dash#	$^1/_4$-20 Dash#	10-32 Dash#	$^1/_4$-28 Dash#
1/4	-13	-26	-41	-59	–	-59	–
5/16	-14	-27	-42	-60	-76	-60	-76
3/8	-15	-28	-43	-61	-77	-61	-77
7/16	-16	-29	-44	-62	-78	-62	-78
1/2	-17	-30	-45	-63	-79	-63	-79
9/16	-120	-123	-126	-129	-132	–	–

NOTE: All dimensions are in inches

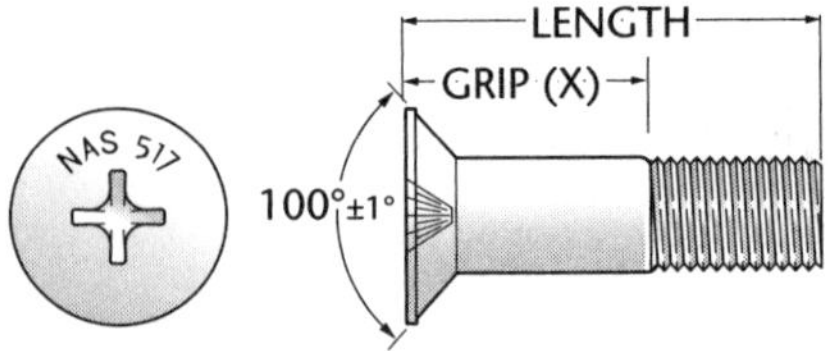

13.35 NAS514P Series Countersunk Head: NAS600 through NAS606 Series: Pan Head

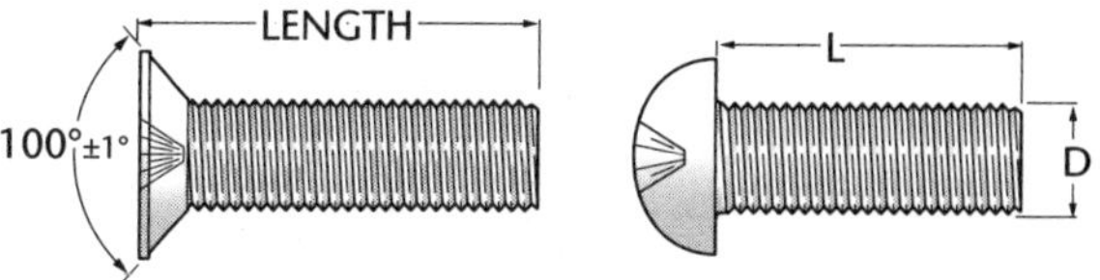

NAS514P832-9P: 8-32 threads, $9/16$" overall length including the countersunk head, Phillips drive, alloy steel, Cad II plated

NAS514P832-9P

Cad plated

Length overall

Threads

Screw, structural, countersunk or pan head, Phillips drive, alloy steel, 125 to 180 K.p.s.i. tensile strength, Cad II plated

Pan Head	Countersunk Head	Thread Size
NAS600-	NAS514P440-	4-40
NAS601-	NAS514P632-	6-32
NAS602-	NAS514P832-	8-32
NAS603-	NAS514P1032-	10-32
NAS604-	NAS514P428-	1/4-28
NAS605-	NAS514P524-	5/16-24
NAS606-	NAS514P624-	3/8-24

NOTE: All dimensions are in inches

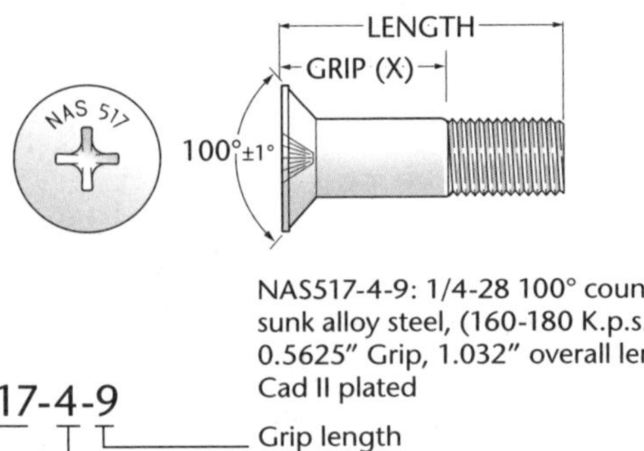

NAS517-4-9: 1/4-28 100° counter-sunk alloy steel, (160-180 K.p.s.i.), 0.5625" Grip, 1.032" overall length, Cad II plated

NAS517-4-9

- Grip length
- Thread and length
- Screw, structural, 100° countersunk, Phillips drive, alloy steel, 160 to 180 K.p.s.i., Cad II plated

Thread Size		8-32	10-32	1/4-28	5/16-24	3/8-24
Shank Diam.		0.161 to 0.164	0.186 to 0.189	0.246 to 0.249	0.3085 to 0.3115	0.371 to 0.374
Part #		NAS517-2-(X)	NAS517-3-(X)	NAS517-4-(X)	NAS517-5-(X)	NAS517-6-(X)
Grip Length	**(X)**			**Overall Lengths**		
0.1250	2	0.531	0.531	0.594	0.656	0.750
0.1875	3	0.594	0.594	0.657	0.719	0.813
0.2500	4	0.656	0.656	0.719	0.781	0.875
0.3125	5	0.719	0.719	0.782	0.844	0.938
0.3750	6	0.781	0.781	0.844	0.906	1.000
0.4375	7	0.844	0.844	0.907	0.969	1.063

NOTE: All dimensions are in inches

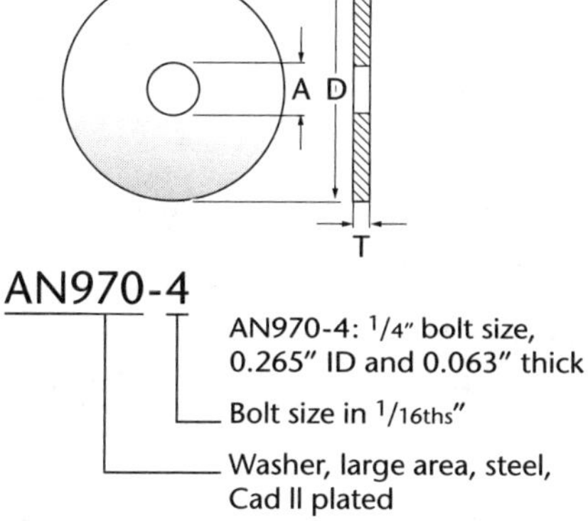

AN970-4

AN970-4: $^1/_4''$ bolt size,
0.265" ID and 0.063" thick

Bolt size in $^1/_{16\text{ths}}''$

Washer, large area, steel,
Cad II plated

Dash Numbers	Bolt Size	A	D	T	Superseded Part #
3	No. 10	0.203	0.875	0.063	MS63040-3
4	1/4	0.265	1.125	0.063	-4
5	5/16	0.328	1.375	0.063	-5
6	3/8	0.390	1.625	0.063	-6
7	7/16	0.453	1.812	0.109	-7
8	1/2	0.515	2.000	0.109	-8
9	9/16	0.578	2.188	0.125	-9
10	5/8	0.640	2.375	0.125	-10

NOTE: All dimensions are in inches

EXTERNAL STAR

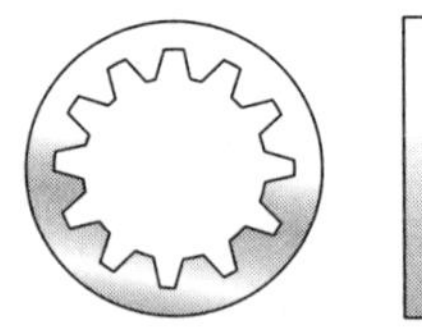

INTERNAL STAR

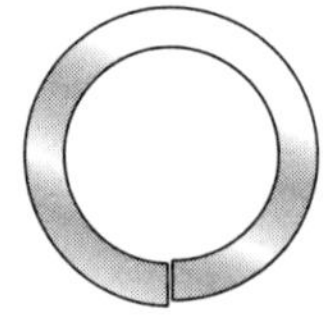

HELICAL SPLIT

Material:	Steel, Cadmium Plated			Stainless
Style:	Internal Star	External Star	Helical Split	Helical Split
Part:	MS35333-(XX)	MS35335-(XX)	MS35338-(XX)	MS35338-(XXX)
Nom ID.				
#2	-35	N/A	-39	-134
#4	-36	-29	-40	-135
#6	-37	-30	-41	-136
#8	-38	-31	-42	-137
#10	-39	-32	-43	-138
1/4	-40	-33	-44	-139
5/16	-41	-34	-45	-140
3/8	-42	-35	-46	-141
7/16	-43	-36	-47	-142
1/2	-44	-37	-48	-143
9/16	N/A	-38	-49	-144
5/8	-46	-39	-50	-145
3/4	-47	-40	-51	-146
7/8	-48	-41	-52	-147
1	-49	-42	-53	-148

NOTE: All dimensions are in inches

MS20002 Washers, Countersunk and Plain

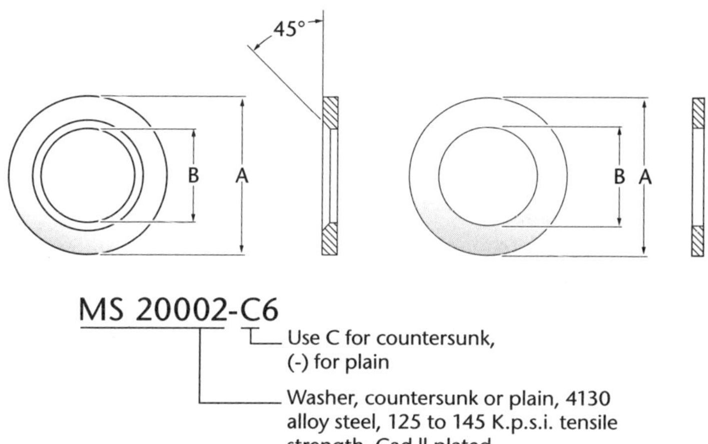

| Thread Size | MS Part No. | | A Diam | B Diam | | Flatness Tolerance |
	Countersunk	Plain		Max	Min	Max
1/4	MS20002C4	MS20002-4	0.531	0.260	0.252	0.007
5/16	MS20002C5	MS20002-5	0.593	0.324	0.315	0.007
3/8	MS20002C6	MS20002-6	0.687	0.388	0.378	0.007
7/16	MS20002C7	MS20002-7	0.781	0.451	0.441	0.007
1/2	MS20002C8	MS20002-8	0.875	0.515	0.504	0.007
9/16	MS20002C9	MS20002-9	0.968	0.579	0.568	0.010
5/8	MS20002C10	MS20002-10	1.062	0.643	0.631	0.010
3/4	MS20002C12	MS20002-12	1.250	0.770	0.757	0.010
7/8	MS20002C14	MS20002-14	1.437	0.897	0.884	0.010
1	MS20002C16	MS20002-16	1.625	1.025	1.010	0.010
1-1/8	MS20002C18	MS20002-18	1.875	1.150	1.135	0.010
1-1/4	MS20002C20	MS20002-20	2.125	1.275	1.260	0.010
1-3/8	MS20002C22	MS20002-22	2.313	1.400	1.385	0.015
1-1/2	MS20002C24	MS20002-24	2.500	1.525	1.510	0.015

NOTE: All dimensions are in inches

13.40 NAS1149 Series: Aircraft Washers

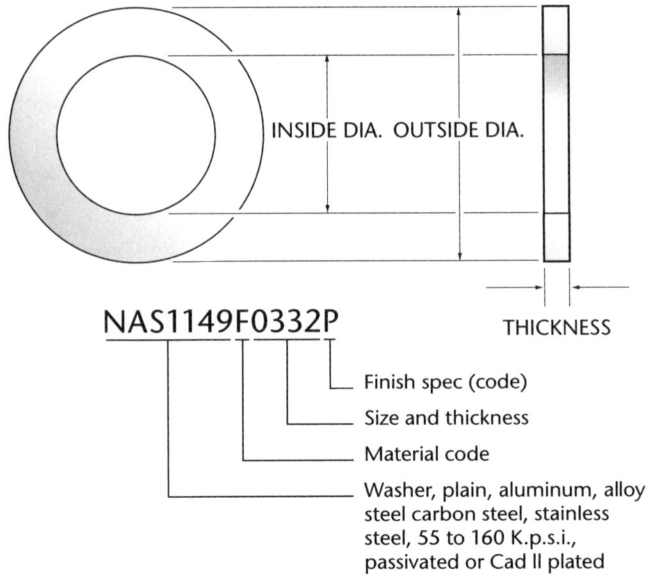

Material Specification	Code	Finish Spec. (Color)	Code
300 Stainless (75 K.p.s.i. MIN UTS) 0.032 through 0.090	C	Passivate plain	R
301 Stainless (125 K.p.s.i. MIN UTS) .016 ONLY	C	Passivate plain	R
2024-T3 Aluminum (58 K.p.s.i. MIN UTS)	D	Chemical treat conductive gold	J
2024-T3 Aluminum (58 K.p.s.i. MIN UTS)	D	Anodize non-conductive gray	K
2024-T3 Aluminum (58 K.p.s.i. MIN UTS)	D	None	H
A28E High Temp Stainless (160 K.p.s.i. MIN UTS)	E	Cadmium plate gold	P
A286 High Temp Stainless (160 K.p.s.i. MIN UTS)	E	Passivate plain	R
1020 Carbon Steel (55 K.p.s.i. MIN UTS)	F	Cadmium plate per qq-p-416. type II class 2. (gold)	P
4130 Alloy Steel (90 K.p.s.i. MIN UTS)	G	Cadmium gold	P

NOTE: All dimensions are in inches, UTS= utimate tensile strength

Fastener Type	Nominal Inside Dia.	Inside Dia. +/- 0.010	Outside Dia. +0.020, -0.005	Size and Thickness Number			
				0.016 Thick	0.032 Thick	0.063 Thick	0.090 Thick
Screws	#2	0.099	0.25	N216	N232	N542 (.042 Thickness)	
	#3	0.105	0.250	N316	N332		
	#4	0.125	0.312	N416	N432		
	#5	0.140	0.438	N516	N532		
	#6	0.149	0.375	N616	N632		
	#8	0.174	0.375	N816	N832		
	#9	0.188	0.500	N949 (.049 Thickness)			
Bolts	#10 or 3/16	0.203	0.438	0316	0332	0363	–
	#11	0.234	0.625	N1165 (.065 Thickness)			
	1/4	0.265	0.500	0416	0432	0463	–
	5/16	0.328	0.562	0516	0532	0563	–
	3/8	0.390	0.625	0616	0632	0663	–
	7/16	0.453	0.750	0716	0732	0763	–
	1/2	0.515	0.875	0816	0832	0863	–
	9/16	0.578	1.062	0916	0932	0963	–
	5/8	0.640	1.188	1016	1032	1063	–
	3/4	0.765	1.312	1216	1232	–	1290
	7/8	0.890	1.500	1416	1432	–	1490
	1	1.015	1.750	1616	1632	–	1690
	1-1/16	1.078	1.812	1716	1732	–	1790
	1-1/8	1.140	1.875	1816	1832	–	1890
	1-1/4	1.265	2.000	2016	2032	–	2090

NOTE: All dimensions are in inches

13.41 **MS20392 Series Clevis Pins**

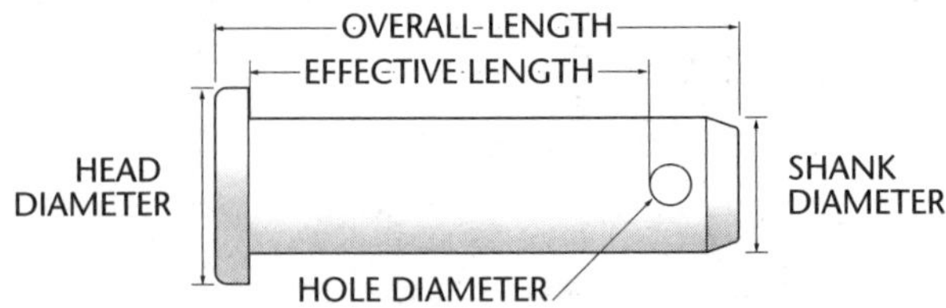

MS20392-3C47: 1/4" diameter pin, 1.469" effective length, 1.672" overall length, was AN394-47

Diam.	Shank Diam.	Diam. (max.)	Diam. (min.)	Hole Diam. (±.010)	Head Diam.	Old AN #
1C	1/8	0.125	0.123	0.070	0.250	AN392-
2C	3/16	0.188	0.186	0.076	0.312	AN393-
3C	1/4	0.250	0.248	0.076	0.375	AN394-
4C	5/16	0.312	0.310	0.106	0.437	AN395-
5C	3/8	0.375	0.373	0.106	0.500	AN396-
6C	7/16	0.438	0.436	0.106	0.562	AN397-
7C	1/2	0.500	0.498	0.106	0.625	AN398-

NOTE: All dimensions are in inches

13.42 **AA55488 Safety Pins**

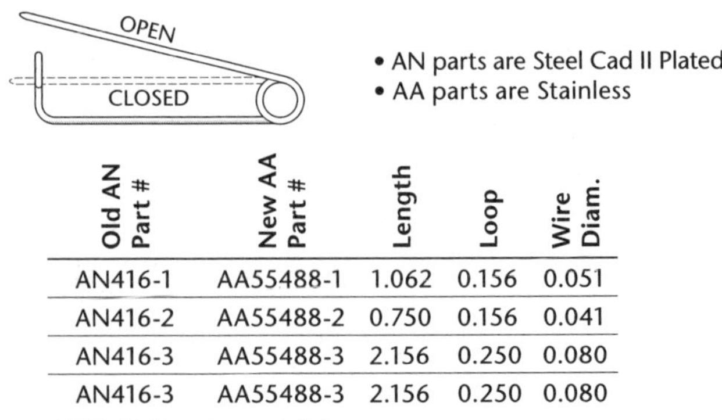

- AN parts are Steel Cad II Plated
- AA parts are Stainless

Old AN Part #	New AA Part #	Length	Loop	Wire Diam.
AN416-1	AA55488-1	1.062	0.156	0.051
AN416-2	AA55488-2	0.750	0.156	0.041
AN416-3	AA55488-3	2.156	0.250	0.080
AN416-3	AA55488-3	2.156	0.250	0.080

NOTE: All dimensions are in inches

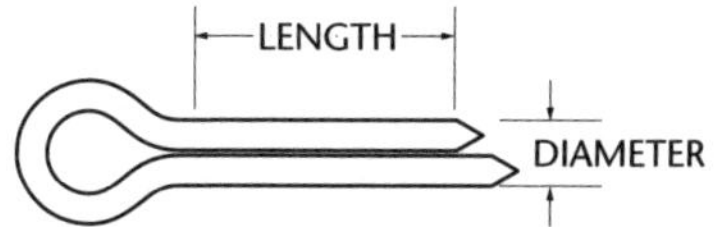

Replaces AN4380 and AN381

Nominal Diameters - Steel Cadmium Plated MS24665-(XXX)

Length	1/32	3/64	1/16	5/64	3/32	1/8	5/32	3/16
1/4	-001	-065	–	–	–	–	–	–
3/8	-003	-067	-130	–	–	–	–	–
1/2	-005	-069	-132	-208	-281	-349	-417	–
3/4	-007	-071	-134	-210	-283	-351	-418	-490
1	-009	-073	-136	-212	-285	-353	-419	-491
3/4	-010	-074	-138	-214	-287	-355	-421	-493

NOTE: All dimensions are in inches

Nominal Diameters - Stainless Steel MS24665-(XXX)

Length	1/32	3/64	1/16	5/64	3/32	1/8	5/32	3/16
1/4	-018	-082	-1010	–	–	–	–	–
5/16	-1001	-083	-1011	–	–	–	–	–
3/8	-1002	-084	-1012	–	–	–	–	–
7/16	-1003	-085	-1013	–	–	–	–	–
1/2	-022	-086	-151	-227	-298	-366	-435	–
5/8	–	-087	-152	–	-299	–	–	–

NOTE: All dimensions are in inches

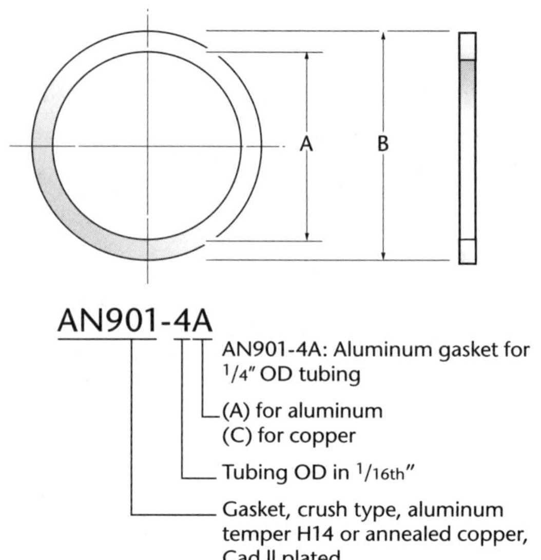

Dash Number		Tubing OD	A (+.010 -.000 Diam.)	B (+.010 -.000 Diam.)
Aluminum	Copper			
4A	4C	1/4	0.443	0.683
5A	5C	5/16	0.505	0.745
6A	6C	3/8	0.568	0.808
8A	8C	1/2	0.755	0.995

NOTE: All dimensions are in inches

13.45 **MS35769 Copper-Asbestos Crush Gaskets**

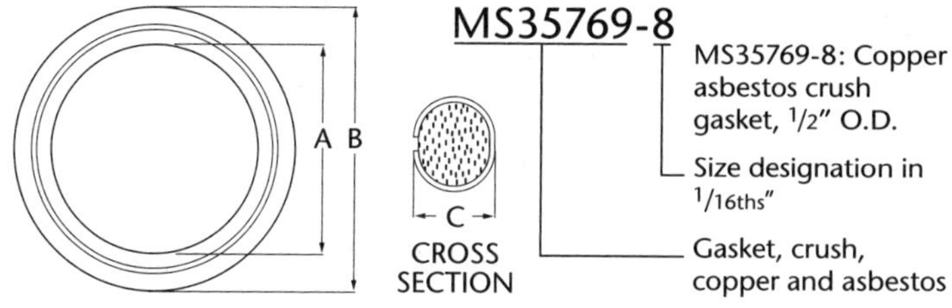

OLD AN900 Dash #	MS35769 Dash #	Inside Diameter A (+1/64, -0)	Outside Diameter B (+1/64, -0)	Thickness C (+1/64, -0)
-6	-6	3/8	5/8	3/32
-7	-8	7/16	11/16	3/32
-8	-9	1/2	3/4	3/32
-9	-10	9/16	13/16	3/32
-10	-11	5/8	7/8	3/32
-11	-13	11/16	15/16	3/32

NOTE: All dimensions are in inches

13.46 **AN804 Tee Bulkhead Fitting**

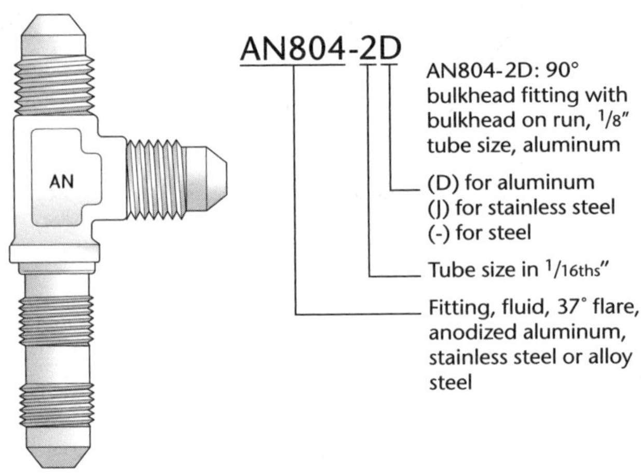

13.47 **AN806 Pressure Plug**

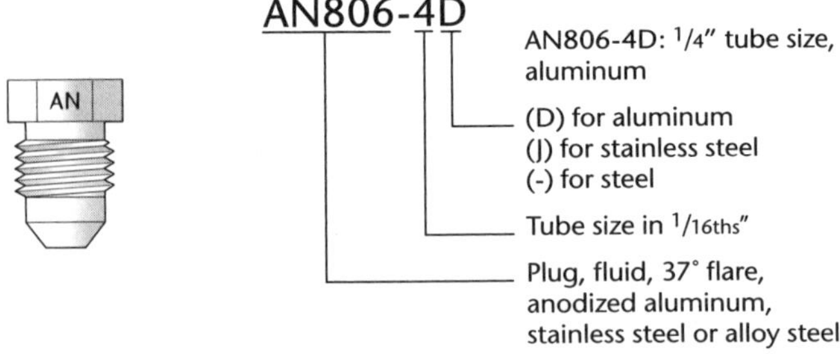

13.48 **AN815 Union**

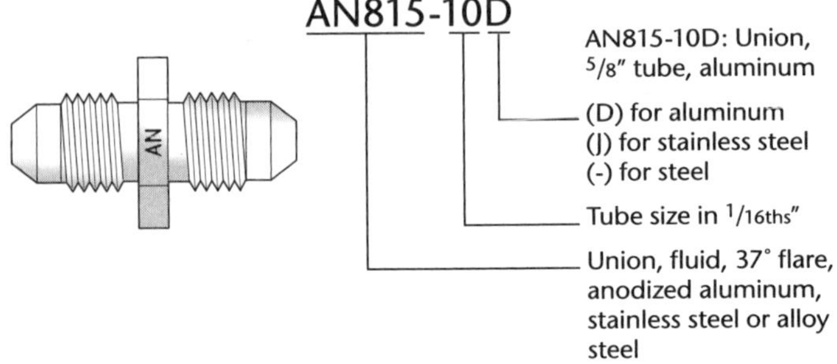

13.49 AN816 Pipe to Flare, Straight Fitting

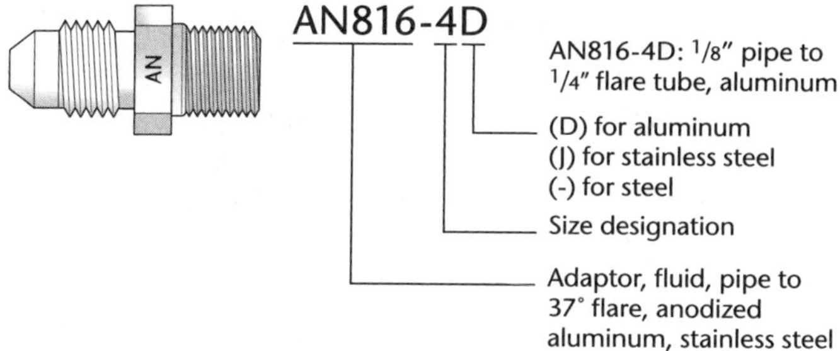

Pipe Size	Tube Size	Material		
		Aluminum	Steel	Stainless
1/8	1/8	-2D	-2	-2J
1/8	3/16	-3D	-3	-3J
1/8	1/4	-4D	-4	-4J
1/4	1/4	-4-4D	-4-4	-4-4J
1/8	5/16	-5D	-5	-5J
1/4	5/16	-5-4D	-5-4	-5-4J

NOTE: All dimensions are in inches

13.50 AN818 Tube Nut

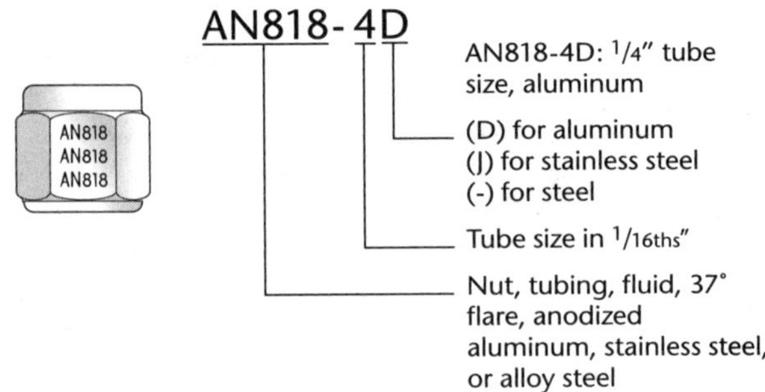

13.51 AN821 90° Elbow Fitting

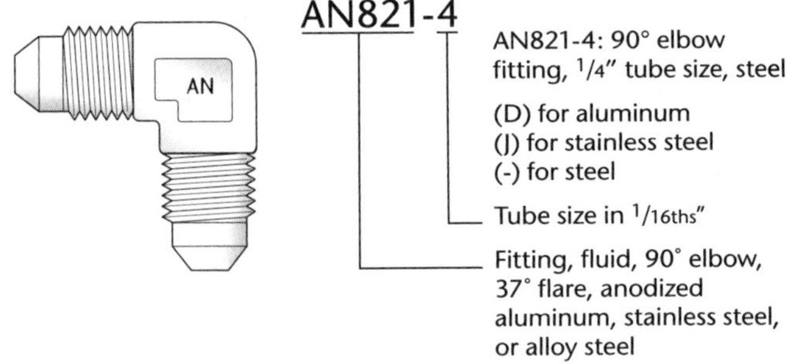

13.52 AN824 Tee Fitting

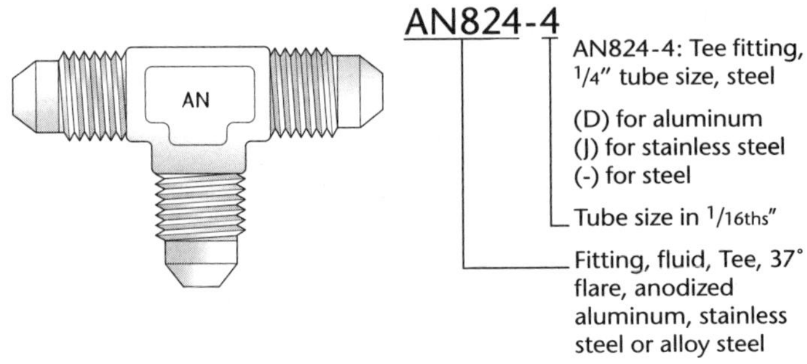

13.53 AN827 Cross Fitting

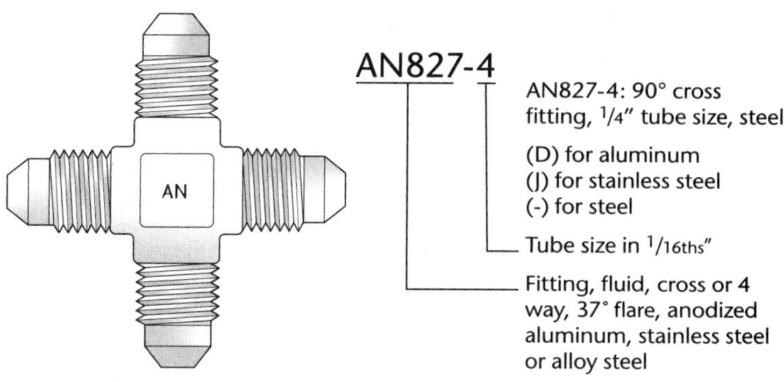

AN827-4

AN827-4: 90° cross fitting, 1/4" tube size, steel

(D) for aluminum
(J) for stainless steel
(-) for steel

Tube size in 1/16ths"

Fitting, fluid, cross or 4 way, 37° flare, anodized aluminum, stainless steel or alloy steel

13.54 AN832 Bulkhead Straight Fitting

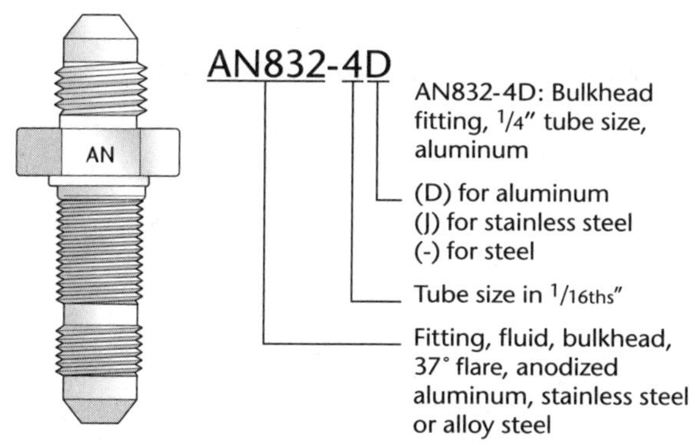

AN832-4D

AN832-4D: Bulkhead fitting, 1/4" tube size, aluminum

(D) for aluminum
(J) for stainless steel
(-) for steel

Tube size in 1/16ths"

Fitting, fluid, bulkhead, 37° flare, anodized aluminum, stainless steel or alloy steel

13.55 AN833 Bulkhead 90° Fitting

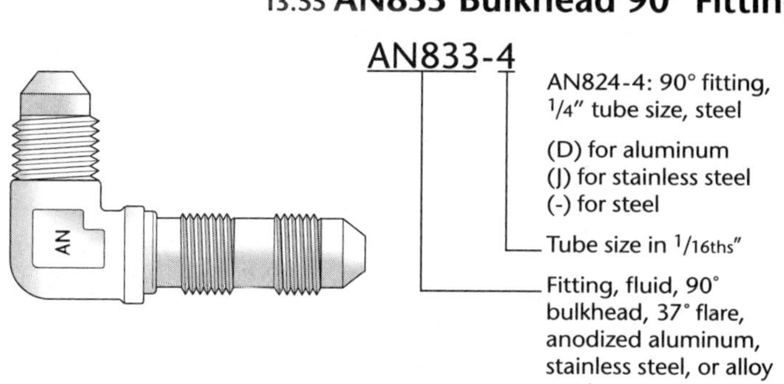

AN833-4

AN824-4: 90° fitting, 1/4" tube size, steel

(D) for aluminum
(J) for stainless steel
(-) for steel

Tube size in 1/16ths"

Fitting, fluid, 90° bulkhead, 37° flare, anodized aluminum, stainless steel, or alloy steel

13.56 AN834 Bulkhead Tee Fitting

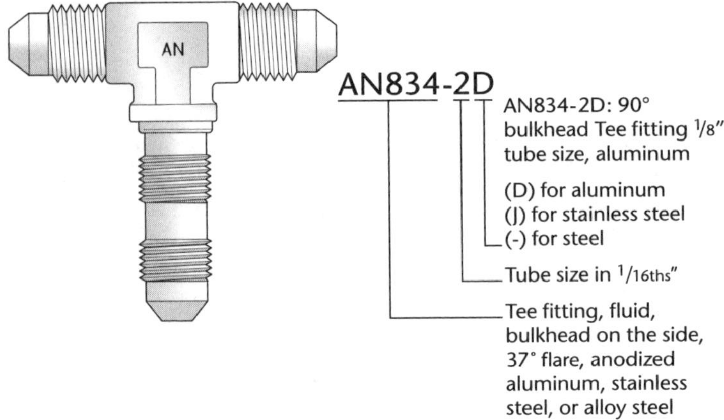

AN834-2D

AN834-2D: 90° bulkhead Tee fitting $\frac{1}{8}$" tube size, aluminum

(D) for aluminum
(J) for stainless steel
(-) for steel

Tube size in $\frac{1}{16}$ths"

Tee fitting, fluid, bulkhead on the side, 37° flare, anodized aluminum, stainless steel, or alloy steel

13.57 AN837 Bulkhead 45° Fitting

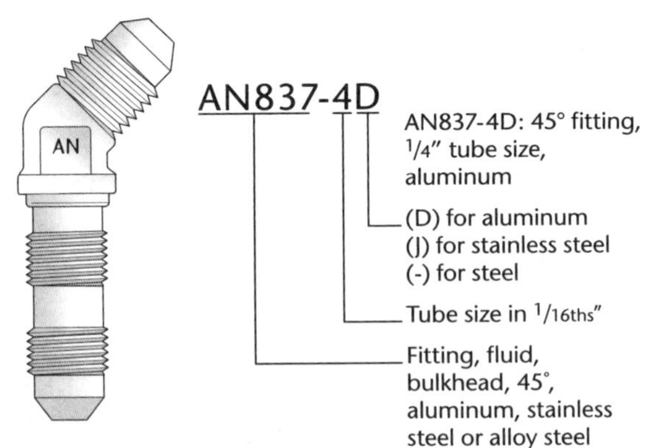

AN837-4D

AN837-4D: 45° fitting, $\frac{1}{4}$" tube size, aluminum

(D) for aluminum
(J) for stainless steel
(-) for steel

Tube size in $\frac{1}{16}$ths"

Fitting, fluid, bulkhead, 45°, aluminum, stainless steel or alloy steel

AN840, AN842, AN844, Pipe to Hose Fittings

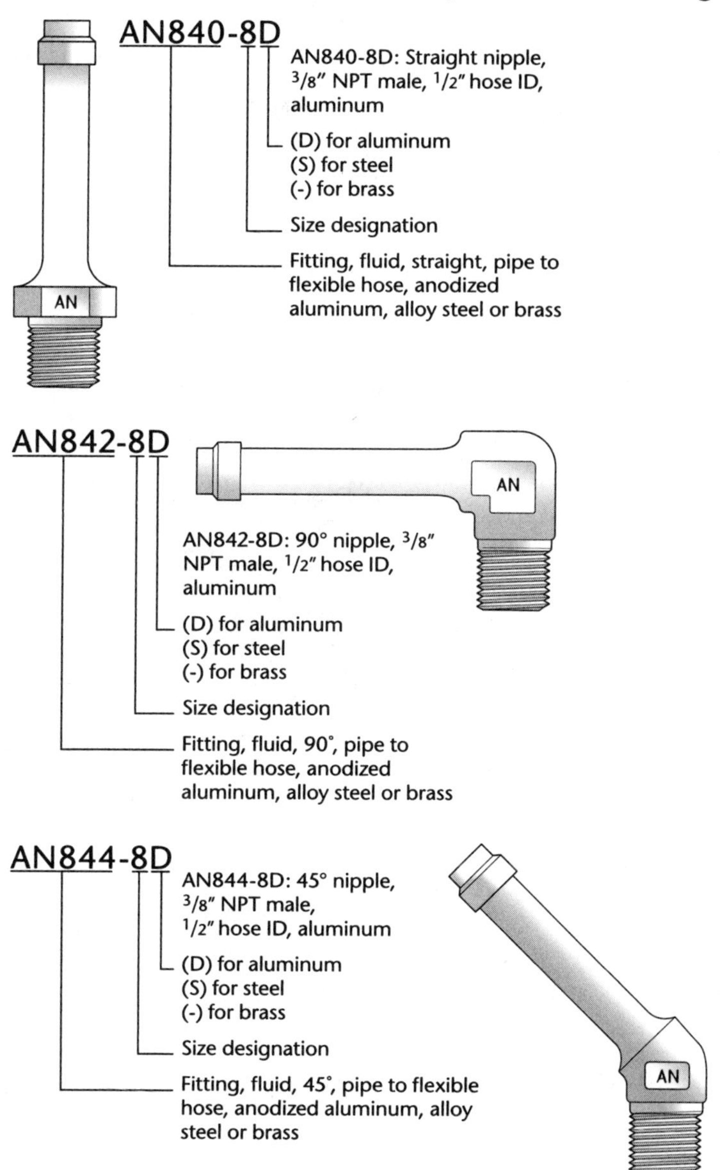

13.59 AN893 Female to Male, Straight Fitting

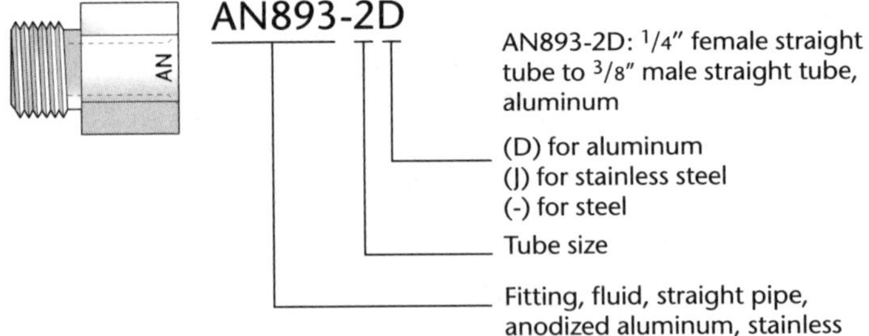

Female Tube Size	Male Tube Size	Material		
		Aluminum	**Steel**	**Stainless**
3/8	1/8	D3-2	-3-2	J3-2
1/4	1/8	D4-2	-4-2	J4-2
1/4	3/16	D4-3	-4-3	J4-3
5/16	1/4	D5-4	-5-4	J5-4
3/8	1/4	D6-4	-6-4	J6-4
3/8	5/16	D6-5	-6-5	J6-5
1/2	1/4	D8-4	-8-4	J8-4
1/2	5/16	D8-5	-8-5	J8-5
1/2	3/8	D8-6	-8-6	J8-6

NOTE: All dimensions are in inches
Female portion to be sealed with boss O-ring or metal gasket

13.60 AN894 Female Straight to Male 37° Flare Adapter

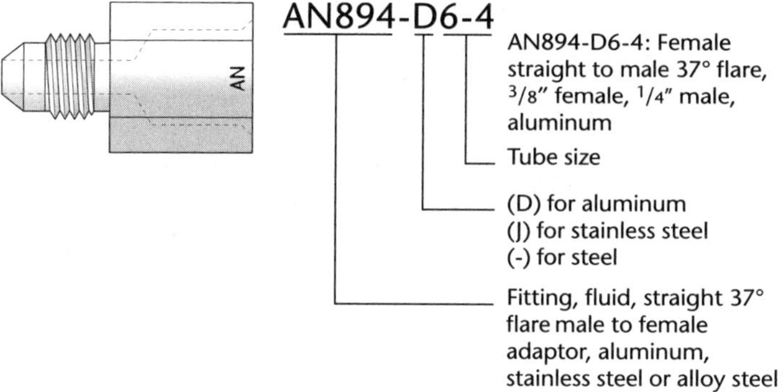

 AN Pipe and Union Fittings

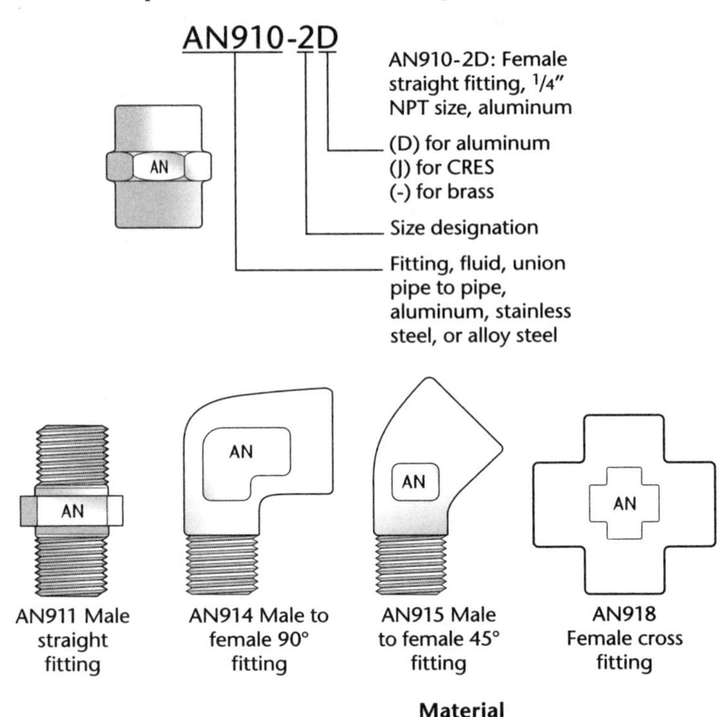

AN911 Male straight fitting

AN914 Male to female 90° fitting

AN915 Male to female 45° fitting

AN918 Female cross fitting

NPT Size	Material		
	Aluminum	Brass	CRES.
1/8	-1D	-1	-1J
1/4	-2D	-2	-2J
3/8	-3D	-3	-3J
1/2	-4D	-4	-4J
3/4	-6D	-6	-6J
1	-8D	-8	-8J

NOTE: All dimensions are in inches

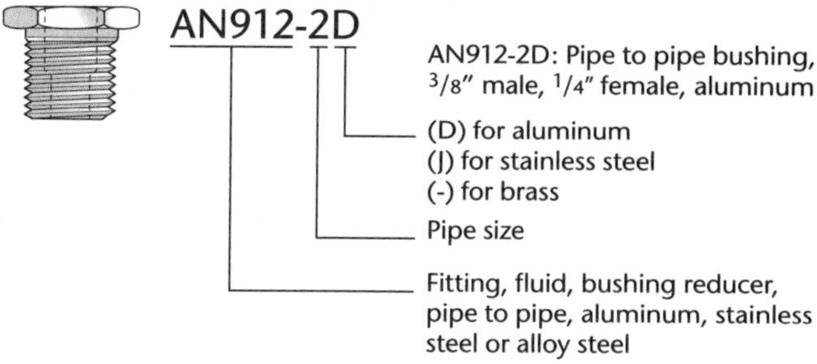

Male Pipe Size	Female Pipe Size	Material		
		Aluminum	Brass	Stainless
1/4	1/8	-1D	-1	-1J
3/8	1/4	-2D	-2	-2J
3/8	1/8	-3D	-3	-3J
1/2	3/8	-4D	-4	-4J
1/2	1/4	-5D	-5	-5J
1/2	1/8	-6D	-6	-6J

NOTE: All dimensions are in inches

13.63 AN919 Male to Male 37° Flare Adapter

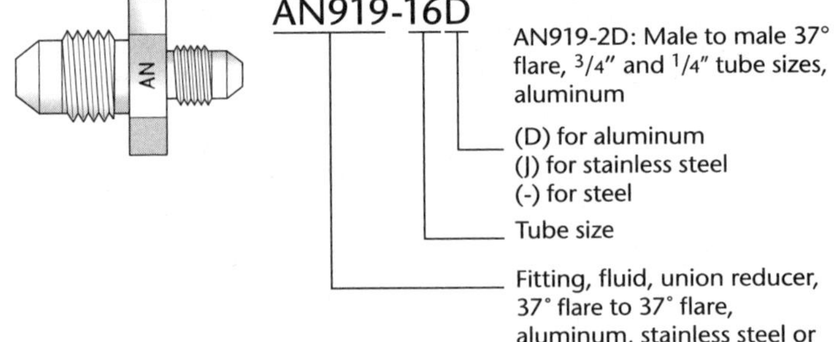

Female Tube Size	Male Tube Size	Material		
		Aluminum	Steel	Stainless
3/16	1/8	-0D	-0	-0J
1/4	1/8	-1D	-1	-1J
1/4	3/16	-2D	-2	-2J
1/16	1/4	-3D	-3	-3J
3/8	1/8	-4D	-4	-4J
3/8	3/16	-5D	-5	-5J

NOTE: All dimensions are in inches

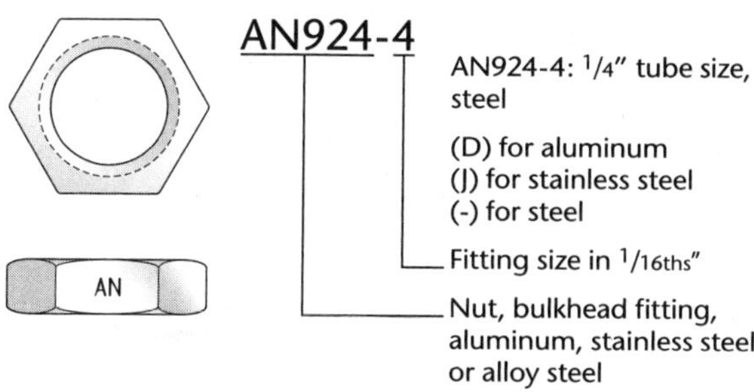

13.65 **AN929 Pressure Cap**

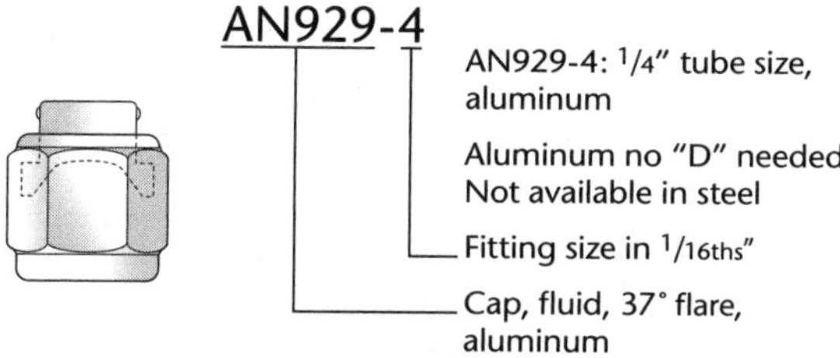

13.66 AN Fittings, Straight Threads O-ring Sealing

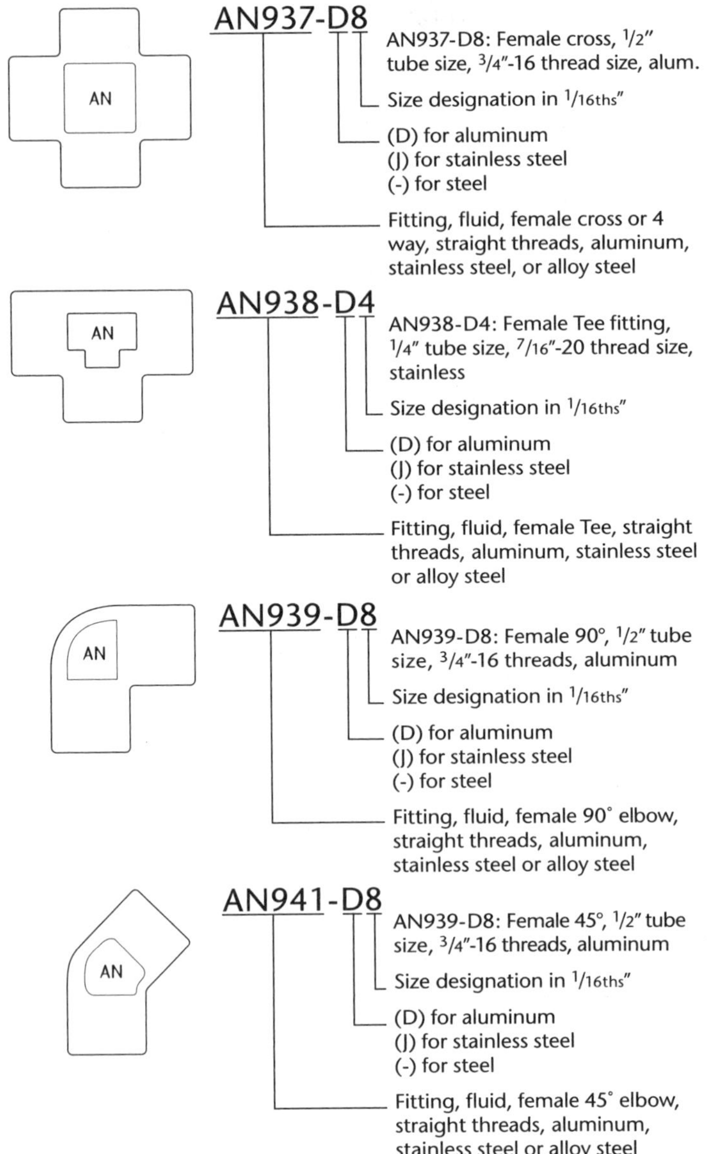

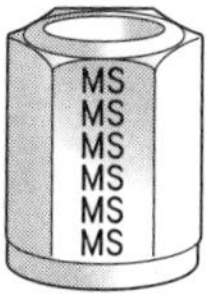

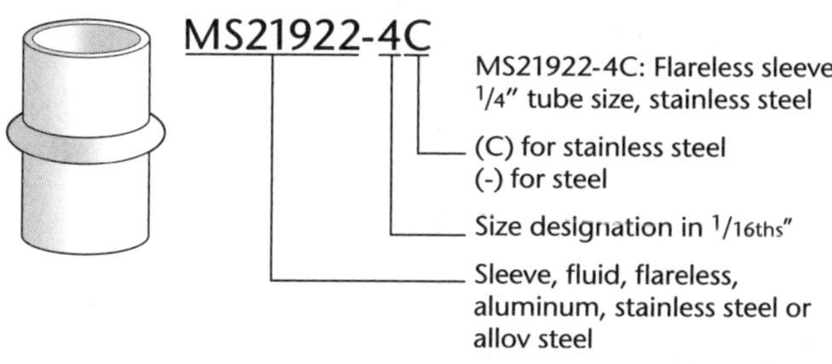

MS21921-D4

MS21921-D4: Flareless nut, 1/4" tube size, aluminum

Size designation in 1/16ths"

(D) for aluminum
(-) for steel
(J) for stainless

Nut, fluid, flareless, aluminum, stainless steel or alloy steel

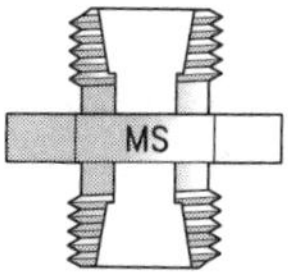

MS21902-D8

MS21902-D8: Flareless union, 1/2" tube size, aluminum

Size designation in 1/16ths"

(D) for aluminum
(-) for steel
(J) for stainless

Union, fluid, flareless, aluminum, stainless steel or alloy steel

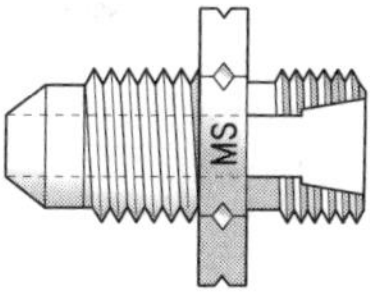

MS21900-D6

MS21900-D6: 37° Flare to flareless union, 3/8" tube size, aluminum

Size designation in 1/16ths"

(D) for aluminum
(-) for steel
(J) for stainless

Union, fluid, flareless to 37° flare, aluminum, stainless steel or alloy steel

13.68 **MS21922 Flareless Sleeve**

MS21922-4C

MS21922-4C: Flareless sleeve, 1/4" tube size, stainless steel

(C) for stainless steel
(-) for steel

Size designation in 1/16ths"

Sleeve, fluid, flareless, aluminum, stainless steel or alloy steel

13.69 **Grease Fittings**

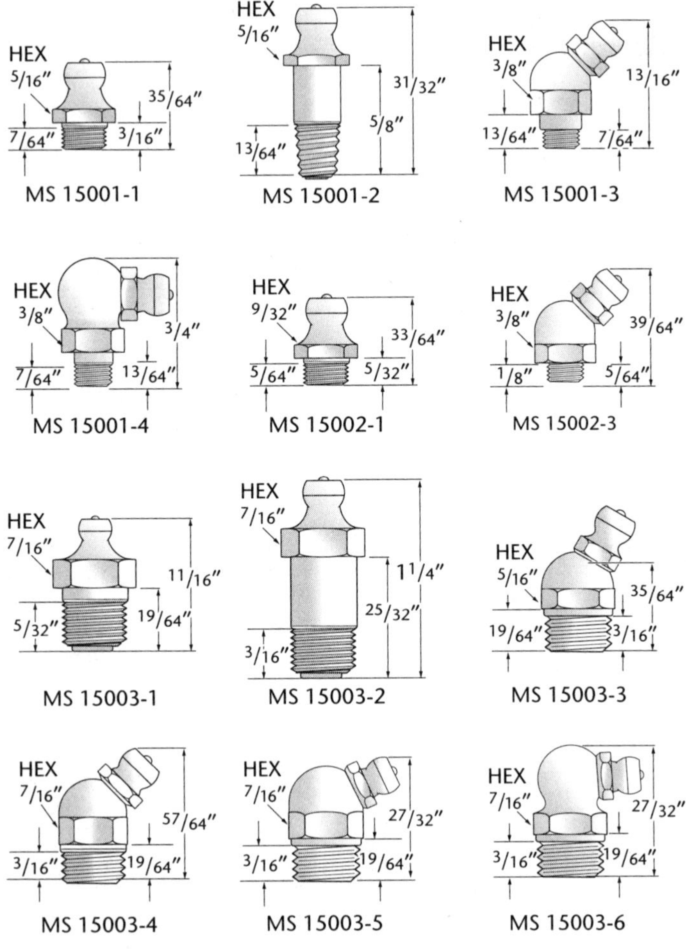

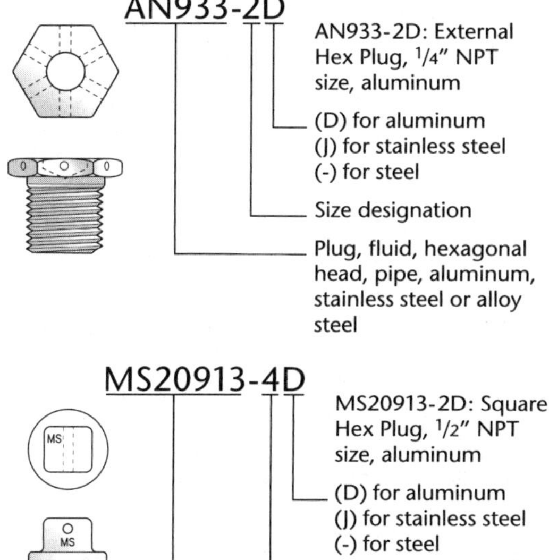

| | Material | | |
NPT Size	Aluminum	Steel	Stainless
1/16	-0D	-0	-0J
1/8	-1D	-1	-1J
1/4	-2D	-2	-2J
3/8	-3D	-3	-3J
1/2	-4D	-4	-4J
3/4	-6D	-5	-6J
1	-8D	-8	-8J

NOTE: All dimensions are in inches

13.71 Primer and Oxygen Hardware

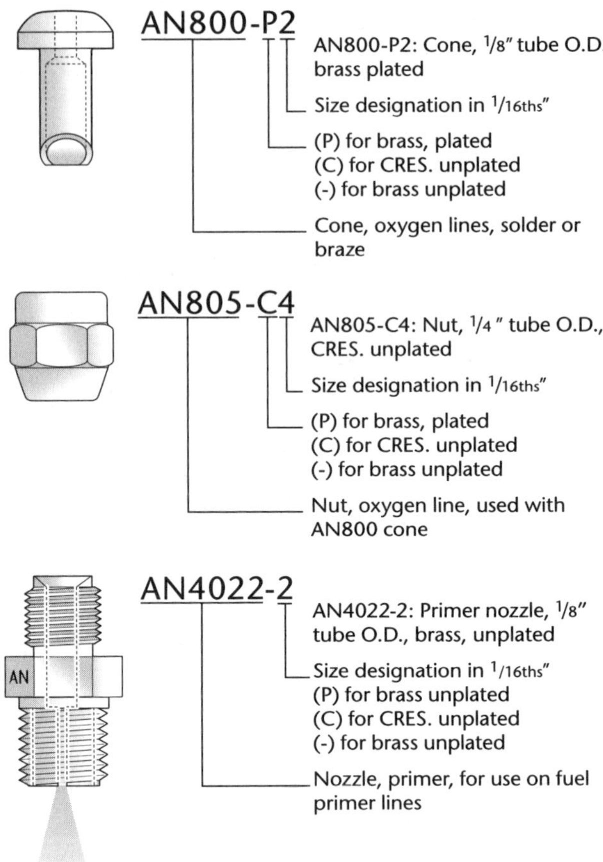

13.72 MS20819 Tubing Sleeve

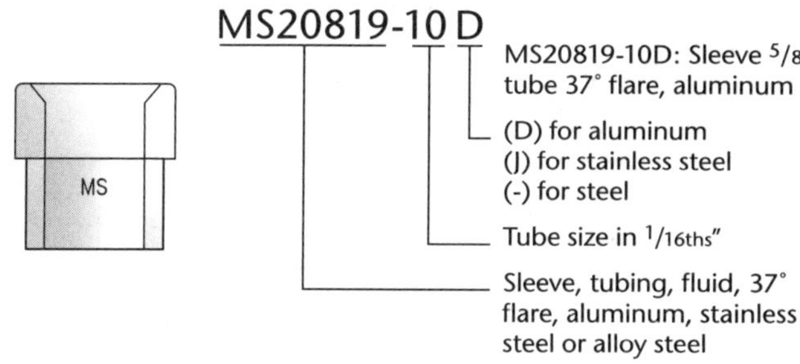

13.73 MS20822 Pipe to Flare, 90° Fitting

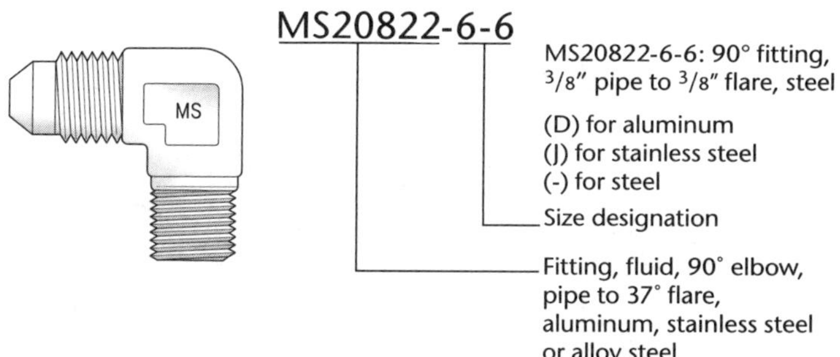

Pipe Size	Tube Size	Material		
		Aluminum	Steel	Stainless
1/8	1/8	-2D	-2	-2J
1/8	3/16	-3D	-3	-3J
1/8	1/4	-4D	-4	-4J
1/4	1/4	-4-4D	-4-4	-4-4J
1/8	5/16	-5D	-5	-5J
1/4	5/16	-5-4D	-5-4	-5-4J

NOTE: All dimensions are in inches

13.74 **MS20823 Pipe to Flare, 45° Fitting**

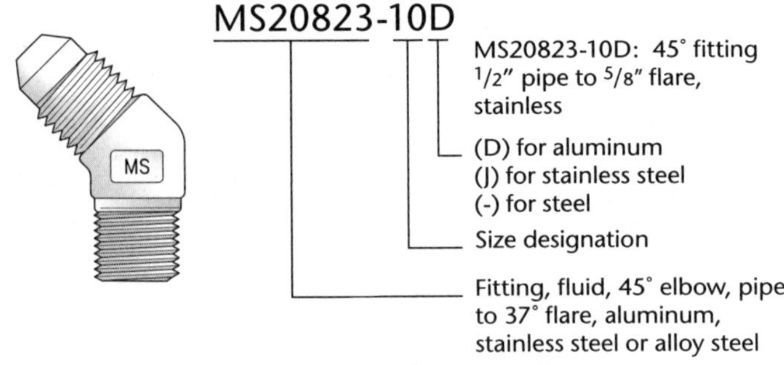

Pipe Size	Tube Size	Material		
		Aluminum	Steel	Stainless
1/8	1/8	-2D	-2	-2J
1/8	3/16	-3D	-3	-3J
1/8	1/4	-4D	-4	-4J
1/8	5/16	-5D	-5	-5J
1/4	3/8	-6D	-6	-6J
3/8	1/2	-8D	-8	-8J

NOTE: All dimensions are in inches

13.75 MS20825 and MS20826 Tee Fittings

MS20825-10D

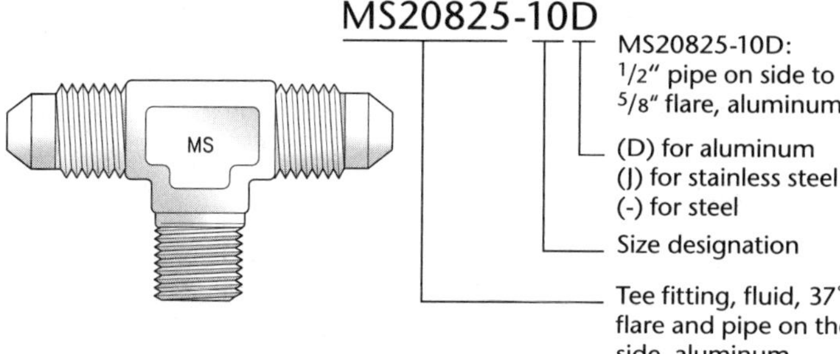

MS20825-10D:
$^1/_2$" pipe on side to
$^5/_8$" flare, aluminum

(D) for aluminum
(J) for stainless steel
(-) for steel

Size designation

Tee fitting, fluid, 37°
flare and pipe on the
side, aluminum,
stainless steel or alloy
steel

MS20826-10D

MS20826-10D $^1/_2$"
pipe on run to $^5/_8$"
flare, aluminum

(D) for aluminum
(J) for stainless steel
(-) for steel

Size designation

Tee fitting, fluid, 37°
flare and pipe on the
run, aluminum,
stainless steel or alloy
steel

Pipe Size	Tube Size	Material		
		Aluminum	Steel	Stainless
1/8	1/8	-2D	-2	-2J
1/8	3/16	-3D	-3	-3J
1/8	1/4	-4D	-4	-4J
1/8	5/16	-5D	-5	-5J
1/4	3/8	-6D	-6	-6J
3/8	1/2	-8D	-8	-8J
1/2	5/8	-10D	-10	-10J
3/4	3/4	-12D	-12	-12J
3/4	1	-16-12D	-16-12	-16-12J
1	1	-16D	-16	-16J

NOTE: All dimensions are in inches

13.76 MS27769 Hex Plug

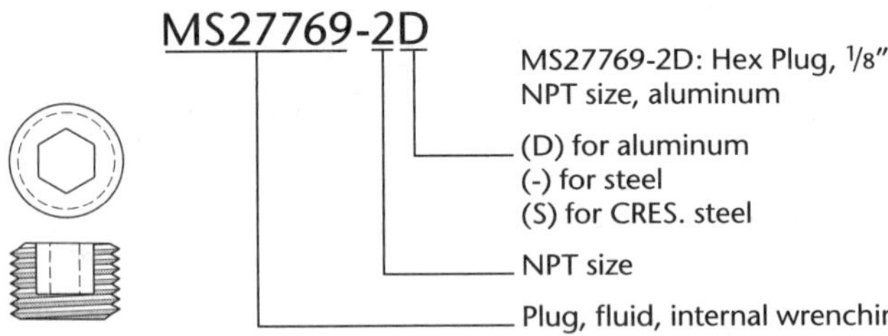

NPT Size	Material		
	Aluminum	Steel	CRES.
1/16	-1D	-1	-1S
1/8	-2D	-2	-2S
1/4	-3D	-3	-3S
3/8	-4D	-4	-4S
1/2	-5D	-5	-5S
3/4	-6D	-6	-6S
1	-7D	-7	-7S

NOTE: All dimensions are in inches

13.77 NAS1564 Female 37° to Male 37°

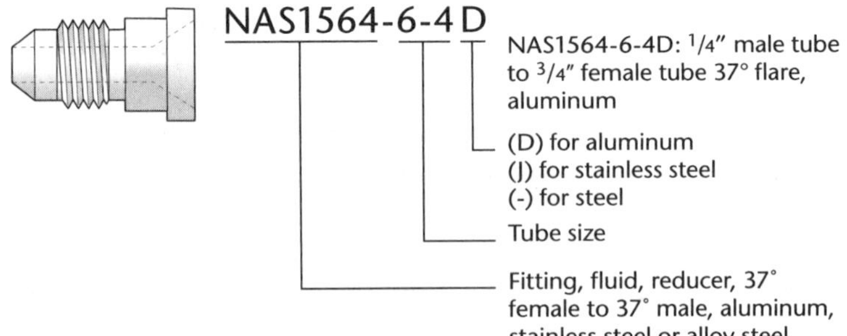

Female Tube Size	Male Tube Size	Material		
		Aluminum	Steel	Stainless
3/8	1/4	-6-4D	-6-4	-6-4J
1/2	1/4	-8-4D	-8-4	-8-4J
1/2	3/8	-8-6D	-8-5	-8-6J
5/8	3/8	-10-61D	-10-6	-10-61J
3/4	1/2	-12-8D	-12-8	-12-8J

NOTE: All dimensions are in inches

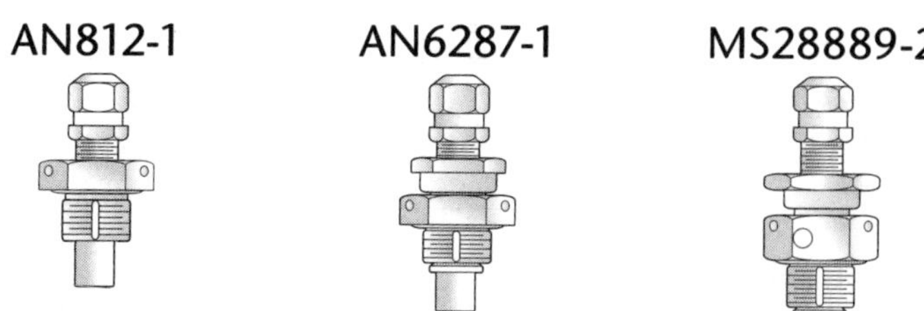

Valve Assy Part #	Pressure Rating	Valve Core Part #	Threads
AN812-1	1,500 p.s.i.	AN809-1	1/2 - 20
AN6287-1	3,000 p.s.i.	AN809-1	1/2 - 20
MS2889-2	5,000 p.s.i.	NONE	1/2 - 20

NOTE: All dimensions are in inches

13.79 **MS28778 O-Ring**

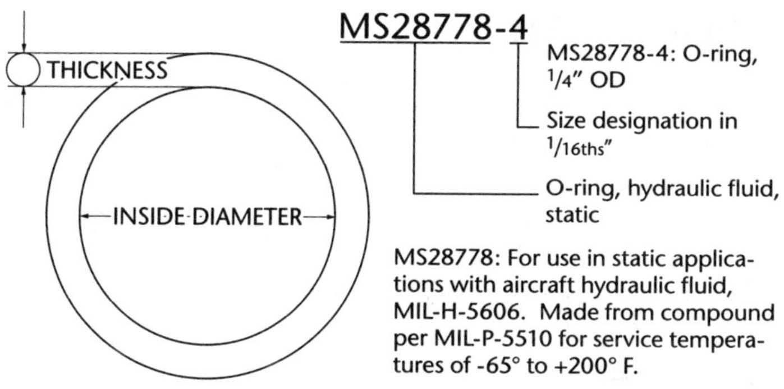

MS28778: For use in static applications with aircraft hydraulic fluid, MIL-H-5606. Made from compound per MIL-P-5510 for service temperatures of -65° to +200° F.

NOTE: Consult the manufacturer's manuals for exact O-ring type, material, size and part number

13.80 MS28775 O-Ring

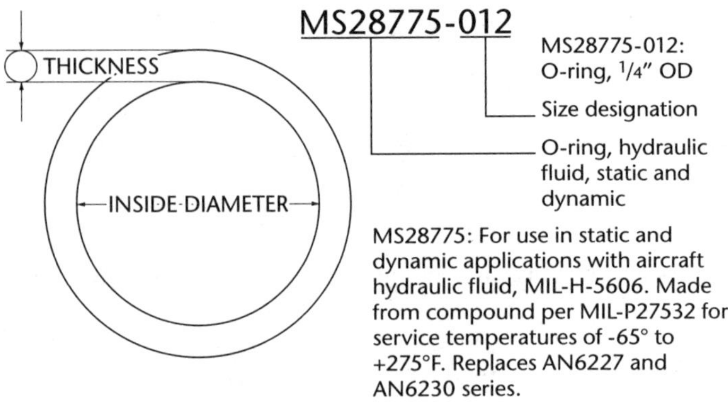

MS28775: For use in static and dynamic applications with aircraft hydraulic fluid, MIL-H-5606. Made from compound per MIL-P27532 for service temperatures of -65° to +275°F. Replaces AN6227 and AN6230 series.

NOTE: Consult the manufacturer's manuals for exact O-ring type, material, size and part number

13.81 Cherry® Rivet

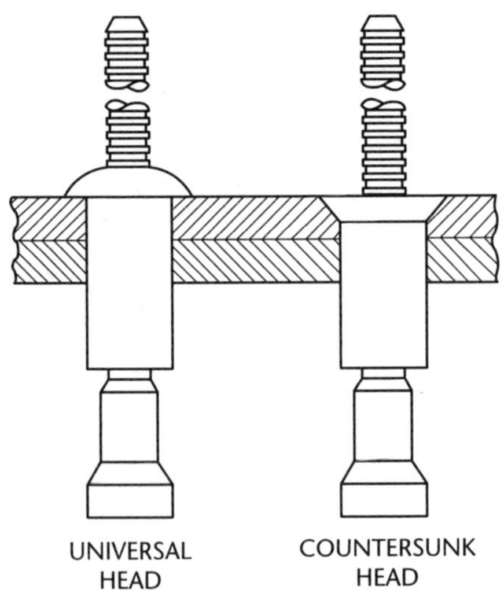

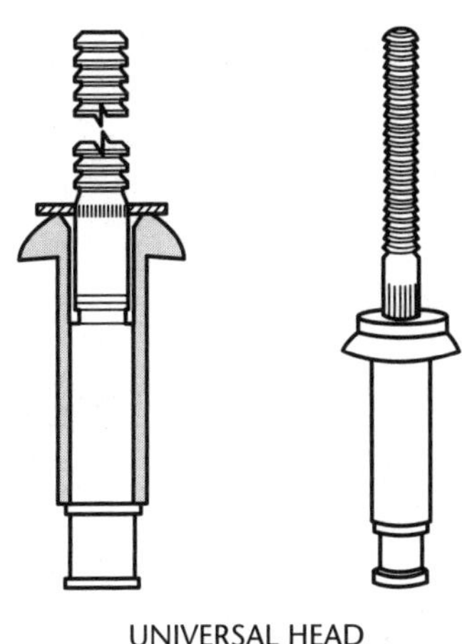

UNIVERSAL HEAD

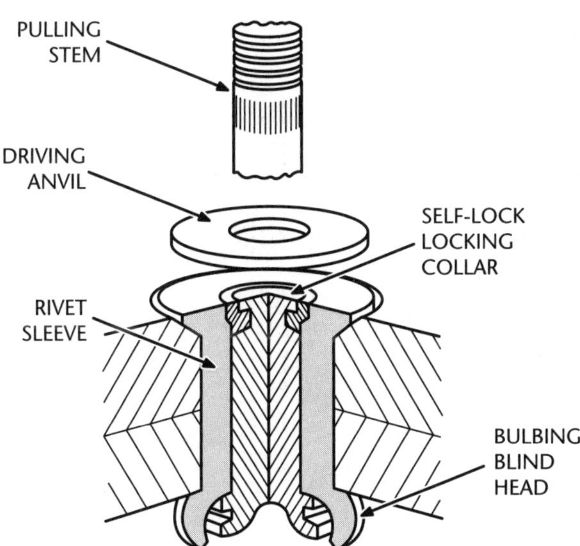

13.83 Hi-Lok® Collars

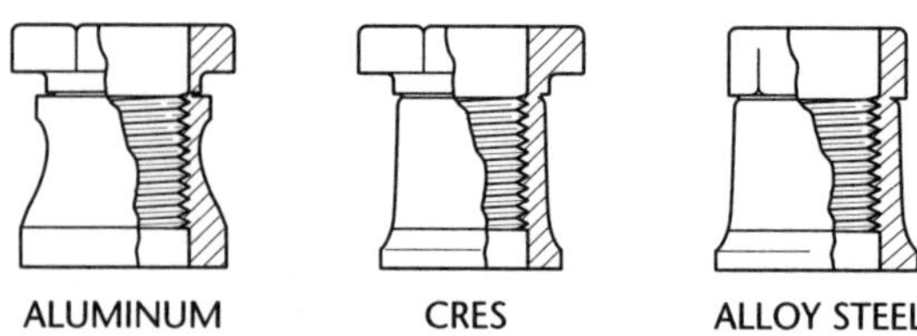

13.84 Hi-Lok® Fasteners

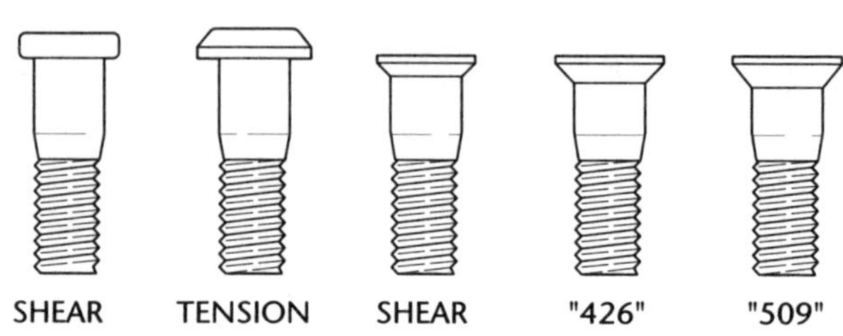

13.85 Huck Rivet

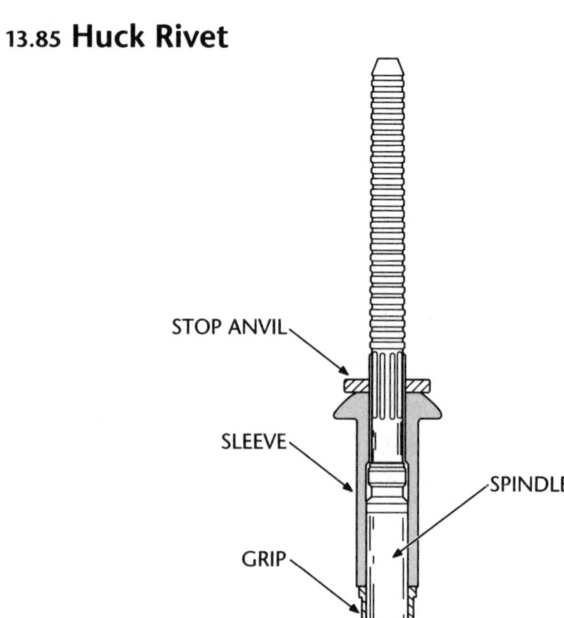

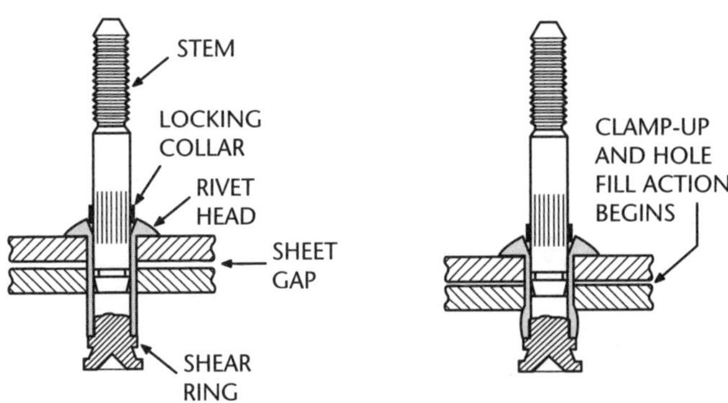

1. Before pulling begins

2. Stem is pulled into rivet sleeve and starts to form bulb blind head

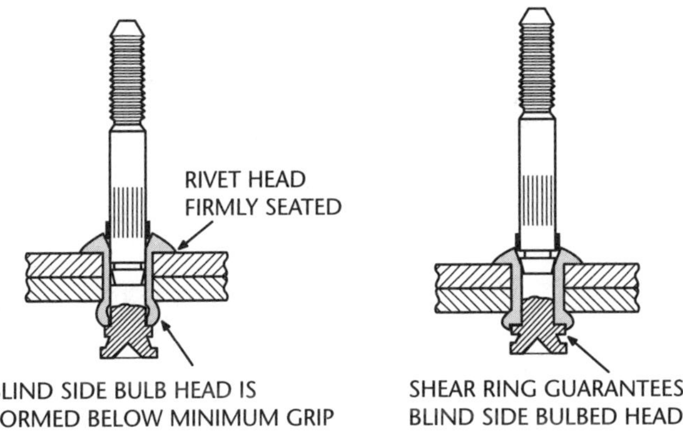

3. Clamp-up completed as stem continues to bulb out blind head

4. Formation of blind head and hole filling are completed

   Shear ring now shears from stem cone to allow stem to pull further into rivet

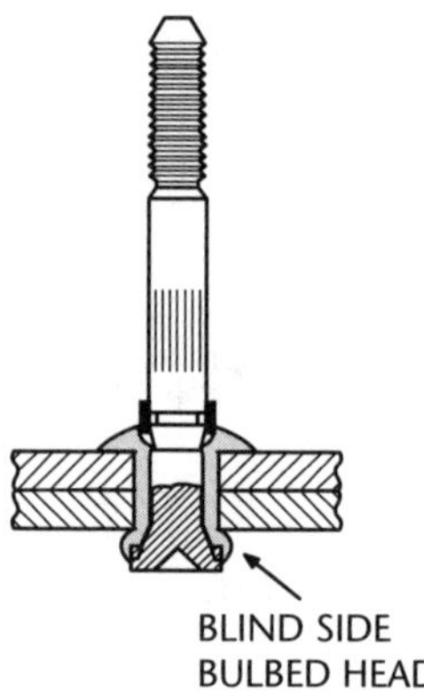

(Maximum grip illustrated)

5. Shear ring has moved down stem cone until pulling head automatically stops stem break notch flush with top of rivet head

   Locking collar is now ready to be inserted

6. Completely installed bulbed cherrylock

   Pulling head has inserted locking collar and stem has fractured flush with rivet head

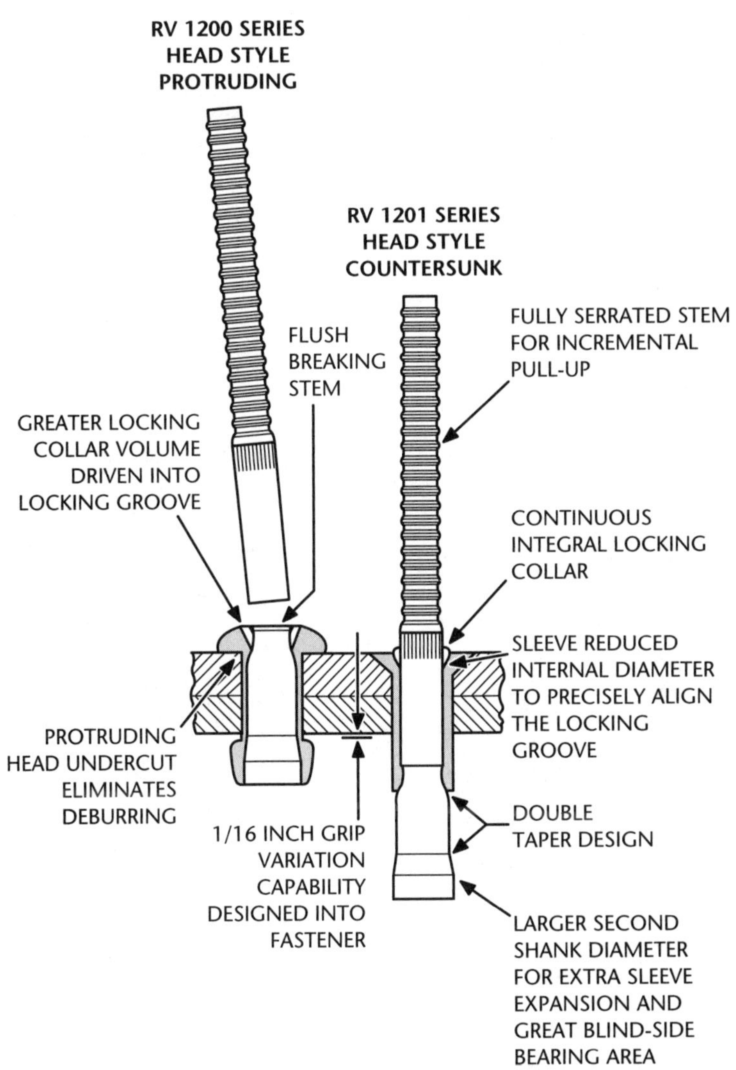
RV 1200 SERIES
HEAD STYLE
PROTRUDING
RV 1201 SERIES
HEAD STYLE
COUNTERSUNK
FLUSH
BREAKING
STEM
FULLY SERRATED STEM
FOR INCREMENTAL
PULL-UP
GREATER LOCKING
COLLAR VOLUME
DRIVEN INTO
LOCKING GROOVE
CONTINUOUS
INTEGRAL LOCKING
COLLAR
SLEEVE REDUCED
INTERNAL DIAMETER
TO PRECISELY ALIGN
THE LOCKING
GROOVE
PROTRUDING
HEAD UNDERCUT
ELIMINATES
DEBURRING
1/16 INCH GRIP
VARIATION
CAPABILITY
DESIGNED INTO
FASTENER
DOUBLE
TAPER DESIGN
LARGER SECOND
SHANK DIAMETER
FOR EXTRA SLEEVE
EXPANSION AND
GREAT BLIND-SIDE
BEARING AREA

13.88 Standard Rivet Alloy Code Markings

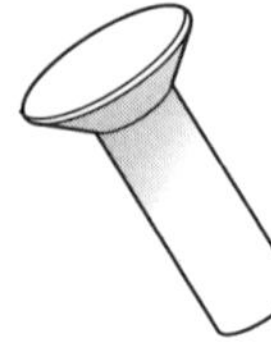

Alloy Code: A
Alloy: 1100 or 3003
  aluminum
Head Marking:
  None
Shear Strength: 10
  K.p.s.i.
(Non-structural
  uses only)

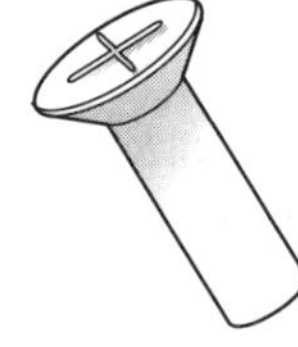

Alloy code: B
Alloy: 5056
  aluminum
Head marking:
  Raised cross
Shear strength:
  28 K.p.s.i.

Alloy code: AD
Alloy: 2117
  aluminum
Head marking:
  Dimple
Shear strength:
  30 K.p.s.i.

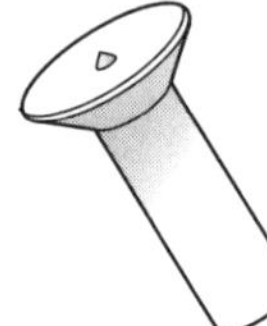

Alloy code: D
Alloy: 2017
  aluminum
Head marking:
  Raised dot
Shear strength:
  38 K.p.s.i.
(when driven as
  received, 34
  K.p.s.i. when
  re-heat treated)

Alloy code: DD
Alloy: 2024
  aluminum
Head marking:
  Two bars
Shear strength:
  41 K.p.s.i.
(Must be driven in
  "W" condition
  (ice-box))

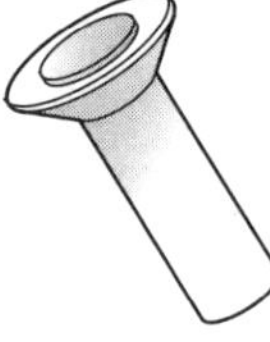

Alloy code: E
Alloy: 7050
  aluminum
Head marking:
  Raised ring
Shear strength:
  43 K.p.s.i.
(Replacement for
  DD rivet to be
  driven in "T"
  condition)

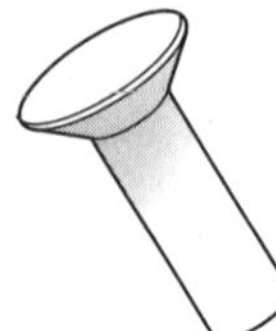

Alloy code: M
Alloy: Monel ®
Head marking:
  None on flush head
Shear strength:
  54 K.p.s.i.

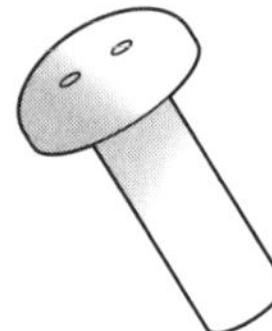

Alloy code: M
Alloy: Monel ®
Head marking:
  Two dimples on
  universal head
Shear strength:
  54 K.p.s.i.

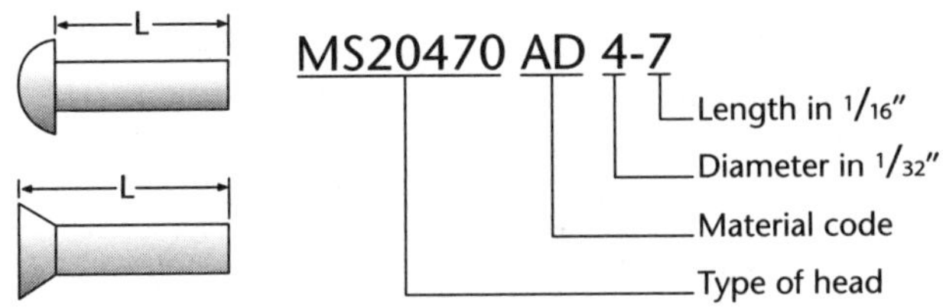

Material Code	Head Marking	Material
A	Plain (Dyed)	1100
AD	Dimpled	2117
D	Raised Dot	2017T
DD	Two Raised Dashes	2024
B	Raised Cross (Dyed)	5056
E	Raised Circle	7050
M	Two Dots	Monel

100° FLUSH

MS20425
BACR15BA

MODIFIED 120° REDUCED HEAD

MS14218
BACR15FV

UNIVERSAL

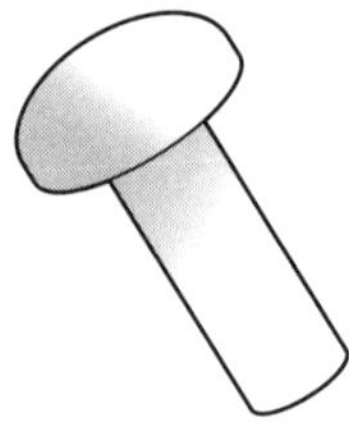

MS20470
BACR15BB

BOEING REDUCED HEAD

BACR15CE

NAS REDUCED HEAD

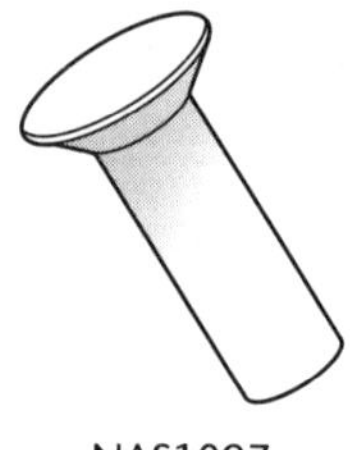

NAS1097

UNIVERSAL REDUCED HEAD

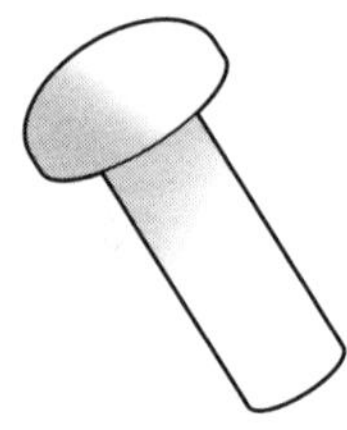

BACR15FT

13.91 **MS20663 and MS20664 Shanks**

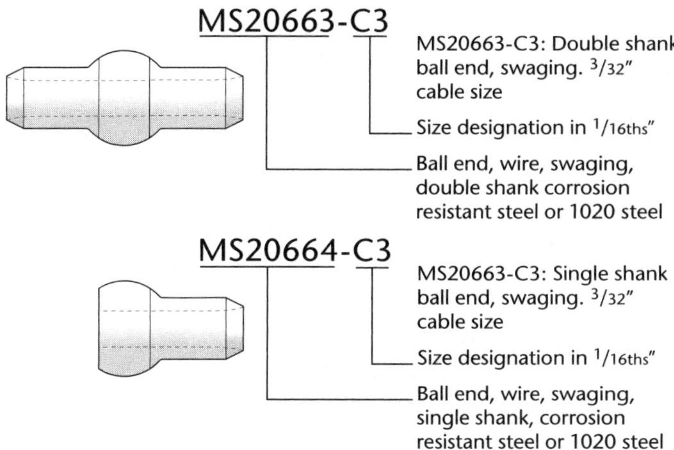

MS20663-C3

MS20663-C3: Double shank ball end, swaging. $3/32''$ cable size

Size designation in $1/16\text{ths}''$

Ball end, wire, swaging, double shank corrosion resistant steel or 1020 steel

MS20664-C3

MS20663-C3: Single shank ball end, swaging. $3/32''$ cable size

Size designation in $1/16\text{ths}''$

Ball end, wire, swaging, single shank, corrosion resistant steel or 1020 steel

13.92 **MS20667 and MS20668 Terminal**

MS20667-3

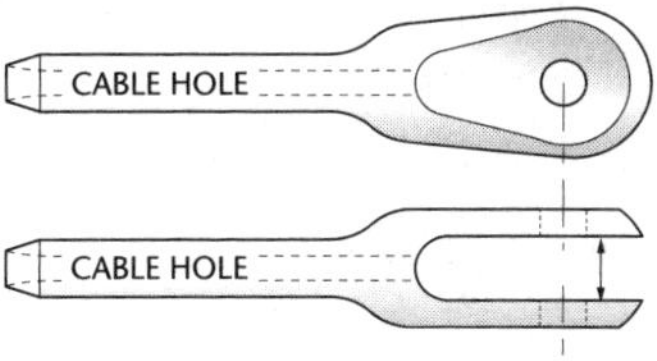

MS20667-3: Terminal, fork end, swaging. $3/32''$ cable size

Size designation in $1/16\text{ths}''$

Terminal, wire, swaging, fork end, corrosion resistant steel or carbon steel

MS20668-3

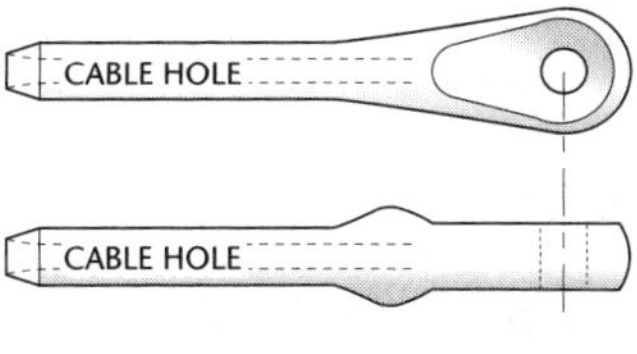

MS20668-3: Terminal, eye end, swaging. $3/32''$ cable size

Size designation in $1/16\text{ths}''$

Terminal, wire, swaging, eye end, corrosion resistant steel or carbon steel

13.93 MS21251 Turnbuckle Barrel

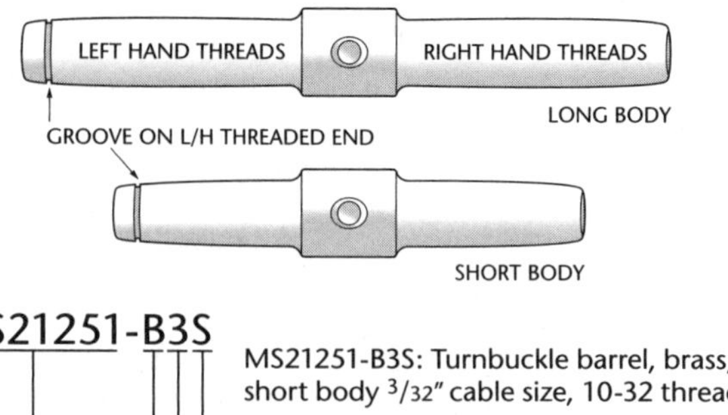

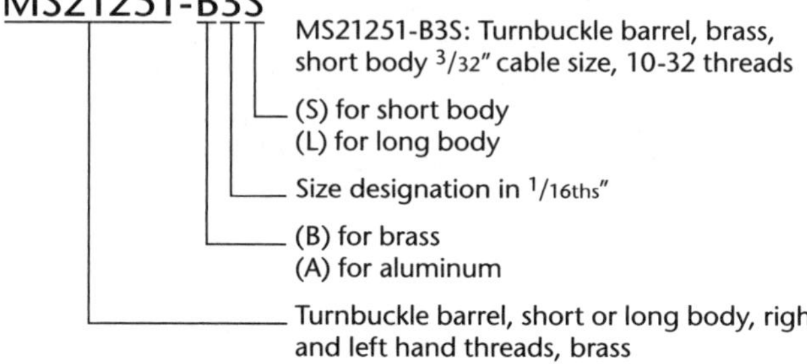

13.94 MS21252 Turnbuckle Clevis

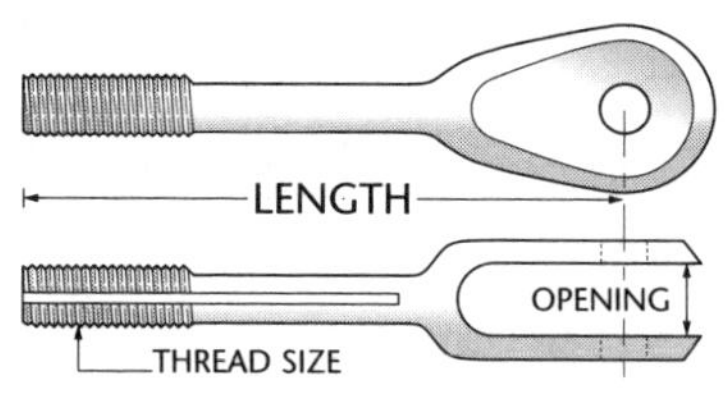

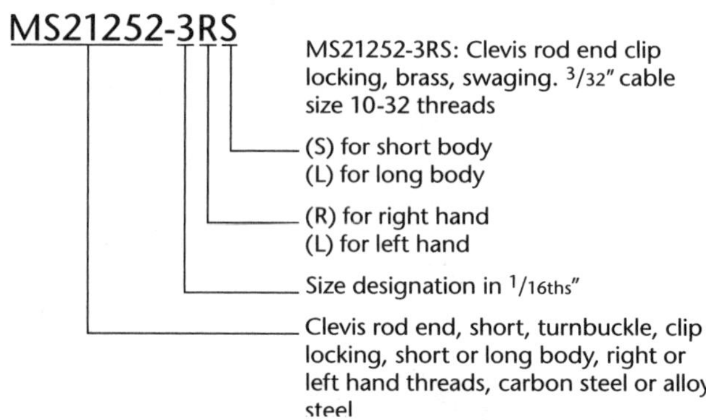

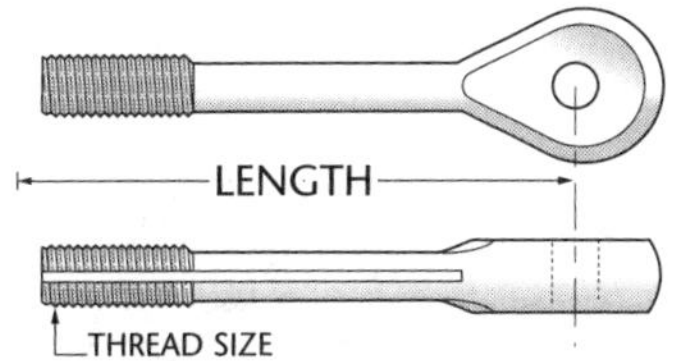

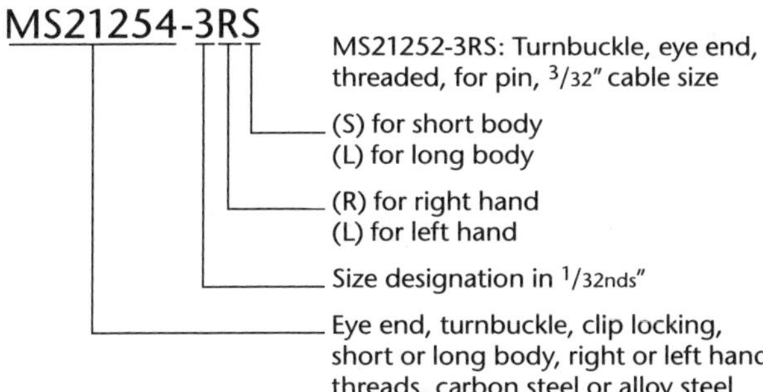

MS21254-3RS

MS21252-3RS: Turnbuckle, eye end, threaded, for pin, $^3/_{32}$" cable size

(S) for short body
(L) for long body

(R) for right hand
(L) for left hand

Size designation in $^1/_{32}$nds"

Eye end, turnbuckle, clip locking, short or long body, right or left hand threads, carbon steel or alloy steel

13.96 **MS21259 and MS21260 Terminals**

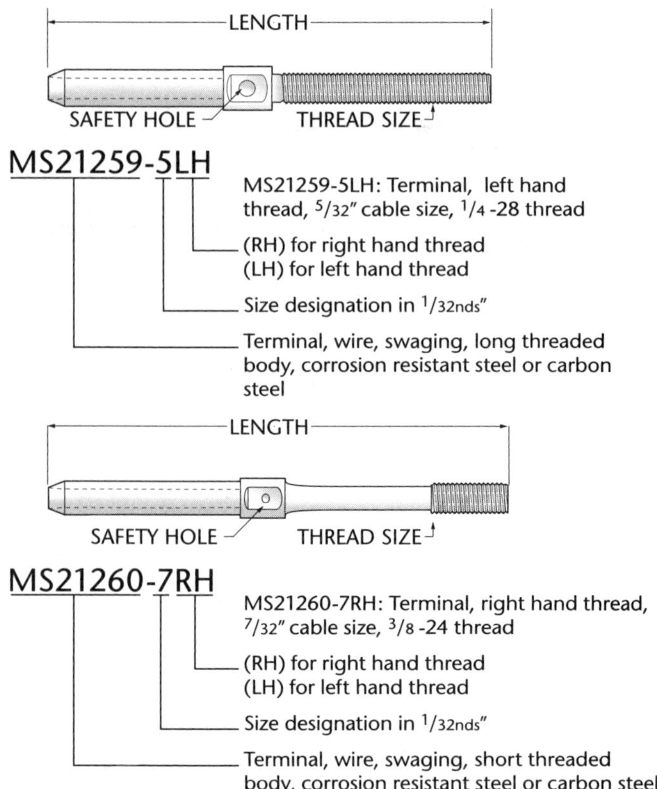

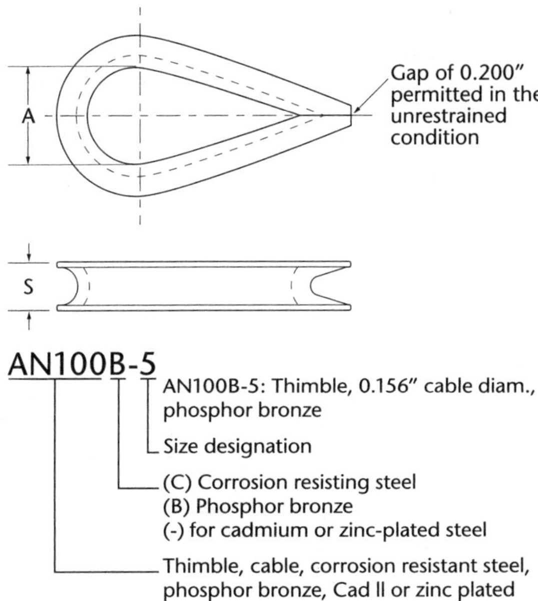

AN100B-5

AN100B-5: Thimble, 0.156" cable diam., phosphor bronze

Size designation

(C) Corrosion resisting steel
(B) Phosphor bronze
(-) for cadmium or zinc-plated steel

Thimble, cable, corrosion resistant steel, phosphor bronze, Cad II or zinc plated

13.98 Safety Wiring Bolts

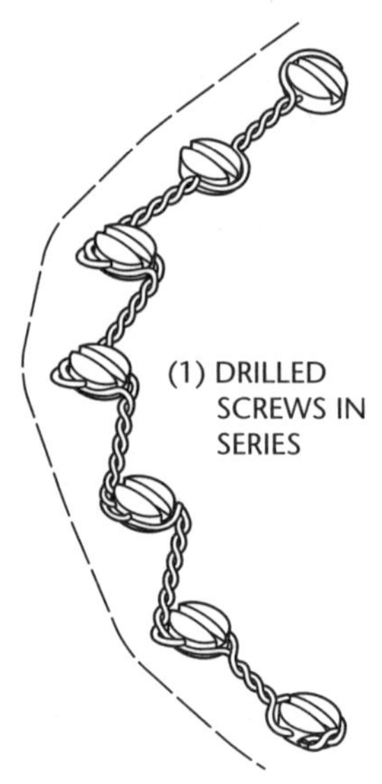

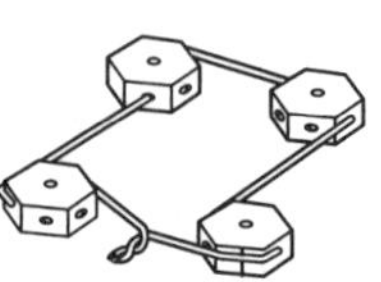

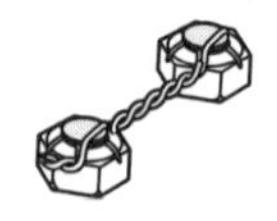

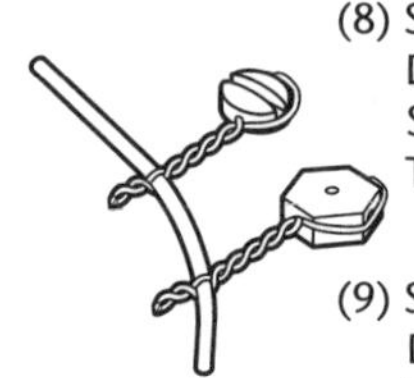

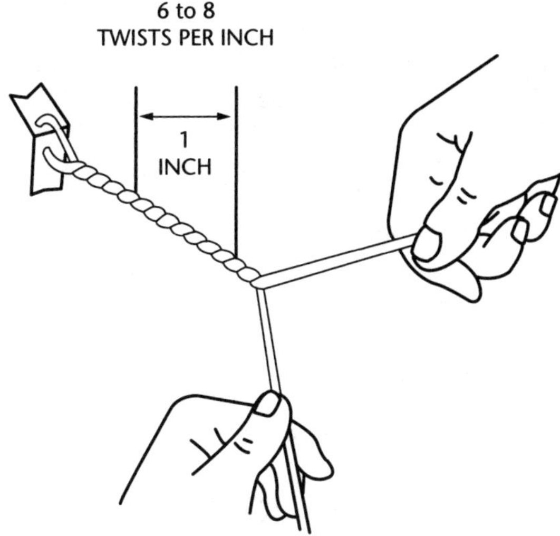
6 to 8
TWISTS PER INCH
1
INCH

13.100 Safety Wiring Fluid Fittings

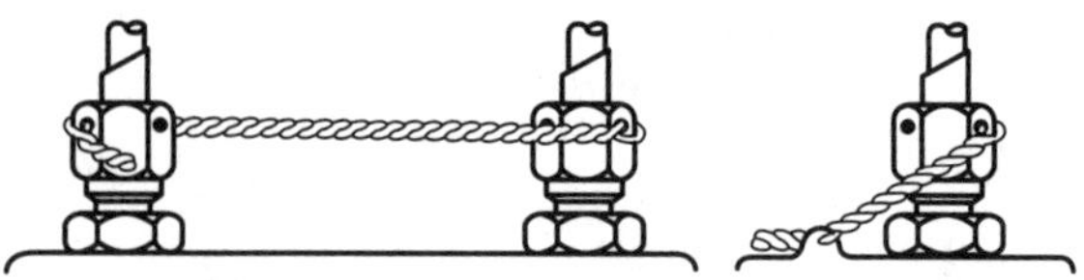

Coupling nuts attached to straight connectors as shown, when hex is an integral part of the connector.

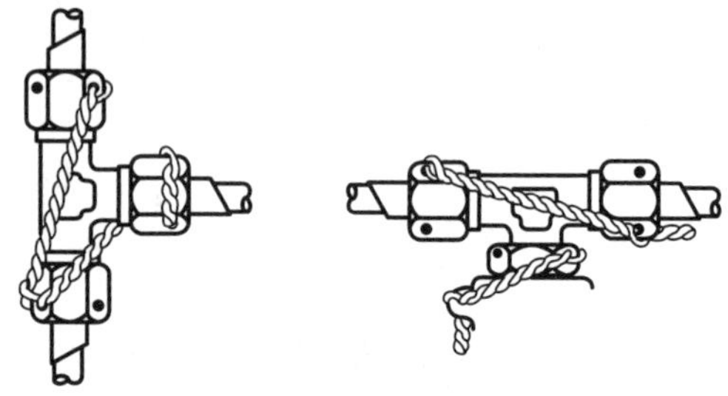

Coupling nuts on a tee wired as shown, so that tension is always in the tightening direction.

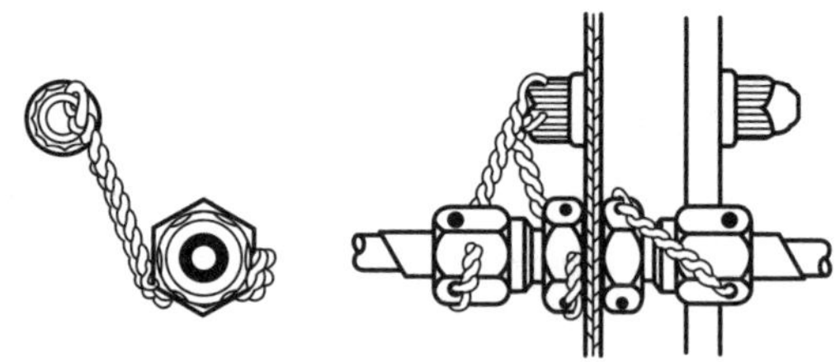

Straight Connector (Bulkhead Type)

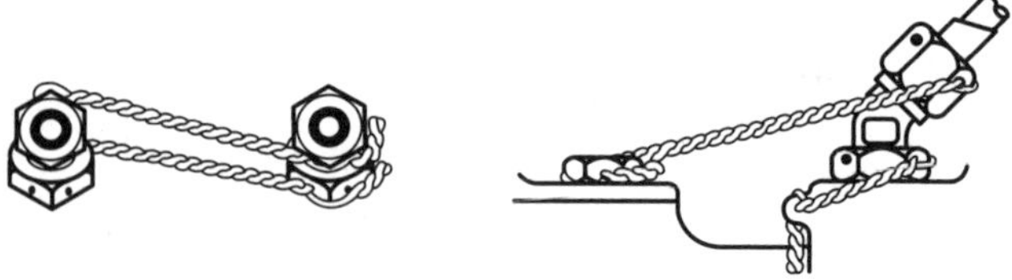

Method for wiring fittings with checknut wired independently so it need not be disturbed when removing the coupling nut.

BREAKER OVERLAY
LOW ANGLE
BREAKERS
TREAD
INNER
LINER
WIRE BEAD
APEX
STRIP

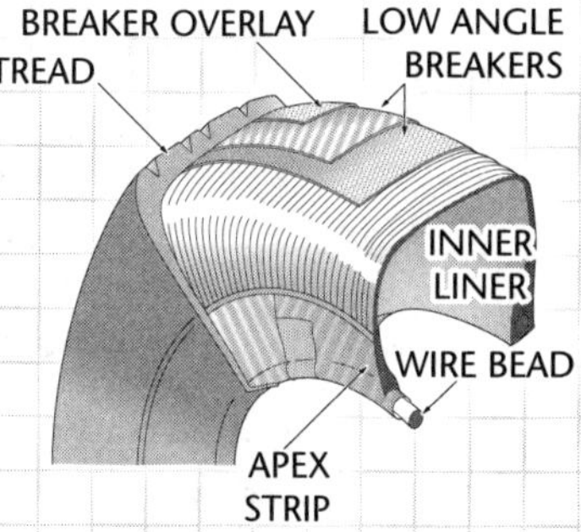

14
Tires

14.1 **Tire Care Terms**

Bead	Multiple strands of high tensile strength steel wire imbedded in rubber and wrapped in strips of open weave fabric. Beads hold the tires firmly on the wheels and serve as an anchor for the fabric plies that are turned up around the bead wires.
Bias tire	Tires made with the carcass plies laid between 30° and 60° to the direction of rotation
Breaker	One or more plies of cord or woven fabric used between the tread rubber and cord body to provide extra reinforcement to prevent damage to the tire.
Chafing strip	One or more plied of rubber-impregnated woven fabric wrapped around the outside of the beads. They provide additional rigidity to the bead and prevent the wheel rim from chafing the tire.
Chine	A chine is a flared ring that protrudes around one or both sides of a tire. Its purpose is to deflect water and debris to the side on aircraft with engines mounted on the rear of the airframe. A nose wheel will normally have a chine on both sides of the tire, while a main gear will have one on the outside only.
Cord body	Multiple layers of nylon with individual cords arranged parallel to each other and completely encased in rubber
Ply rating	Used to identify a tire's maximum recommended load for specific types of service.
Radial tire	Tires made with the carcass plies laid 90° to the direction of rotation
Sidewall	A layer of rubber adjoining the tread and extending to the beads. It protects the cord body from damage.
Tread	Layer of rubber on the outside of the tire. It protects the chords from abrasion, cuts, bruises and moisture. The surface that contacts the ground.

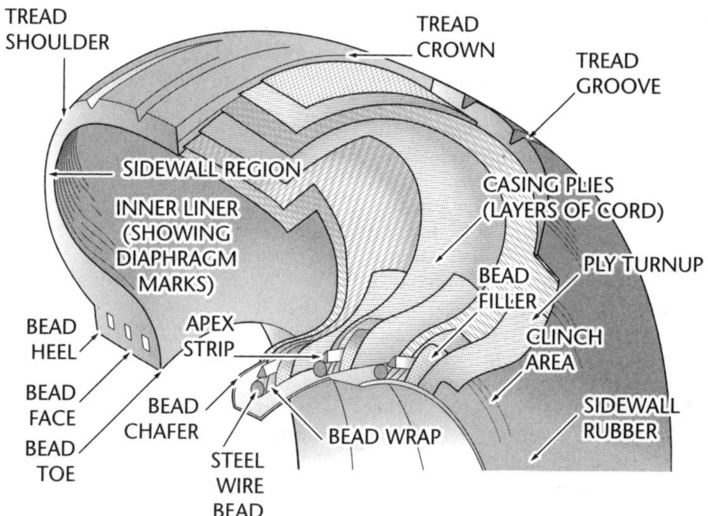

14.3 **Tire Safety**

Aircraft tires and wheels operate with high inflation pressures in order to withstand the operational loads imposed on them. Observe all safety precautions recommended by the manufacturer and in the applicable maintenance manual.

- When inflating tires always use a safety cage
- When using high-pressure nitrogen make sure the regulator is backed off before opening the bottle(s)
- Leave a tire in the cage for several minutes after inflating
- Keep all hoses, gauges and regulators in good condition
- Always approach an in service tire and wheel from an oblique angle to the shoulder
- Mark all foreign objects clearly and remove once the tire is deflated
- Roll tires rather than lifting and carrying
- Use proper equipment to move and handle large tires and wheels to avoid back injury
- Deflate tires before removing them from the aircraft
- Use caution when removing valve cores since they can become propelled from the stem by high-pressure air

14.4 **Tire Inspection**

Mounted Tires
- Check tire inflation daily
- Check tire inflation 3 hours after a flight
- Use calibrated dial or digital gauges when checking tire pressures
- For dual or boogie arrangements check that inflation pressures

14.4 **Tire Inspection (cont'd)**

are within the manufacturer's recommendations
- For dual or boogie arrangements check that the tire heights and combinations are within the manufacturer's recommendations
- Check tread wear patterns for signs of under inflation and over inflation
- Check for flat spots, cracks, missing tread rubber, and sidewall damage in accordance with the maintenance manual
- Inspect tire for imbedded objects
- Check for cut limits in accordance with the maintenance manual
- Verify chevron cutting to be within limits
- Clean any fluid contamination with alcohol followed by soap and water
- On newly mounted tires check for tire pressure changes due to tire growth in accordance with the manufacturer manual

Demounted Tires
- Bead seat distortions
- Debris or cuts on the bead seating surfaces
- Cracking that reaches the cords
- Contamination from oil, grease or other fluids that softens any area of the tire
- Wear limits for retreading are with the manufacturer's limits
- Damage from imbedded objects is within limits and does not reach the cords
- Inspect the inside for damage and loose material

14.5 **Tire Wear Limits**

Guidelines for wear limits are specific to the airframe manufacturer. General criteria can be used in the absence of any specific limits set by the maintenance manual. A tire and wheel should be removed if:
- Any time the aircraft has made a hard, rough or aborted take off, the tire, tube and wheel should be removed for inspection
- Flat spotting due to skids or heavy braking turns are found
- When wear levels reach the bottom of any groove along more than 1/8th of the tire circumference
- Operating a tire that has been underinflated and shows wear in the shoulder area
- Operating a tire that has been over inflated will increase the wear in the center of the tire
- Asymmetrical wear patterns due to improper landing gear alignment
- Any wear that exposes the carcass plies, reduces the tire strength

MISALIGNMENT

OUT OF BALANCE

CUT SIDEWALL

WEATHER CHECKING

When the maintenance manual does not specify the damage limits, the following guidelines may be used:

Bulges and Separations
- Any bulge or separation on any part of the tire is an immediate cause for removal

Cuts to the Tread or Sidewall
- Any cut or injury that exposes the carcass plies
- A cut that extends across a tread rib
- Undercutting at the base of any tread rib
- Any cut to the sidewall that exposes the underlying plies

Damage the Exposed Carcass Plies
- Any tread chunking or peeled treads
- Any groove cracking
- Weather or ozone cracks

14.7 **Tire Wear Conditions**

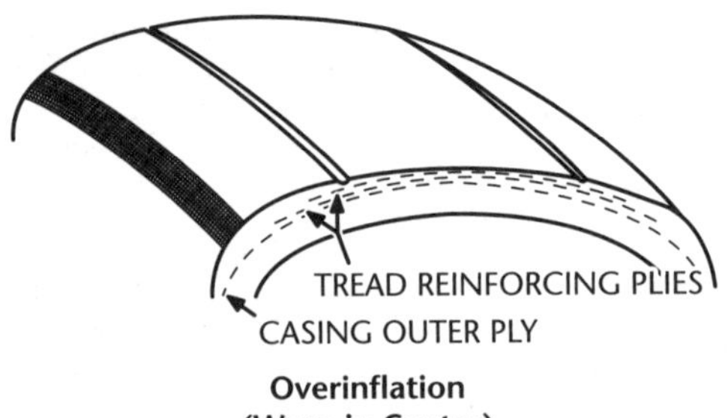

**Overinflation
(Worn in Center)**

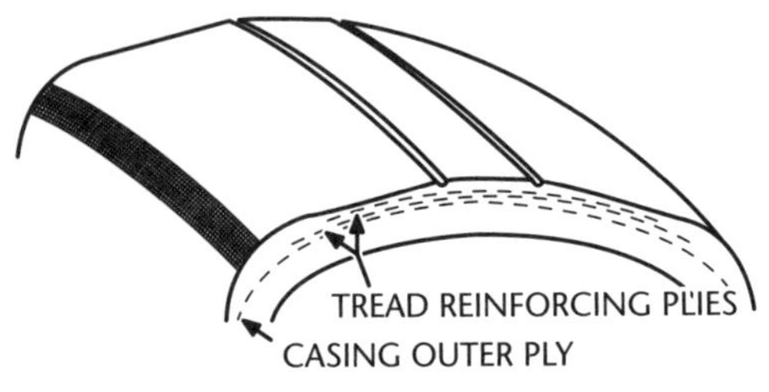

**Underinflation
(Worn at Shoulders)**

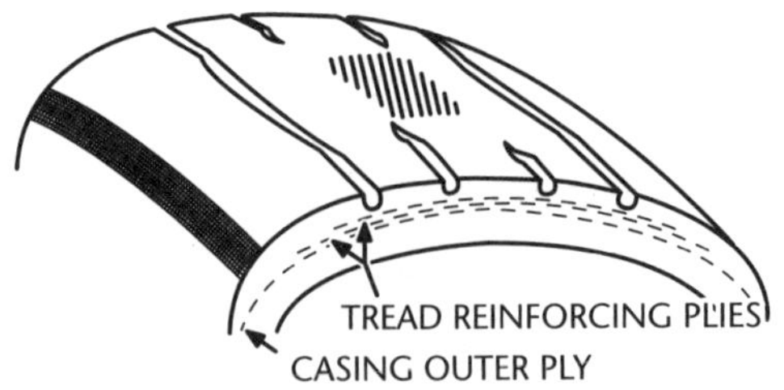

**Worn Beyond Recommended Limits
(Reinforcing Plies Showing)**

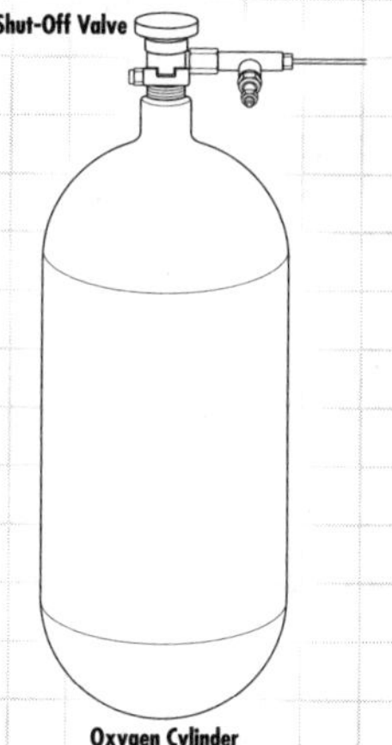

15

Oxygen

15.1 Basic Components

Aircraft oxygen systems typically include the following basic components:
- **Cylinders.** These are containers for the storage of oxygen.
- **Plumbing.** This term is sometimes used to include the tubing, valves, and fittings necessary to interconnect the fixed components of the system, and to permit recharging of the cylinders.
- **Regulators.** These govern the flow of oxygen to the flyer.
- **Indicators.** Oxygen supply pressure is shown by a pressure gage. Action of the regulator is shown by a flow indicator.
- **Delivery Apparatus.** This usually consists of a mask and a flexible tube connecting it to the regulator.

15.2 Types of Assemblies

Portable and Emergency Equipment. Walk-around assemblies are provided in aircraft, for movements of personnel from station to station within the airplane. Emergency cylinders furnish a source of oxygen in the event that the normal oxygen supply is lost.

Flight Station Equipment. Regulators, indicators, delivery apparatus, portable and emergency assemblies may be referred to collectively as flight station equipment. There are three types of flight station equipment: demand, pressure-demand, and continuous-flow. Cylinders and plumbing are essentially similar in almost all aircraft, varying mainly in arrangement.

15.3 Storage

Protect cylinders from excessive heat, and from the direct rays of the sun. Oxygen cylinders must be segregated from cylinders of other gases, and must not be stored near inflammable material of any kind. Cylinders depleted to a pressure approaching 50 psi are to be marked "EMPTY" and segregated from other cylinders.

15.4 Oxygen Safety

CYLINDERS

- Never allow any type of oil or petroleum product anywhere near excess oxygen. The atmosphere produced by excess oxygen can self-ignite and cause an intense fire.
- Handle oxygen cylinders carefully, and open the valves slowly.
- If opened too quickly, it is possible for a regulator diaphragm to rupture, allowing high-pressure gas to escape through a damaged regulator.
- When replacing a storage cylinder, keep the cylinder protective cap screwed onto the cylinder until it is firmly secured.
- Before attaching a regulator to a full cylinder, briefly crack the cylinder valve to blow dust and debris from the fitting.
- When storing high-pressure cylinders, always chain or strap them to something stable, like the beam of a building.
- Never use oxygen to inflate anything.

GENERATORS

- Never remove the safety cap when handling oxygen candles until the maintenance instructions tell you to do so.
- Follow the aircraft maintenance instructions for replacing all solid oxygen candles.
- It is safer to store oxygen candles in their shipping container than to just put them on the shelf.
- There are specific regulations for shipping oxygen candles. They are considered a hazardous material.
- NEVER ship an oxygen candle in an aircraft cargo compartment. To do so can, and has, caused at least one violent airplane accident.
- During an inspection, always follow the established procedure. To vary from it could cause you to trip the trigger on the squib, starting the irreversible oxygen generation process to start.

15.5 Servicing Oxygen Systems

Gaseous oxygen systems are serviced using a special procedure that helps conserve oxygen. Special oxygen service carts using the cascade system are used for filling aircraft systems. A typical cart mounts six oxygen bottles, all connected to a manifold. Because of prior usage, each bottle has a different pressure, and each bottle has its pressure recorded on a logbook system.

To start the filling operation, the bottle with the lowest pressure is turned on just enough to purge the filler hose with oxygen and blow out any accumulation of debris. After purging, the fill hose is connected to the system fill fitting.

Once connected, the cylinder with the lowest pressure is slowly opened and oxygen is allowed to transfer to the aircraft system until all flow stops. Then the cylinder valve is closed and the current bottle pressure is recorded, superseding the previous log entry. The next lowest-pressure bottle is now slowly opened and it, too, is allowed to flow until all flow stops. This stair-stepping, or cascading, system is repeated until the aircraft system reaches its proper pressure. By using this system, the higher-pressure supply cylinders are drawn down less. Their higher pressure is used to boost the system pressure, instead of supplying the majority of the volume.

Because all supply cylinders are connected to a manifold, there is no requirement that higher-pressure cylinders be in a specific location on the service cart. All you have to do as an A&P technician is to be sure and purge the line, fill the system to the correct pressure, and re-record the remaining cylinder pressures in the log for the next refill.

15.6 Oxygen CFRs

The federal regulations dealing with oxygen systems for both reciprocating and turbine aircraft are:

23.1441	Oxygen equipment and supply
23.1443	Minimum mass flow of supplemental oxygen
23.1445	Oxygen distribution system
23.1447	Equipment standards
23.1449	Means of determining use of oxygen
23.1450	Chemical oxygen generators
23.1451	Protection of oxygen equipment
125.219	Oxygen for medical use by passengers
135.91	Oxygen for medical use by passengers
135.157	Oxygen equipment requirements